A
Creed
forMy
Profession

Missouri
Biography
Series

William E. Foley,
Editor

A
Creed
forMy
Profession

Walter Williams,
Journalist to
the World

RONALD T. FARRAR

University of Missouri Press
COLUMBIA AND LONDON

Copyright © 1998 by
The Curators of the University of Missouri
University of Missouri Press, Columbia, Missouri 65201
Printed and bound in the United States of America
All rights reserved
5 4 3 2 1   02 0 1   00 9 9 98

Library of Congress Cataloging-in-Publication Data

Farrar, Ronald T.
    A creed for my profession : Walter Williams, journalist to the
world / Ronald T. Farrar.
        p.   cm. — (Missouri biography series)
    Includes index.
    ISBN 0-8262-1188-7 (alk. paper)
    1. Williams, Walter, 1864–1935.   2. Journalists—United States–
Biography.   3. College presidents—United States—Biography.
4. Historians—United Sates—Biography.   5. Missouri—Biography.
I. Title.   II. Series.
PN4874.W634F67   1998
070'.92—dc21
[B]   98-39815
                                                                CIP

♾™ This paper meets the requirements of the
American National Standard for Permanence of Paper
for Printed Library Materials, Z39.48, 1984.

Text design: Elizabeth K. Young
Jacket design: Susan Ferber
Typesetter: Bookcomp, Inc.
Printer and binder: Thomson-Shore, Inc.
Typefaces: Times

For Gayla Dennis Farrar
and Janet and Mark,
Bradley and Carole

Contents

Acknowledgments

I began this book at the suggestion of Beverly Jarrett, director and editor-in-chief of the University of Missouri Press. She and her editorial board felt that Walter Williams belonged in the Press's Missouri Biography Series, and that I might enjoy writing about this uniquely interesting man. They were right on both counts. I never met Walter Williams—he died the summer I was born—but I owe him a great deal, for he invented the academic discipline in which I've made my living for a very long time now. I hope this biography begins to do the man justice. Whether it does or not, a great many people helped along the way with this project and they should be thanked.

High on the list is Dr. William Howard Taft, professor emeritus at the University of Missouri. If I had only drawn upon his own prodigious scholarship, his books and articles about Missouri journalism, my debt to him would be enormous. But Bill Taft also shared with me his own papers, which included many letters from former students at the School of Journalism and others whose recollections of Walter Williams found their way into these pages. He also introduced me to Francis Pike, able biographer of Ed Watson, and a number of other sprightly octogenarians with firsthand knowledge of the Walter Williams family. Indeed, to this entire project Bill Taft committed the same wonderful encouragement and insight he had devoted more than a generation ago to the supervision of my doctoral dissertation.

Two full-length biographies of Walter Williams were written earlier. The first, never published, was by his widow, Sara Lockwood Williams. The other, by a friend and former student of Williams, Frank Rucker, was brought out by the Missourian Publishing Company in 1964. I've drawn heavily and gratefully upon both works, and if some of my interpretations are somewhat harsher than theirs, my respect for Williams, and for his earlier biographers, remains intact.

Archivists and reference librarians, as always, were uncommonly helpful. I'm especially beholden to D. J. Wade, Senior Manuscript Specialist at the University of Missouri Archives—she opened up the shop on Saturdays, when necessary, to accommodate a hard-pressed researcher from far away—and to Randy Roberts, Senior Manuscript Specialist at the Western Historical Manuscript Collection at the University of Missouri. That marvelous repository houses the extensive papers of both Walter and Sara Lockwood Williams as well as those of dozens of political and journalistic leaders with whom they corresponded. The manuscript collection is a very rich source, and Randy Roberts was a splendid guide to it.

Charles Overby, who heads the Freedom Forum, provided funding for a number of my research errands to Columbia, Missouri. I'm grateful also for smaller travel grants from the University of South Carolina Foundation and the Southern Regional Education Board.

I owe at least two debts to Dean Mills, an old friend who now sits at Walter Williams's desk. First, he kept his distance while this manuscript was being researched and written. While I would have welcomed his thoughtful observations and his sharp editorial eye, it seemed important to both of us that this manuscript be developed quite apart from the present-day operations of the School of Journalism at the University of Missouri. But, and this is the second debt, Dean Mills did place at my disposal a bright and energetic research assistant, a young graduate student from Russia named Pavel Chernyshev. Pavel attacked those voluminous papers in the Western Historical Manuscript Collection with an intelligent ferocity that makes me glad the Cold War ended when it did.

I likewise deeply appreciate the patience of Beverly Jarrett at the Missouri Press—this manuscript should have been completed long before it was—and for her talented editorial team, notably John Brenner, a skilled and sensitive editor. Bill Foley, professor of history at Central Missouri State University and general editor of the Missouri Biography Series, gave the manuscript an especially thorough and authoritative reading. His comments were very helpful. Needless to add, however, any errors that might appear in this text are not the fault of anyone but me.

My faculty colleagues in the College of Journalism and Mass Communications at the University of South Carolina, as they have in the past, proved a great source of support. My dean, Judy VanSlyke Turk, came through with a sabbatical leave for me at a critical point in the project, and my fellow professors, close friends as well as respected colleagues, picked up the slack at other times, particularly during the author's two prolonged medical absences.

Finally: about thirty years ago, in acknowledging the help that made possible the first book I ever wrote, there was this paragraph:

> The greatest debt, of course, is to my wife, Gayla Dennis Farrar, not only for her aid and comfort throughout, but for the grace and delight she brings . . . to whatever she does. Dedicating this to her, in return, is a wholehearted, but utterly inadequate, gesture of thanks.

The same holds true today. The words may not have gotten any better with time, but she has.

A
Creed
forMy
Profession

Introduction

The old roadway winds through the southern highlands of Guatemala to the Pacific coast. It was one of the worst Scott Norvell had ever traveled in Central America, a region he knew well enough to write about for *Time* as well as the *New York Times,* the *Los Angeles Times,* and the *Journal of Commerce.* The old road skirts the base of Aqua Volcano, south of Antigua, and leads eventually to Palin, where it will link up with newer and better highway. Often little more now than an unpaved path, this long-neglected route was broken by frequent washouts and rocks the size of footballs. It was far better suited to the horse traffic of its day, Norvell thought, than to his rented Nissan. Before long the road would become impassable because of frequent clashes between government troops and the guerrillas who maintained a stronghold in these remote, forboding hills. The threat of violence was clear and present. Armed extremist groups, procommunist and anticommunist, were poised at any time for yet another terrorist raid. In an attempt to head off more violence, the government in 1951 had taken over thousands of acres of private property, much of it belonging to the United Fruit Company, and parceled it out to landless *campesinos.* But no lasting peace had yet been found. The army had seized control of the government again in 1963. In 1967 three Guatemalan congressmen and three U.S. Embassy officials, including the ambassador, were assassinated. There was another presidential election in 1970, and the winner was an army colonel. Times remained tense.

On that warm, muggy day in 1977, Scott Norvell was stopped four or five times by roaming patrols of seventeen-year-old soldiers who pointed expensive Galil assault rifles at him and asked lots of questions. Had he seen any guerrillas? No, he said. *Nada.*

But during that otherwise uncomfortable journey he did run across something he found far more interesting. It was a monument beside the dusty roadway. Larger and more imposing than a highway marker, the monument must have impressed passersby in the old days when there was brisk traffic along the road. Now the shrine was chipped and eroding, its lettering badly rusted. Worse yet, it was situated directly in the path of the lush, creeping vegetation that had already engulfed huge sections of the old roadbed. The monument had been erected long ago to commemorate the belated christening of the highway, in honor not of a Guatemalan politician, but of a visitor from North America. Norvell recognized the name. Swiftly, he translated the rust-covered text:

WALTER WILLIAMS HIGHWAY, 1925
The Government of the Republic, in tribute to the memory of the North American citizen Walter Williams, President of the University of Missouri and founder of the first school of journalism and the World Press Congress, who with his presence on the inauguration of this highway in 1925 cordially fostered relations between the great people of North America and our own, is disposed to designate it in his name in recognition of his merits.[1]

Like the monument, the name and reputation of Walter Williams have been dimmed a bit by the passing years. The World Press Congress, which had met once in Guatemala, during 1925, was a utopian dream that if peoples could only communicate better then international tensions would disappear. Perhaps its only tangible legacy, for Guatemala at least, was the crumbling monument alongside the all-but-abandoned roadway. But the World Press Congress had met in other places at other times—San Francisco, Honolulu, Mexico City, Geneva, Zurich—and, if only for a little while, journalists had shared their concerns as well as their knowledge and their dreams of a world at peace. The organization died when Williams did; as one editor put it, Walter Williams *was* the World Press Congress. He founded it and served as its president or honorary president as long as he lived. He believed that America could teach the rest of the world much about journalism, but he also knew that Americans could learn from others. He was a student of the press of every nation, and no one had ever been a more visible or articulate spokesman for good journalistic values and for the free flow of information and ideas across the globe.

Some listen to him still. During the early 1990s, just after the collapse of communism in Eastern Europe, newly emancipated nations such as Romania found themselves in the midst of a lovely, bewildering profusion of uncensored newspapers and magazines. The press was courageous and sensational, high-minded and tawdry, unstable, wildly uneven, fragile at best, but editorially free. After three-quarters of a century of totalitarian control, Romanians were uncertain of how best to cope with their newfound liberties. In a burst of idealism, the University of Bucharest moved swiftly to establish a Faculty of Journalism, hoping it could instill in a few bright young men and women the professional ethics and skills and leadership training their country's newspapers and magazines and broadcast operations now so urgently needed. Mihai Coman, a sociologist who knew something about U.S. journalism, was chosen

1. Scott Norvell to William H. Taft, undated letter, c. 1977.

dean. Like his hero Walter Williams, the energetic Coman built his curriculum around a laboratory publication designed to afford realistic practice for his students and, equally important, a continuing example of a temperate, responsible newspaper for the community. The paper would be written and edited by the students. But for the first issue the dean asked for, and got, permission to use all of page one for a message he particularly wanted to impart: it was *The Journalist's Creed,* by Walter Williams. "I believe," the translation began, "in the profession of journalism . . . I believe that a public journal is a public trust; that all connected with it are, to the full measure of their responsibility, trustees for the public; that acceptance of lesser service than the public service is betrayal of this trust . . ."

A visitor from America noted that *The Journalist's Creed* had been written a long time ago. "In Romania," Dean Coman replied, his smile a little sad, "it is still a long time ago. But more than anything I could think of to set the tone for a free and decent press in Romania, that Creed expresses it best."[2]

Walter Williams probably did more for the elevation of journalism than anyone of his time. "And the full fruits of his labor are yet to appear," wrote a distinguished editor after Williams's death in 1935, "for he did more perhaps than any other to raise journalism from a nondescript vocation to a professional level."[3]

Williams had a vision of a greater, finer, and more useful journalism, and he applied himself with a passionate and yet pragmatic devotion to the realization of that dream.[4] He was convinced that journalism was indeed a profession, or could be, and that if it were ever to rank with law, medicine, and theology it must, first of all, establish a base on the university campus— at a school which provided rigorous training in skills and ethical practice, a school which symbolized a degree of recognition and acceptance within the intellectual community. Other editors before him—not many, but a few—had also campaigned for the founding of a school of journalism. But where they had tried and failed, Williams had succeeded.

Others had written professional codes of ethics for journalists, too, but it would be Williams's *The Journalist's Creed* that would be displayed on the walls of many hundreds of newspaper offices—including, as of May 1993, the newly established student newspaper at the University of Bucharest— and be translated into more than a hundred languages throughout the world.

---

2. Conversation with the author, June 12, 1994.
3. Casper S. Yost, *St. Louis Globe-Democrat,* August 3, 1935.
4. Ibid.

"Journalism owes a great deal, a very great deal, to Walter Williams," wrote Casper S. Yost of the *St. Louis Globe-Democrat,* "and because journalism is distinctively an instrument of public service, the indebtedness of the public to him is no less."[5]

What made Walter Williams important was his lifelong conviction that journalism really mattered, that nothing bolstered freedom and brotherhood more than information that was honestly and intelligently presented by men and women who had the knowledge, judgment, and skill to do their jobs right. What made him succeed was a complex formula of discipline and charm, idealism and pragmatism.

He also knew a thing or two about publicity.

5. Ibid.

1

Boonville

 Next to a good woman on the farm is a good road to get to the farm. The whole problem of country life is a transportation problem.

—Missouri farmer, interviewed near Boon's Lick Road

In the summer of 1805, two sons of Daniel Boone, driven as he had been by restless energy and adventurous spirit, pressed beyond the thin line of civilization along the Mississippi River and into the wilds of what would become central Missouri. Their objective was to find salt, which was both scarce and precious in that remote part of the world. For some months they tramped through the woods alongside unmapped waterways, sometimes following faint paths of the region's Indian occupants, more often cutting their own trail. Well over a hundred miles west of their starting point, the tiny Femme Osage district settlement near St. Charles, young Nathan and Daniel Morgan Boone would find the resources they needed: a series of springs so strongly impregnated with salt that deer and other wild animals convened there to drink the waters and lick the salty concentrate off the rocks jutting out of the stream. The Boones boiled the brine from the springs and loaded the salty residue into hollowed-out logs, which they then floated down the Missouri River to St. Louis, where merchants were laying out as much as $250 a hundredweight for good-quality salt.

The Boones gave their name to the salt lick and to the overland pathway, Boon's Lick Trail, they had created to locate it, and to much else that would need to be named thereabouts. The Boones spelled their name differently; some used the final "e" and some did not. Thus were born Boon's Lick and, eventually, Boonville, situated just outside what would become Boone County, Missouri.

Much of the background material in this chapter, as well as the chapter's epigraph, is from a lengthy series of articles published in the *Columbia Herald* and other newspapers by Walter Williams in 1911, and based on his remarkable travels along the Boon's Lick Road and the Santa Fe Trail. Williams spent several weeks researching this series, retracing the whole of the route from St. Charles to Franklin to Santa Fe. The best source for this, and other matters related to the Boones, is John Mack Faragher, *Daniel Boone: The Life and Legend of an American Pioneer* (Henry Holt and Co., 1992). The author is especially grateful to Professor William Foley, a leading authority on Missouri history, for his thoughtful and knowing review of this chapter.

Each was named with equal authority after the most celebrated pioneer family in America.

The Boone brothers were not the first white men to investigate the Missouri wilderness. Before them had come trappers and hunters, even a fort or two. Colonel Benjamin Cooper had led a group of hardy Kentucky rangers on a prolonged exploration of Upper Louisiana, as it was then called, perhaps with a view toward claiming additional territory for their new state. But Kentucky's governor, James Garrard, wearied of financing the costly venture and sent word to his rangers to return. They brought home with them vivid reports of what they called "The New Eden" of the Missouri territory, tales that would later inspire hopeful Kentuckians and Virginians to pick up stakes and head for the fertile lands to the west.

For the most part, the early settlers and the Native American tribes coexisted peaceably. There was, however, some resentment, notably from the Missouri Indians as well as the Fox and Sauk tribes, over the loss of their ancient hunting grounds. Raids on the frontier outposts near St. Louis, though infrequent, were nevertheless bloody. The situation worsened in 1812, when war broke out between the United States and Britain. British troops joined forces with the tribes, helpfully supplying weapons to the warriors and goading them into gruesome attacks on the Missouri pioneers. The opposition began to crumble in 1813, with the death of Tecumseh, the great Shawnee chief who led the alliance of tribes, and upon whom the British had conferred the rank of brigadier general. Hostilities officially ended in 1815, when representatives of the U.S. government signed a peace treaty at Portage des Sioux. The Native American tribes retreated farther to the west, to lands Europeans did not yet want, and settlers by the thousands began pouring into Missouri Territory.

Many of them traveled via the Boon's Lick route, which had been surveyed and mapped by Nathan Boone, and which quickly became Missouri Territory's most famous thoroughfare. Boon's Lick Road originally spanned from St. Charles, on the northwest bank of the Missouri River not far from St. Louis, to Franklin, an enterprising community also on the low north bank of the Missouri near the center of the territory, and within a few miles of Boon's Lick. The road had been a "trace," or narrow pathway, until Nathan Boone, now a colonel in the U.S. Army, took fifty men, widened and straightened it, and marked it with some degree of clarity. (He also, according to legend, rerouted it somewhat, at the urging of a young maiden of the area, Olive Van Bibber, so that it would pass directly by a roadhouse/tavern owned by her uncle, where she lived; later scholarship suggests that sixteen-year-old Olive had already married Nathan Boone back in Kentucky in 1799, long before the move to Upper Louisiana, but attributing the rerouting of Boon's Lick to a wilderness romance made a better story.)

Improvements notwithstanding, the Boon's Lick Road still afforded only the roughest of rides; it was never more than a dirt road, packed down by wagon wheels and kept in only fair condition by crude and irregular supervision. But it would turn the tide of Missouri's settlement. Soon there would be stagecoaches running regularly between St. Louis and Franklin, a grinding, twisting, precarious journey of 173 miles. The fare was steep, $10.50 per person, but many passengers happily paid it. Their patronage, plus lucrative mail contracts, enabled the stage-line owners to dispatch as many as five coaches a day between St. Charles and Franklin and to amass sizable fortunes in the process.

The Boon's Lick Road also became the father of the Santa Fe Trail, one of the longest and most lucrative trade routes of the era. William Becknell was the first of many to exploit the commercial possibilities of the Santa Fe Trail, setting out from Franklin in 1821 with a train of packhorses laden with goods for trading with the merchants of the Mexican empire. At least two similar expeditions followed a few months later. The following year, some eighty Missouri merchants, mostly from Franklin, formally organized much of the commerce with New Mexico, moving an average of more than eighty wagonloads of manufactured goods a year to exchange for mules, furs, gold, and silver. In just one such venture, the traders departed from Franklin bearing ten thousand dollars' worth of goods; they returned with silver and other valuables worth two hundred thousand dollars. Other caravans were typically less profitable, but a great deal of money came out of them. One hard-driving trader was said to have made the sixteen-hundred-mile round trip in a month's time, averaging more than fifty miles a day across difficult terrain that included both the Cimarron Desert and the Raton Pass. By 1819, before the yellow waters of the Missouri River changed course and washed it away, Franklin had grown rich enough to invite comparisons with St. Louis as a hub of politics, education, commerce, and culture.

But for the most part central Missouri was farming country, lush land on the edge of the great prairies, ripe for the working by men who were most comfortable when under open skies. Such men prized their cornfields and fishing streams and hunting grounds far more than commercial gain. Beyond their doorstep was a freedom that made life less sordid and more sensible. "The yellow of the primrose is not suggestive of the yellow of gold," waxed one emotional defender of farm life in that region. "The sheen of the moon gives no thought of the dollar's silver. One cannot live long out of doors, drink deep from the spring, or gather wild flowers from the meadows without losing some

of the cruelties of commercialism, which shuts up men's souls to selfishness."[1]
While shrewd and enterprising merchants brought great fortunes to Franklin,
the robust pioneer farmers who lived in the fields brought a different, and far
more permanent, kind of abundance.

Now with a population of two thousand—this while the whole vast Missouri
Territory had only sixty thousand—Franklin could also boast of its own
newspaper, the first to be established west of St. Louis. Like many western
newspapers founded by itinerant printers with a rude press and a shirttail full
of type, Franklin's *Missouri Intelligencer and Boon's Lick Advertiser* was
there to boost the community, filling its columns with propaganda to keep
the immigration flowing. "Every particular locality is the garden spot of the
Union," sniffed one Eastern journalist of the period after examining numerous
examples of the pioneer press. "Every little community is the most energetic
and intelligent; every State the most patriotic, and every city a true exemplar
of public virtue."[2] Measured by those criteria, the *Intelligencer* was more
restrained than most. Still, the paper found much to brag about. On April 23,
1819, for example, it proclaimed:

> The immigration to this territory, and particularly to this county, during the present
> season almost exceeds belief. Those who have arrived in this quarter are primarily
> from Kentucky, Tennessee, etc. Immense numbers of wagons, carriages, carts,
> etc., with families, have for some time past been daily arriving. During the month
> of October it is stated that no less than 271 wagons and 4-wheeled carriages and
> fifty-five 2-wheeled carriages and carts passed near St. Charles, bound probably
> for Boon's Lick. It is calculated that the number of persons accompanying these
> wagons, etc., could not be less than three thousand. It is stated in the St. Louis
> *Enquirer* of the 19th instant that about twenty wagons, etc., per week had passed
> through St. Charles for the last nine or ten weeks, with wealthy and respectable
> immigrants from various states. These united numbers are supposed to amount
> to twelve thousand. The county of Howard, already respectable in numbers, will
> soon possess a vast population, and no section of our country presents a fairer
> prospect to the immigrant.

One of the earliest immigrants had been Hannah Cole. The Cole family
left Kentucky for Missouri Territory in 1807. They had traveled as far as
Loutre Island when her husband, William Temple Cole, was killed by a band
of Indians. Too stubborn to turn back, Hannah dealt with her grief by forging
ahead, with her nine children, to settle near Boon's Lick. Arriving not long
after the Boone brothers had gone into the salt business, Hannah Cole and
her children built themselves a sturdy log home, a place so well constructed
it would later be pressed into service as a fort for U.S. troops during the War

---

1. Ibid.
2. Frank Luther Mott, *American Journalism,* 3d ed. (New York: Macmillan, 1962), 282.

of 1812.[3] It was the first structure on the high ground just across the Missouri River from Franklin, an area that would come to be called Boonville.

The territory of Missouri was named for the Missouri River, which winds across it from west to east in broad and impressive fashion. Any community that sprang up on the banks of the Missouri River would be born with better than average prospects, assuming it could survive a flood, and Boonville was no exception. Its development, modest at first, surged ahead dramatically after 1826, filling the void created when the Missouri flooded the lowlands on the north banks and wiped out all of Franklin. The Santa Fe Trailhead, the focal point for what had been Franklin's far-flung commercial interests, was lost forever to more stable communities farther west. The town of Franklin would later be rebuilt, back from the water in a higher and safer place, but New Franklin, as it would be called, never achieved the shining success that attended Old Franklin in its heyday. Directly across the river, however, on hillier terrain far less prone to flooding, Boonville would pick up much of the slack. The new town had its rough edges, at least initially, and was something less of a cultural and commercial center than Old Franklin had been. But Boonville was alive and confident and not without a certain style of its own. One observer, who signed his name only as "A. Fuller," wrote from Boonville to a friend back in Virginia:

> I tell you, Tom, there is an independence and nobleness in the bearing of the young folks here, dressed in their homemade clothing,—the case of gait and carriage—that puts affectation and fine dresses in the shade. I am not carried away entirely by the nobleness of the wild frontier people, but there is a frank generosity with them that you in the East know nothing of, therefore you cannot appreciate it.[4]

But another early visitor, taken aback by the steep land prices and hastily distilled whiskey he encountered in Boonville, was somewhat less impressed:

> They have laid out a town here on the river, called Boonville, which they think will eclipse [Franklin] and I think likewise if the river will let it alone. I went over the river last summer to attend a sale of lots, intending to purchase some to build on, but they were run up to a fabulous price beyond my reach. There were some of the voters who appeared to be affected by patriotism acquired at the only tavern in the place, kept by a hard-looking old fellow named Reames, who bowed politely to all who came in and asked for something to drink, and I was told the whiskey had actually not had time to cool before it was dealt out to customers . . .

---

3. From "Boonville, Missouri: A Great Place to Visit, A Better Place to Live," booklet published by the Boonville Area Chamber of Commerce, 1993.
4. Williams, Santa Fe Trail series.

The distinguished author Washington Irving, however, found Boonville most agreeable. In journals of his remarkable travels along Boon's Lick Road, he wrote of the Boonville area:

> The hospitality of those upon whose kindness we were daily cast was a source of constant admiration, and nothing in the life and surroundings of the 'settlers' escaped their notice and kindly comment. The double loghouse, with kitchen at a distance; the zigzag fence of rails, inclosing a tall growth of Indian corn; cattle, swine and poultry, supplemented by wild game—deer, turkeys and squirrels—all in abundance, enabling the good housewives on shortest notice to spread a plentiful meal of tame or wild meats, fried chicken, eggs, milk, honey, delicious butter, boiled maize and hot wheaten bread.[5]

Boonville did indeed have much to recommend it, and dozens of families, including many who had lived in Old Franklin, decided to stake their futures there. One of these was the family of young George Caleb Bingham, who had immigrated to Missouri Territory from Virginia when he was eight. When floodwaters washed away their home in Old Franklin, the Binghams moved across the river and apprenticed their precocious son to a local cabinetmaker, Justinian Williams—a stouthearted pioneer who, just a few months earlier, had led a wagon train of new settlers from Richmond to Boonville. In Williams's shop, George Caleb Bingham first began to develop the draftsmanship skills that would characterize his magnificent paintings of river life and frontier towns and earn him the distinction of being the country's most important painter of the American scene in the mid–nineteenth century. Before leaving for Philadelphia to study at the Pennsylvania Academy of Fine Arts, Bingham married a Boonville girl, Sarah Elizabeth Hutchinson. Her father, Nathaniel Hutchinson, was a successful druggist and de facto physician who had also established Boonville's first newspaper, the *Herald,* in 1834. That newspaper gave additional credibility to the town, and on February 8, 1839, Boonville was officially awarded a charter by the Missouri legislature.

The great majority of Boonville's earliest citizens, like those who lived elsewhere in central and western Missouri, were farmers, Protestants, tenacious workers, often illiterate, more often deeply religious. One perceptive observer described the migrants to Missouri this way:

> They were Baptists and they were Democrats, and like Thomas Jefferson they believed that those who labored in the earth were the chosen people of God. They saw themselves as the true Americans . . .
> With their Bibles, farm tools, and rifles, their potent corn whiskey, their black slaves, they brought from Kentucky a hidebound loathing for taxes, Roman Catholics, and eastern ways. Their trust was in the Lord and common sense. That

---

5. Ibid.

they and their forebears had survived at all in backwoods Kentucky—or earlier in upland Virginia and the Carolinas—was due primarily to "good, hard sense," as they said, and no end of hard work . . . They could be tough, courageous, blunt, touchy, narrow-minded, intolerant, and quarrelsome. And obstinate. "Lord, grant that I may always be right, for Thou knowest I am hard to turn," was a line from an old Scotch-Irish prayer.[6]

Not all were like that. Some were gentler folk, such as the wagon train of Virginians who formed up at Richmond in the spring of 1837, bound from the Old Dominion to the West. Justinian Williams, the cabinetmaker, was the wagonmaster and led the procession. Just behind him rode his brother, a middle-aged man named Marcus Williams. In the same covered wagon was a stripling—in his mid-twenties, but he looked younger—Marcus Williams, Jr., who had abandoned his farm in Rockbridge County to join his father and uncle for the long journey.

Farther back in the train came the wagon of Mary Jane Littlepage, a soft-spoken, gentle girl from a distinguished family in the Tidewater country of eastern Virginia, traveling with her widowed mother. Mary Jane was the grandniece of a mysterious soldier and adventurer, Louis Littlepage, who was then on an escapade in an undisclosed part of Europe.[7] The first known Littlepage in the New World, Richard Littlepage, had been granted land in New Kent County, Virginia, in 1660; he went on to be appointed sheriff of the county a few years later. His son likewise received a substantial land grant, 2,367 acres, in New Kent, as well as permission to employ Indian servants, including a woman for housework and a man to hunt game for him. Mary Jane was the granddaughter of John Carter Littlepage, who had been elected attorney general of Virginia in 1792 and had served as a captain of the Virginia militia during the Revolutionary War. Later promoted to colonel, Littlepage had been elected to Virginia's House of Burgesses in 1764. His opponent, Nathaniel West Dandridge, charged that Littlepage had won the election through fraud. He filed a lawsuit and hired Patrick Henry to plead his case. Henry's soaring oratory captivated the courtroom audience, but the jury was not persuaded. Colonel

---

6. David McCullough, *Truman* (New York: Simon and Schuster, 1992), 16. This superlative biography of Harry S. Truman is, among much else, a splendid chronicle of life in early Missouri.

7. The passages that follow are drawn largely from three works that have been invaluable to the present author: Frank W. Rucker, *Walter Williams* (Columbia: Missourian Publishing Association, Inc., 1964), 1–11; an unpublished biography of Walter Williams by Sara Lockwood Williams; and Elizabeth Williams Cosgrove, *An Old House Speaks* (St. Louis: Horace Barks Printing Co., 1943). The unpublished biography, a rich source document, is housed at the Western Historical Manuscript Collection at the University of Missouri in Columbia. Cosgrove was the granddaughter of Marcus and Mary Jane Littlepage Williams. She compiled not only a history of the Williams home on Morgan Street in Boonville, but also a history of the Williams family.

Littlepage held his seat and, indeed, was reelected two years later. Records at the Bureau of Pensions in Washington reveal that Littlepage had earlier saved Patrick Henry from being detained by British authorities by alerting him to the location of a hostile British patrol while Henry was en route to attend the First Continental Congress at Philadelphia in 1774. Branches of the Littlepage family tree intertwined with those of the Byrds, the Randolphs, and others so prominently involved in Virginia's formative years. But the family fortunes had declined somewhat by the time Mary Jane Littlepage was born, in Powhatan County, near Richmond, in 1822. She never saw her father, Lewis Byrd Littlepage, who died before she was born, well before his fortieth birthday. Eventually his widow decided to forsake her native Virginia and to invest her modest inheritance in a new and uncertain life for herself and her daughter in Missouri.[8]

"With laughter and joke, songs and stories," as one family member re-called, the Virginians wended their way over the Appalachian hills, camping around blazing fires, sleeping under the stars, doggedly driving their wagons toward the west. The trek, which took the better part of a year, eventually led them to the rich plains and rolling hills of central Missouri. There, amid flourishing orchards of grapes and with the powerful Missouri River just below—"unwinding like a blue ribbon," a pioneer said, lay Boonville and their journey's end.[9]

It was a harsh trip, but not unrewarding. Along the way, young Miss Littlepage got to know another expatriate Virginian, Marcus Williams, Jr., and within a year she would become his bride.

Not as much is known about his forebears, but Marcus Williams, Jr., had been born in Albemarle County, near Charlottesville, on August 7, 1816, and had spent his youth in nearby Rockbridge County. Though he never referred to himself as "Junior," his father was also named Marcus Williams.

Rich in farmland and scenic beauty, Rockbridge was one of Virginia's most populous and well-to-do counties. Within its borders was the famed Natural Bridge, for which the county was named, and hundreds of farms, many of them prosperous. The county's population exceeded fourteen thousand in the 1830s. By that time one native son of Rockbridge County, Cyrus H. McCormick, had already patented a reaping machine that would come to symbolize the mechanical revolution in agriculture, and another, Sam Houston, was about to be inaugurated as the first president of the Republic of Texas. Surrounding counties in Virginia had already given the United States four presidents, and

---

8. Cosgrove, *An Old House Speaks,* 32–34.
9. Ibid., 21.

four more would follow. For all its rich tradition, however, Virginia also had had to endure its share of frustrations. An economic recession swept across the Eastern seaboard, and Virginia was hit especially hard. The political mood was likewise depressed. A controversial new state constitution, adopted in 1830 in an attempt to placate the growing contentiousness of the western counties, helped distribute power within the state somewhat more equitably, but eastern leaders were able to hang on to state office anyway. The resulting reorganization left relatively few Virginians satisfied, and a spirit of discontent spread across the commonwealth. "In most revolutions, the people overthrow the aristocrats and take over," one Virginia historian wrote of this period, "but in the Virginia revolution, the aristocrats overthrew themselves and the people got out."[10] In 1838, Marcus Williams, then twenty-six years old and with limited means, decided to join the exodus from Virginia to "The New Eden" of Missouri. Perhaps his reasons were much the same as those which had prompted the widow Littlepage and her daughter to quit Virginia at the same time. But while the Littlepages were quiet and gentle, the Williams clan were movers and shakers. Marcus Williams, Sr., would become an influential local leader and was elected Boonville's first mayor. He also made the brick for the first brick home in Boonville, a house that still stood 120 years later.

Brimming with energy but strangely without a clear and specific vocational calling, young Marcus Williams, Jr., threw himself into life at Boonville, jumping at first one commercial opportunity and then another. He captained a steamboat, piloting cargo and passengers up and down the Missouri River; he bought an interest in, and frequently operated, a ferryboat across the Missouri between Boonville and New Franklin; he was a contractor and builder; he worked as a miller; at one point in his life he dug clay from a place south of town, built a kiln, and crafted enough vases and dishes to open a pottery, the first pottery in Missouri. He even left Boonville once, traveling alone to California after gold had been discovered there in 1849. Little is known of that mission, except that it didn't last long and Marcus Williams returned to Boonville empty-handed. None of his local ventures would make him wealthy either, but somehow he always seemed to keep his family in comfortable, if modest, circumstances. He was a quiet and thoughtful man, strong in his convictions, popular with his neighbors, active in community affairs, a devout and valued member of the Presbyterian church. And if Marcus Williams's business ventures were sometimes shaky, his personal life was stability itself: it was devoted to, and revolved around, Mary Jane Littlepage, whom he had courted and married within months of his arrival in the New Eden.

---

10. Clifford Dowdry, *The Great Plantation* (New York: Rinehart and Co., 1957), 211.

Boonville, meanwhile, was by now established and comfortable. Its business climate may have been more conservative and less lucrative than Old Franklin's had been, back when nervy, resourceful traders operated on the grand scale. But the boom days for mid-Missouri were ended. The jump-off points for the Santa Fe and Oregon Trails and the other westward passages had shifted to Independence and St. Joseph, rough, energetic new towns near the Kansas border. Boonville was left to grow in less spectacular fashion, but grow it did, evolving nicely into a progressive riverport town, farm community, and trade center for its immediate region. When Cooper County was surveyed and named—for the Kentucky colonel who had led the first expedition of rangers into the area early in the century—Boonville was chosen its county seat. Other communities within the county were far more centrally located, but Boonville was on the river.

As early as 1807, Robert Fulton had shown upstate New Yorkers how to harness the steam engine to propel watercraft, and to do so at a profit. Ten years later steamboats had been deployed as far west as St. Louis, and by 1819 they were traveling up the Missouri. The *Independence* reached Franklin that year, even though regular steamboat traffic on the Missouri was still a decade away. By the 1840s shallow-draft vessels were consistently able, with luck, to negotiate the twisting currents upstream from St. Louis to within a few miles of Independence. Packed with goods and wagons and passengers, the steamers pushed their way up "The Big Muddy," passing slowly alongside thick forests and occasional open fields, bringing more trappings of civilization with them. A historian of the period wrote of one ill-fated side-wheeler which sank in the treacherous waters east of Independence; its cargo, recovered years later, consisted of twenty-five hundred pairs of boots and shoes, ax handles, whale oil lanterns, rifles, school slates, doorknobs, saddles and harnesses, beeswax candles, and thousands of beads, buttons, and spangles, most likely for the Indian trade.[11] Midway between St. Louis and Independence, Boonville developed into an important port of call servicing dozens of boats each month at its docks near Wharf Street Hill. For most of the steamers, Boonville was merely a stopover, a reliable place to take on more cordwood for fueling the engines. But many of the vessels began and ended their runs there, transporting tobacco, wheat, corn, bacon, and other Cooper County products to market, hauling in the manufactured goods for distribution from Boonville's warehouses to central and southern Missouri.

The steamers did a lively business in passengers, too, especially among the Germans, who were then settling in large numbers along river towns. Only

---

11. McCullough, *Truman,* 17.

the first generation of Germans was truly German; the second was American, coexisting easily with the Scotch-Irish Southerners who had settled Boonville. Some of the old ways remained: a keen interest in beer and winemaking, for example, which added a brisk new dimension to the commercial and social sides of Cooper County. Merchants, artisans, lawyers, and property developers of German descent were quickly integrated into the life of the town. Frederick J. Kemper in 1844 opened a private academy that would become well known as a military school and private college. German influence was prominent, too, in establishing the Thespian Society, formed in 1838—a year before Boonville was even an incorporated town—by sixty locals whose first theater was a hewn log structure thirty by sixty feet in size on the brow of a river hill. The society's magnificent permanent home, Thespian Hall, built in 1857, would be acclaimed throughout the region. Boonville street names, many of them, reflected the German influence: Alpine, Mueller, Gmelich, Poertner, Stegner, Knabe. The first pedigreed Shorthorn bull to be imported into Missouri would become head of the herd on the Leonard farm, just outside Boonville.

Much of the best farmland in the area was already being cultivated, but thousands of acres remained for sale at low cost, a bargain ardently promoted by local developers. Their boosterism was matched by that of Boonville's early newspapers. One of them, the *Western Emigrant,* in a January 10, 1839, news report that read like paid advertising, and might well have been, asserted:

> The most splendid advantages which this [Boonville] country presents to new settlers is the ease and cheapness of raising stock, such as horses, mules, cattle and hogs . . . A farmer on a quarter section, 160 acres, with the advantage of prairie range, can raise more stock than he could on 500 acres in the old states. Land can be obtained either by entry at Congress prices [then starting at $1.25 per acre], abounding with timber and prairies, or by purchasing an improved quarter section at from $5 to $8 an acre, or he can buy farms improved with tolerable log houses and enough land to work upon at $5 to $10 an acre.[12]

From all over the East, but especially from Kentucky and Virginia, farmers bought land and moved to Missouri. Many brought their slaves with them.

As early as 1818, Missouri had asked to be admitted to the Union.[13] The application, though recognized as appropriate and timely, nevertheless triggered a prolonged and fateful national debate. At that point in the emerging nation, six of the original thirteen states and five of the newly admitted ones still permitted slavery. Seven of the original states and four new states had abolished it. The U.S. Senate was evenly divided, with twenty-two senators

---

12. Williams, Santa Fe Trail series.

13. An especially useful and far more detailed interpretation of the Missouri Compromise is G. G. Van Deusen's *The Life of Henry Clay* (Boston: Little, Brown and Co., 1937).

on either side of the slavery question. When Missouri applied for admission to the Union it asked to come in as a slave state—understandable, given the fact that more than ten thousand slaves, a sixth of the total population, were already living in Missouri. Two new proslavery senators from Missouri would break the deadlock in a way that abolitionist forces found intolerable. The Senate balance had been tilted, temporarily, in previous years, but always there had been an understanding that the Mason and Dixon Line and the Ohio River would form the north-south line, influencing the admission status of each new applicant as a slave or a free state. No such line, however, existed west of the Mississippi River, where many more states, of which Missouri would be merely the first, prepared to seek admission. Worse yet, if the Ohio River/Mason-Dixon Line could be extended to the west, parts of Missouri would lay north of it and part to the south. A disputatious session of the House produced a proposed amendment to the Missouri statehood bill that would have allowed Missouri slaveowners to keep their slaves, but require them to grant children of slaves their freedom and to prohibit importation of any other slaves into Missouri. The House amendment was defeated in the Senate. During the next session of the Congress, Maine applied for admission to the Union, as a free state, and Missouri thus could be admitted at the same time to preserve the equilibrium. The Missouri Compromise, as it was called, required all territories that had been part of the Louisiana Purchase to become free states, as they were ready to join the Union—except for Missouri. But voters in Missouri insisted upon defining their slavery question for themselves; a defiant Missouri territorial legislature wrote into the new constitution a clause forbidding any free blacks from entering the state, a proviso the Congress found unacceptable. At this critical juncture Henry Clay of Kentucky developed a second Missouri Compromise and steered it gingerly through the Congress: it was silent on the subject of Missourians owning slaves, but did stipulate that the constitutional rights of free black citizens of other states must be respected. Consequently, Missouri in 1821 became the twenty-fourth state. It represented the western frontier, but in its tortured handling of the slavery issue, Missouri was not unlike the Union itself.

The political divisions did not end with statehood. By 1860 each of four national parties had substantial followers in Missouri: the Republicans, who took a hard-line position in opposition to the extension of slavery; the Breckenridge Democrats, equally hard-line advocates of slavery; the Constitutional Union, a conciliatory party which advocated compromise on the slavery question; and the Douglas Democrats, who favored local option votes on whether to allow slavery.[14]

_____

14. Rucker, *Walter Williams,* 23. The Whig party was gone, having collapsed in 1855.

For his part, however, Marcus Williams kept his pro-Confederacy views pretty much to himself. Perhaps his own financial position, never really robust, rendered him cautious about making enemies that could hurt his business. Or possibly his quiet demeanor precluded him from political activism. Or it could have been that he was simply too busy trying to make a living and provide for the children he and Mary Jane brought into the world. Susan Ann was born in 1840 (twins, Douglas and Carrie, first-born, died in infancy). Joseph Howard was born in 1843, William Muir in 1850, Elizabeth in 1852, and Louis Littlepage in 1855. Then, on July 2, 1864, when Marcus Williams was forty-eight and his wife Mary Jane was forty-two, their youngest child was born. Sensing this would be the last, they took the opportunity to name him Marcus Walter Williams. It was an eloquent, if belated, tribute to father and grandfather alike. The middle name, almost as an afterthought, honored Dr. John Walter, beloved Sunday school teacher of Susan Ann Williams.[15] The family expected to call the child Marcus. But the child never wanted to be called anything but Walter.

---

15. Cosgrove, *An Old House Speaks,* 50.

2

Young Walter

 A large part of virtue consists in good habits.

—William Paley, British theologian

The Civil War reduced the economic station of the Williams family from middle-class to poor, as it did most of Boonville.[1] The fighting was intense, and it was local: two significant battles and numerous raids and skirmishes were fought in the immediate region of Boonville, draining the manpower and the economy of the town and the spirits of those who were left there to cope as best they could with adversity, shortage, and, often, despair. When Walter Williams was born in 1864, the war had already been going on for three years—longer than that, if one counts the wildcat violence associated with the proslavery Missouri Bushwhackers, who were known to have launched terrorist attacks on abolitionist strongholds in Missouri and Kansas as early as 1856. Retaliatory strikes by Kansas Jayhawkers turned the Missouri-Kansas border into a bloody battleground over slavery long before there was a Confederate States of America, much less a rebel army and an Emancipation Proclamation. On April 12, 1861, hostilities officially commenced when Confederate artillery shelled Fort Sumter, a tiny island outpost strategically positioned just outside the entrance to Charleston harbor. Weeks later, a land battle, one of the earliest of the Civil War, would be fought for control of another port: the river town of Boonville, Missouri.

After months of anguished debate, Missourians had opted against secession. But considerable proslavery sentiment existed throughout the state, and after the Fort Sumter attack, federal forces headquartered in St. Louis moved swiftly, if clumsily, to rid the Missouri River valley of the threat that might be posed by Southern sympathizers. A secondary objective, but far more important for the long pull, would be to show the U.S. flag and make certain that

---

1. This assessment, along with a few other details about his early years, is from an unpublished manuscript written by Walter Williams and found among his papers in the Western Historical Manuscript Collection, University of Missouri. The undated typewritten manuscript, seven pages long, is clearly a tentative and preliminary start on an autobiography, a project presumably begun late in his life, and one which he soon abandoned. The works of Robert Dyer, notably *Jesse James and the Civil War in Missouri* (University of Missouri Press, 1992), contain the best modern account of Boonville's history.

Missouri remained in the Union. The clearing party was headed by General—
only a month before he had been a captain—Nathaniel Lyon, described by
one historian as "a little man, hard-bitten of feature, red of hair and beard,
with the burning eye of the zealot."[2] Meeting with practically no organized
resistance as they marched up the valley of the Missouri, Lyon's forces drove
the state government, rife with Confederate sympathizers, from the capital
at Jefferson City. On June 17 they advanced a few miles north, to the hills
below Boonville, where, for the first time, they ran into a fight. It came from
an untrained volunteer militia, then thirteen hundred strong, that Missouri
Governor Claiborne F. Jackson had hurriedly assembled to defend what he
thought were the state's interests and autonomy. The rebel forces fought
gamely, but they were poorly armed and only half-organized, and were soon
overwhelmed. The battle began at 6 A.M. and ended a few hours later when
the town mayor, James H. O'Brian, surrendered Boonville to General Lyon.
Though there was ferocious shooting and unnumbered wounded on both sides,
only one person was killed: Dr. John Walter, a gentle soul tragically miscast
as a fighting man, the Sunday school teacher for whom Walter Williams
was named.[3]

The defeated Missouri militiamen beat a hasty withdrawal from the rich river
valley toward the Ozarks to the south. The secessionist cause in general, and
the governor's prestige in particular, had been dealt a punishing blow. There
would be a rematch, of sorts, farther south seven weeks later at Wilson's Creek;
resurgent rebel forces, better prepared, won this one, and General Nathaniel
Lyon, a brave man if a driven one, was killed.

Throughout the months that followed, the people of Boonville lived in
dread that their town, now occupied by Union forces, would become another
battleground. On October 8, 1863, it did. The invading rebel force, eight
hundred Missouri cavalry supported by only two small cannon, was under the
command of Colonel Joseph O. Shelby. Less an army than a large raiding party
that moved swiftly and lived off the land, Shelby's hit-and-run troops earlier
had fought their way into southern Arkansas, reclaiming that state's capital
for the Confederacy. In late September, they turned back north. Charging
hard through the Ozarks into southwestern Missouri, Shelby captured Neosho
and a number of smaller towns before pushing on to Waverly, his home
community on the Missouri River a few miles upstream from Boonville.

---

2. This quote, along with some background on the Battle of Boonville, is from Robert Selph
Henry, *The Story of the Confederacy* (New York: Grosset and Dunlap, 1936), 33 ff. Also helpful
here was a brief historical sketch of Boonville prepared by that city's Chamber of Commerce
and published as part of "Boonville, Missouri: A Great Place to Visit, A Better Place to Live."

3. Cosgrove, *An Old House Speaks,* 50.

From there he launched an attack on Boonville, blowing past the barricades on the roadways, surrounding enemy headquarters in a fortified courthouse building, and forcing the Union troops to surrender. This skirmish, too, was over quickly. But the second Battle of Boonville turned out to be something other than a joyous deliverance. It was merely a nightmare of a different kind: once the shooting stopped, Shelby's raiders plundered the stores and warehouses, commandeering food and supplies for the battles ahead, and unnerving the townspeople in the process. And this would not be Boonville's last brush with the Civil War. In the autumn of 1864, while General William Tecumseh Sherman was leading his victorious army on a scorched-earth campaign through Dixie, a large Confederate force, under the command of a former governor of Missouri, Sterling Price, mounted one final Confederate attempt to drive Federal forces out of Missouri. When his soldiers, twelve thousand strong, were repulsed by Union defenses at St. Louis, Price pushed them westward, up the rich Missouri valley toward Independence, destroying bridges, railroads, telegraph lines. Their line of march carried them through Boonville. The scars would not heal for a long time.

Marcus and Mary Jane Williams, who had brought their Virginia heritage to the frontier with them, were Southern sympathizers, so apprehensive about the blue-clad Federal troops occupying Boonville that they had buried the family silver under the grape arbor of their place to protect it from Yankee marauders.[4] At one point during the occupation, Marcus and Mary Jane took in three terrified Confederate soldiers, Missouri militiamen separated from their unit, and hid them for a time in a secret room in the attic of their home. Frightened townspeople never knew when more armed forces, regulars or guerrillas, Federals or Confederates, would turn up. At one point a row of houses overlooking the river caught fire, and a bucket brigade of women, children, and old men—virtually all who were left in the town—formed to fight it. But then word swept through town that William Quantrill's raiders, a murderous proslavery guerrilla band, were just then crossing the river into Boonville. The horsemen proceeded silently through the town and disappeared, but the volunteer bucket brigade had already dispersed in a panic and the house fires raged unabated. The fighting was never far away. Some weeks after the fire, when Boonville was threatened by another attack from the Federals, a one-armed, wild-eyed Presbyterian preacher named Painter, who had been run

---

4. Ibid., 53. Also Sara Lockwood Williams, unpublished Walter Williams biography, written in the late 1930s and housed in the Western Historical Manuscript Collection, University of Missouri. This manuscript, along with the Cosgrove memoir, was drawn upon extensively for this chapter. Both are especially valuable for their detailed insights about the members of the Walter Williams family.

out of Maine because of his overzealous interest in the Confederacy, together
with Marcus Williams and eight other Southern sympathizers were deployed to
hastily erected breastworks to defend the town. The attack did not materialize.
If it had, Boonville had precious few able-bodied men to put up a defense. When
the war finally ended, Boonville's shaken economy, depleted by shortages and
high taxes, defaulted loans and worthless construction bonds, and saddled with
its share of the state's massive war debt, would take years to recover.

On the surface, however, the Williams family seemed somehow to manage.
Marcus's business interests were all but ruined, but despite their modest means
the family lived in a handsome place, at 711 Morgan Street, near the Missouri
River but on a bluff high above it, only two blocks from Main Street and
the downtown shops. Morgan is reported to have been the first street laid out
when Boonville was platted—by the pioneer promoter Asa Morgan. The house
was brick, painted white, and was the pride of Marcus Williams, who had it
built during a period of genuine, if temporary, prosperity in 1852. Some of his
offspring were nearly grown by now. They had been born in a smallish cottage
about a block away. Walter, the youngest, would be the only child to be born
on Morgan Street.

Surrounded by a white picket fence, the house stood on a lot large enough
to accommodate several lesser dwellings, including a pottery, a storage shed, a
workshop, a stand-alone detached summer kitchen, and, later, a frame cottage
constructed when Willie, the second son, and his new bride elected to move in
with his parents. The main dwelling was called "The Big House," mostly to
differentiate it from the outbuildings, but the home was not as large as it may
have appeared to passersby and, in fact, the family more often than not felt
cramped in it.

The first floor contained a dining room, kitchen, and spacious parlor with
Axminster carpet, a mantle decorated by hand-painted China plates, rocking
chairs, and a large table usually piled high with reading matter. A tiny vestibule
gave onto a long porch, beyond which sloped beds of roses and a grape arbor.
The second floor contained only two large rooms, one shared by the four sons,
the other by the two daughters. Calico curtains provided a partition of sorts for
hanging up clothes; there were no closets, as such, nor were there yet indoor
bathrooms. Each bedroom was equipped with a wash basin and pitcher. Full
baths, required of all the children at least once each week, were endured in
a sturdy wooden tub that was dragged onto the kitchen floor on Saturdays.
Marcus and Mary Jane slept downstairs in the high-ceilinged parlor. This
arrangement, although largely dictated by circumstances, had its advantages.
Marcus could start the day by stoking up the morning fires in the front room

and for the kitchen stove, and in the evenings the parents were strategically positioned to note the arrivals and departures of their active young brood.

Susan Ann was the eldest of the Williams siblings, and in many ways the strongest. Bored by housework—as was her mother—and an indifferent dresser, she threw herself into civic and religious projects, her activist ways making her something of a youthful celebrity throughout the community. A voracious reader, she became the first in Boonville to complete the ambitious Chautauqua Circle reading course—a forerunner of the Chautauqua Literary and Scientific Circle, one of the oldest correspondence schools in the country— when it was offered in the area. She later organized other Chautauqua courses in surrounding towns. Sister Sue, as she was known, was admired by her brothers and sister for her intellectual brilliance, forgiven by them for her relentlessly Puritanical views and her perennial bossiness. Brother Willie, even when he was married and living in his own home, was afraid to be seen by her reading the Sunday newspaper, filled as it was with colorful features and entertainment sections; when Sister Sue was visiting him Willie hid the Sunday paper under his coat as he brought it into the house rather than face the withering lecture he would get from her if she saw him with it. Years later, when Walter Williams was invited to dinner at the London apartment of an old friend and her husband from Boonville days, the woman declined her usual after-dinner cigarette. "You notice I am not smoking," she announced. "I wouldn't want a brother of Sue Williams to see me smoking for I know she would disapprove of it."[5] Walter himself referred to her as "The Boss Man." Twenty-four years old when he was born, Sister Sue was still living at home at the time, but not for long. She was being courted by Emilius P. Lamkin, a huge man with close-cropped hair who taught school. His intellectual gifts were comparable to hers, but his personality was far less intimidating. They soon were married, and the home they moved into, a scholarly refuge of a house where every room was crowded with books, would become an important part of Walter Williams's boyhood.

The personality of Elizabeth Williams, the other daughter, was distinctly different from that of her peremptory older sister. Where Sue Ann was brittle and introverted, Betty Williams was a gracious, lovely girl who enjoyed wearing pretty things and making visitors feel welcome. As a child, Elizabeth delighted in housework as much as her elder sister and mother loathed it. She kept the pillows and chairs straight and picked the boys' clothing off the floor, usually while Sue was stretched out prone on the sofa absorbed in a historical novel or a religious magazine. She would later marry a Presbyterian minister,

---

5. Ibid.

the Reverend Horace Bushnell Banks, whom young Walter admired as "the most saintly man I have ever known." But without Betty Williams's leavening influence, a niece would write, "this minister of the Gospel might have been too visionary, too impractical, too unworldly; but she, with her keen sense of fun and her fervent love of family and kin, supplied the earthy, human elements so needed in country parsonages."[6]

Joseph Howard Williams, the oldest son, was likewise outgoing and friendly, an industrious lad who enjoyed running errands for his father, making new friends, visiting with townspeople. Never in robust health, he was the only one of the Williams clan of acceptable age for joining the Confederate army. But he did not. Perhaps, as a family member wrote, "it was on account of his bodily frailty."[7] For a time he lived in Clinton, Missouri, where he was a railroad freight agent. Later he would sell insurance for a time, then become a guard at the Missouri Penitentiary. His career would be cut short, however. He contracted tuberculosis and would die while in his fifties.

Willie—William Muir Williams—was more like Sister Sue, reflective, serious-minded, concerned about civic matters and current issues. He read a great deal about politics, was fond of argumentation, and was totally uninterested in any of his father's commercial ventures. Though it was a costly outlay for the family, Marcus managed to send the bright and promising young Willie to the Kemper school in Boonville for a time. At seventeen, Willie landed an appointment as deputy collector of Cooper County, a post he would retain for five years while reading law in the office of William Muir, a cousin for whom he had been named. Upon William Muir's death, Willie—now called Billy—took over much of his practice and expanded it, developing the firm into one of the most successful in the state. Billy himself became known as a lawyer's lawyer; attorneys from throughout the region consulted with him. His extensive, wide-ranging client list included the Presbyterian-Cumberland Church and the vast International Harvester Co., both of which he represented, among others, in cases before the Supreme Court of the United States. Though he was not regarded primarily as a criminal lawyer, he did defend Edward Butler, the St. Louis political boss, in what was then considered the largest criminal trial in Missouri history. And when Frank James, brother of Jesse, was arrested for robbing a train passing through central Missouri, Williams defended him.

Willie would be elected president of the Missouri Bar Association and Grand Master of the Missouri Masonic Lodge, and was appointed to fill a number

---

6. Cosgrove, *An Old House Speaks,* 95.
7. Ibid., 61.

of positions in state government, including the presidency of the Board of Managers of the Missouri Training School for Boys. In 1898, an unexpected vacancy occurred on the Missouri Supreme Court and Williams was named to the bench. He later declined to run for election to the court, preferring instead to return to his prosperous law practice in Boonville, but he was continually referred to thereafter as "Judge Billy."

While other members of the Williams family would become engaged in political causes, they did so mostly out of a sober sense of duty. Not so the third son, Louis Littlepage Williams, who got into politics for the sheer joy of it. From his early childhood, he was popular with his contemporaries and, naturally and effortlessly, a leader among them. He could organize a neighborhood athletic competition or an evening hayride with equal efficiency and zeal. An unusually large person with a great zest for living, Louis early on would get into law enforcement, first as a deputy U.S. marshal in Springfield and later as a deputy sheriff of Cooper County. He, too, studied law and was admitted to the Missouri bar, developing any number of successful contacts throughout the region. Later he ran for sheriff of Cooper County. In an intense, bitter campaign, he was defeated. A political chasm had developed in central Missouri by that time, a division of warring factions among the Democrats, and Louis Williams was simply swallowed up by it, as, indeed, his younger brother Walter would be in the years to come. In a way, however, the defeat proved a blessing in disguise, for it led Louis Williams to horizons far beyond Cooper County. After the campaign Louis Williams was approached by a Missouri senator and family friend, George G. Vest, with an invitation to the White House; there, following an amiable meeting with President Grover Cleveland, Louis was offered an appointment as United States Commissioner to the Territory of Alaska. Though his knowledge of Alaska was virtually nil, Louis accepted at once. Afterward, he scurried around for an atlas to ascertain where Alaska was situated. Arriving in Juneau, he was distraught at the remoteness and bleakness of the place. But his spirits were never down for long. He became one of Alaska's most ardent boosters, and would live there for twenty years.[8]

Louis, the second-youngest child, was eleven years old when Walter was born. Thus the new baby in the house was more than a blessed event, it was a renewal. The five other brothers and sisters and their aging parents doted on Walter, attending to him with a collective affection that bordered on reverence. Blond, blue-eyed, precocious, and with features that were almost delicate,

8. Ibid., 101.

young Walter delighted in their attention. On his third birthday, he was outfitted in a handsome new plaid kilt suit and placed on display at an afternoon tea party his mother had convened for the occasion. As the matrons of Boonville were making a great to-do over the child, one of them drew him to her knee. "Walter," she inquired, "when you grow up, which would you rather be, pretty or smart?" "Smart, of course," he replied promptly. "I'm already pretty." That family story, which was retold many times over the years, and which invariably would embarrass him to hear it, may have reflected a conceit on his part—or perhaps it was merely an accurate summary of what had been reported so often to him by his brothers and sisters and parents.

From the moment Walter was old enough to understand it—perhaps long before—his mother and Susan Ann read to him from the Bible. His mother's soft accents, still with a trace of the Virginia Tidewater country in them, contrasted vividly with the earnest, proprietary renditions of the Scriptures by Sister Sue. The entire family read and discussed a Bible passage each morning, and Sunday school lessons were taken seriously. Grace preceded every meal. Religious faith, rigorously practiced, kept the Williams family close.

As did conversation. Every member of the family was a capable and entertaining storyteller, and despite the great differences in age and temperament, each could usually find something in the day's activities to tell the others about in a way they would find interesting. Mealtimes were lively events, and the discussions that began around the dinner table often continued afterward before the fireplace in the parlor or, during the long summer evenings, on the white-columned porch that extended the breadth of the front of the Big House. Frequently friends and neighbors of varying ages joined in. There was much to talk about, with politics and government the most prominent of topics. As the harsh memories of the Civil War began to fade, there were further discomforts imposed by the Reconstruction; one provision of the new Missouri constitution adopted in 1865, for example, was a clause that denied the right to vote to anyone who refused to swear he had not sympathized with the South. That clause, especially unpopular in such pro-South communities as Boonville, was repealed in 1870, and two years later, when the election of a Democratic governor, Silas Woodson, signaled that Reconstruction was ending in Missouri, there was rejoicing throughout the community, and especially in the home of the Marcus Williams family.

The history of Boonville's formative period, meanwhile, was still being written. The town had been incorporated only twenty-five years before Walter was born. He and his brothers and sisters were personally acquainted with the children of Hannah Cole, the resolute widow from Kentucky who had been Boonville's first settler. Some Native Americans still lived in the vicinity, mostly in the woods by the old Boone Salt Lick. George Caleb Bingham, by now active in Missouri and national politics, owned a home nearby, on the river just upstream at Arrow Rock, and was a frequent visitor to Boonville. Indeed, most of the work on one of his most famous portraits, of Mrs. James T. Burch, was done at Boonville during the summer of 1877. The locals heard often of Bingham's anger during the war at his commanding officer, General Thomas Ewing, commander of the Eleventh Kansas Infantry Volunteers; after Quantrill's raiders had sacked the town of Lawrence in 1863, Ewing vowed revenge, and organized a search-and-destroy mission to be launched by his Federals against Confederate sympathizers and their homes in the region. Then a junior officer on his staff, Bingham begged Ewing to cancel the order, known as "Order Number Eleven." When he did not, the artist swore he would one day do what he could to bring Ewing's name into disrepute. This he did, with his powerful painting depicting the havoc wreaked on the civilians by Ewing's troops as they savaged the region. Entitled "Order Number Eleven," the work proved enormously popular, and lithographed copies of it were sold across the land. There were stories about other Civil War figures, too, and, especially, tales of former Confederate guerrillas living in the area who had turned to crime after the war.

Robberies of stagecoaches, trains, and banks in Missouri were commonplace. The notorious Jesse James was among many outlaws who roamed more or less freely throughout the region. One of his more successful outings came in Boonville's own Cooper County, near the town of Otterville, in 1876; the James gang held up a Missouri Pacific train, getting away with more than twenty thousand dollars in cash and whatever valuables the passengers had with them.[9] Sheriffs and their posses crisscrossed the hills and prairies in hot pursuit, but to no avail. Jesse James's career of lawlessness did not end until 1882, in St. Joseph; he was not brought to justice by the authorities, but assassinated by a member of his own gang. These were exciting stories of more than passing interest at the Williams dinner table: lawyer Billy, still living at home, had any number of illustrious clients, including Frank James. Much of the talk was about politics, and a number of county political leaders and state politicians were personal friends of Marcus and Billy Williams and visitors to the Big House on Morgan Street.

From the porch steps it was possible to observe other, less well-known, persons as well—the warm-hearted neighbor, Peter Selby, for instance, whose

---

9. Here, as elsewhere, the author has drawn upon Rucker, *Walter Williams,* 7 ff. A monument commemorating and explaining this railway heist by the James gang may be found near Highway 50 just east of Otterville, in southwestern Cooper County.

compassion for his fellow townspeople seemed boundless. In the darkness, the Williamses often observed a man with a lantern striding purposefully past their house. "There goes Peter Selby," one of them would say. "Wonder who's sick tonight?" And they could admire the industry of another neighbor, a tiny, wrinkled African American woman named Liza, who each morning swept not only her own sidewalk but also the half of Morgan Street in front of her property.

During the day, Walter found much to keep himself occupied. His mother's flowers and his father's fern garden, for instance, fascinated him. He asked endless questions about the plants, then astonished his parents later by re-membering, and repeating, all that he had heard. His brothers and sisters were much too old to be his playmates, but Walter was rarely alone unless he wanted to be: the Williams property, which included Marcus's backyard pottery among its wonders, drew the surrounding children like a magnet. So did his woodworking shop, and on any given afternoon the chances were good that Mr. Williams could be observed in action, molding clay into a bowl or fashioning an oak plank into a table leaf. There was an additional payoff from the carpentry shop: at the end of the day, the shavings were swept into a pile of what would become perfect kindling for the kitchen stoves and fireplaces in the neighborhood. Acting on instructions from their parents, the children armed themselves with baskets as they proceeded to the Williams property, then returned home with their share of the day's shavings. Often they would be invited into Mrs. Williams's kitchen for fresh-baked biscuits, which she would serve along with comb honey carefully extracted from the beehives that were situated near the backyard fence.

The Missouri River was the big attraction, of course. Steamboat traffic, which had peaked in the 1860s, remained brisk during the years when Walter was a boy. Some of the sidewheelers ranged up to 250 feet in length and were able to carry several hundred tons of freight and as many as four hundred passengers. The piercing whistle of an arriving steamboat set off a rush of town boys to the levee at the foot of Wharf Street Hill where they could see the cargo being unloaded as well as get a good look at the passengers, each of whom had paid sixteen dollars, cabin class, for the voyage from St. Louis to St. Joseph. Then there was the ferryboat, the *Birdie Brent,* commanded by Captain John Porter, who befriended the young people of Boonville and let them cross the Missouri with him for free whenever they chose. His was a brief voyage, from his sandy beach of a landing near the end of Water Street on the Boonville side, over to New Franklin and back again. The crossing was nothing if not routine, but Captain Porter never tired of it or of his humble vessel. Like another Missourian of the era, Mark Twain, he found the challenge of piloting a boat through swirling river currents an endlessly thrilling exercise. Of the *Birdie Brent,* Captain Porter once said,

> She's a living, moving thing that has more sense than many a man I have known. Why, you can hear her voice, her heart throb, her muscles expand and contract, hear her very blood circulating through her pipes.[10]

Unlike most of his contemporaries, Walter was but faintly interested in games and sports. He learned ice skating as a small boy, but his technique was never good and he often crashed. On one such outing, while attempting some fancy footwork to elude a branch protruding through the ice, he tumbled hard and broke his arm. Weeks later, on the first day he was able to play outside without benefit of cast and sling, he fell from an apple tree and broke the other arm. In a sandlot baseball game, he was struck by a fly ball and suffered a broken nose. Swimming, a sport that came naturally to most lads born in a river town, was never much fun for him either. Indeed, he may never have gotten into the water at all had not his exuberant brother Louis and some buddies tossed him into the Missouri River and watched as sheer instinct took over and he dogpaddled his way back to the bank. Bathing suits were unknown, at least in this circle, and the boys usually swam in the buff, a condition that dictated that most of the swimming be done at night. There was an unwritten rule that they wouldn't undress until three stars were visible. Walter eventually became an adequate swimmer, but never an enthusiastic one.

What Walter did love to do was read. Introduced to magazines and books by his mother and Sister Sue long before he started school, Walter found his greatest pleasures in the printed page. Before he learned to talk he learned his letters, from wooden toy blocks, and soon he was able to compare the block letters with those he saw in newspaper headlines. He pored over newspapers.

One evening, when he was eight years old, neighbors heard him crying so long and so loud that they worried about it. The next morning one of them asked what had been the matter. "Walter was angry," his mother replied, "because his father wouldn't let him read the President's message (in the *Boonville Advertiser*) until he had finished with it."

There were a few books in the Big House—"not many of them, but good ones," as he would recall later. Nearby, however, the holdings were much better. A kinsman, James Muir, had collected volumes of the classics. Most were beyond his years, but Walter pursued them with avidity. Sister Sue was by now married to the schoolteacher, Emilius Lamkin, and between them they had accumulated enough books to fill their small house. Encouraged to browse and

---

10. Emile R. Paillou, *Home Town Sketches* (Boston: The Stratford Co., 1926), 5 ff.

read to his heart's content, Walter discovered many works associated with Sue's Chautauqua Literary and Scientific Circle courses—*Recreations in Astronomy* and *Introduction to the Study of Latin and Greek Literature*—books that were far too advanced for him at the time, but which posed a challenge for the future. Sister Sue, whose missionary zeal matched her impressive intellect, coached the boy enthusiastically, and found in her studious youngest brother a promising and willing pupil.

Lessons of a different sort were learned outside the confines of the Boonville free school, which Walter would attend faithfully only until he was thirteen. Motivated by an elementary science class, young Walter and two close pals, Emile Paillou and Charlie Swap, decided to set up their own private chemistry laboratory in a corner of Marcus Williams's shop. Pooling their resources, the boys ordered apparatuses from a Philadelphia supply house—a few crucibles, a glass retort, various chemicals—from which they hoped to create certain gasses and other arcane compounds and to conduct numerous experiments with them. All the money the boys possessed was sunk into ordering the supplies; no allowance was made for the shipping costs—$1.95, cash on delivery—and the enterprise very nearly ended before it was begun. But their parents came to the rescue, donating enough to cover the shortfall, and the boys confidently began their work. In one sinister round of tests, they were able to soak corn seeds with poisons, thus growing ears of corn that could, and did, immediately kill any chicken that ate from them. On the other hand, they were able to lace hog feed with arsenic without liquidating livestock in the process. Most of their experiments, however, dealt with the creation of gasses, a risky business that often brought the lab to the edge of destruction. A number of the gaseous compounds they created were massively unstable, and one of them exploded. No one was injured, but a wall of Marcus Williams's workshop was blown out. Stoically, he rebuilt it, and the pursuit of science resumed. The chemicals themselves were acquired cheaply enough, either donated or sold at cost by friendly Boonville pharmacists. So excited were the young chemists about their experiments that other boys in the neighborhood grew resentful and jealous. As young Paillou would later recall, a delegation of them once slipped into the lab while it was unoccupied and vandalized it, overturning bottles and jars, emptying the contents on the floor. Anticipating that this would not be the end of it, the young chemists concocted an irritating chlorine gas, filled their jars and bottles with it, then conspicuously left the lab unattended. Some time later they had the satisfaction of seeing their tormentors flee from the lab, coughing and gasping for breath.[11]

---

11. Ibid.

By his twelfth birthday, Walter Williams was still a smallish lad, frail, slender, and somewhat effeminate, with a high, squeaky voice and a childish beauty. Indeed, die-hard members of the embittered political faction that had defeated Louis Williams for sheriff referred to young Walter as "Miss Williams."[12] In the view of his family, he was in pressing need of more physical activity than the reading couch or the chemistry lab could provide. Sister Sue, whose wishes carried great weight where Walter's upbringing was concerned, arranged for him to be sent for the summer to her father-in-law's farm near Jefferson City. The venture met with only mixed success. While appreciating the fresh air and the exercise, Walter found farm life, and particularly plowing, a difficult challenge. "I had difficulty making the mules go where I wanted them," he admitted. "In desperation, I urged them on and they bumped into a ravine, taking the plow and me with them. I never liked farming."[13]

He did, however, begin to like girls. His first love, from afar and totally unrequited, was Grace Kemper. Much older than Walter and widely conceded to be the most beautiful woman in Boonville, she wore her dark hair parted in the center and carried herself with a presence that captivated hearts throughout the town. Willie Williams, who was her contemporary, could give his smitten younger brother no encouragement: "No Boonville youth's life seemed complete until he had fallen in love with Grace Kemper," he said. Girls his own age were less remote, however, and Walter, in his own shy and reserved way, was popular with them. They liked his manners and his ability to talk about a rich variety of subjects and, especially, his thoughtfulness in complimenting a new costume or hair style. He would not go out on his first date until he was seventeen, but during the years before that occasion he attended numerous parties with girls and boys of his age group. A popular game was something called "Your Mental Photograph," in which the young guests were given cards upon which to respond to personality questions. One such card contained the following:

> Your name?. . . . . . . .Walter Williams
> If not yourself, who would you rather be?. . . . . . . .The sultan of Turkey
> Who is your favorite poet?. . . . . . . .T. B. Aldrich
> Your favorite prose writer?. . . . . . . .Washington Irving
> Your favorite slang phrase?. . . . . . . .I'll eat my hat raw.

As he entered his teen years, Walter stoutly continued to resist most sports activity, but he did become fond of bicycling. Riding his high-wheeler was, in fact, virtually the only rigorous physical exercise he ever truly enjoyed. He

---

12. Quoted in Sara Lockwood Williams, unpublished Walter Williams biography.
13. Ibid.

even promoted cycling expeditions to nearby towns, entered races—some of which he won—and became an avid reader of *Wheeling* magazine, through which he was able to locate pen pals among other cycling enthusiasts around the country. Then, in more characteristic fashion, he took up chess. Delighting in the intense intellectual problems posed by the game, he soon developed into a resourceful and proficient player.

When not reading or otherwise occupied in private pursuits, he could usually be found with his closest of close friends, Emile Paillou, Charlie Swap, and, latterly, George Russell. The four were of the same age and their interests and grand ambitions coincided to an astonishing degree. "What high ideals we had cultivated!" wrote Paillou later. "How we planned lives and service and honorable dealings while we were children . . . There was no formality in our association, no stated meetings, no rules. But it was taken for granted that we stood 'all for one and one for all.' "[14] At least some of their activities, however, concerned more earthly matters. "Many a card game ran into the small hours at Swap's office [Dr. Charles Swap, Charlie's father]," Paillou recalled. "We would send Walter Williams home at midnight in order that he might not be contaminated by the poker game that followed."

Walter also identified, in his own way, with the strong dramatic tradition that was so much a part of Boonville's history. The town's munificent Thespian Hall, built in 1857, replaced the Thespian Society's original log house, and served as Boonville's theater and auditorium, museum, library, and clubhouse. During the Civil War it became a hospital; a latter-day journalist visitor to Boonville found Thespian Hall "redolent with the age-old chain of swaying dances of nineteenth century peasants, pent-up with stirring memories and pain during the Civil War when men lay dying within its portals."[15] By his own admission, Walter was an undistinguished actor in his school's plays, mostly performed on the Thespian Hall stage: "I always had the insignificant parts," he would recall. "I was Hamlet's ghost, the butler, the watchman or policeman or whoever had the least to say and do." In terms of oratory and debate, however, he performed very well indeed, making up in preparation and conviction what he then lacked in presence and voice quality. Sharpening rhetorical skills he had had to develop, in the interest of self-preservation, to hold up his end at any Williams dinner table discussion, he was a nimble-witted debater. Additionally, he proved, before the footlamps at Thespian Hall and

---

14. Paillou, *Home Town Sketches,* 49–50. Obviously influenced by Alexandre Dumas, the youths nicknamed each other after the swashbuckling musketeers of French fiction. Walter Williams was Aramis.

15. *Kansas City Times,* January 16, 1937.

elsewhere, that he could deliver speeches and classical recitations with skill, if not yet with flair.

It was this interest in public speaking that was especially served by the T.P.C.,[16] an organization that, during this period, would become particularly meaningful in his social development, and which would do much to prepare him for the years ahead. What the initials "T.P.C." identified was supposed to be a secret, but most young people in Boonville knew they stood for the Time Passing Club. Though it had some of the mysterious trappings of a fraternal society—closed meetings, which only insiders who could remember that month's password could attend—the T.P.C. was, in fact, a self-improvement club devoted to uplifting its members "morally, mentally, and physically." Walter Williams was not a charter member when the club was founded, but he joined a few months later, and a number of the weekly meetings were held behind drawn curtains in the parlor of the Big House on Morgan Street.

The club had a no-nonsense constitution that, among much else, forbade members from chewing or smoking tobacco or eating during the business meetings, and the programs were usually devoted to serious matters. Each meeting included a ten-minute presentation by one member, followed by a twenty-minute discussion, to which each member was required to contribute. Walter Williams was known to have addressed the group on a number of occasions, once on the topic, "America's Great Statesmen," and another time on his reasons for believing in the Bible.

As membership swiftly grew from the original five to thirty, the T.P.C. became less secretive and, in fact, brought in outside speakers and opened up some of its meetings to the public. The Boonville YMCA, which had never quite succeeded, abruptly decided to disband, on the condition that the T.P.C. be incorporated and become a civic organization devoted to the community's good. Thus on March 6, 1883, Walter became a charter member of the revitalized T.P.C., which now openly called itself the "True Principles Club," and helped write the new constitution and by-laws. The reborn T.P.C. was largely devoted to things literary. No longer secret, the meetings were frequently held in Thespian Hall, and the club's mission was expanded. Perhaps the members' goals of self-improvement had already been attained, and it was now time to work on the community. In any event, the T.P.C. took as its project the development of a public library for Boonville, collecting books donated from private collections and raising funds to purchase new ones.

---

16. The minutes and other records of the T.P.C. are housed among the Walter Williams Papers at the Western Historical Manuscript Collection at the University of Missouri.

Encouraged by their heady initial successes, the T.P.C. members then adopted an ambitious scheme to raise still more money by sponsoring a lecture series, scheduling three celebrities of national reputation for talks in Boonville. Attendance turned out to be generally less than anticipated, however, and handling the details proved to be an unrewarding experience. T.P.C. members were shocked, for example, when one visiting speaker, a Rabbi Sonneschein of St. Louis, submitted to the club an expense account that included ten cents for "two glasses of beer." And Mrs. Belva Lockwood, then the first woman ever to run for president of the United States, drew an audience so small that T.P.C. members had to chip in $37.50 apiece—a princely sum—to cover the box office deficit. Through it all, Walter Williams labored tirelessly in the T.P.C.'s behalf. From the outset, he was a valuable worker in each of the club's projects; increasingly, he became a leader of most of them.

The T.P.C. lasted seven years. By 1887 the Boonville public library was on reasonably solid footing, and T.P.C. members decided the club should be disbanded, "its mission being ended," as one of them wrote at the time. The closing ceremony was a formal dinner held at Boonville's leading restaurant. There were two items of business: one was to adopt a resolution of sympathy for members who were about to get married; the other, more serious, was to present Walter Williams with a gold-headed walking cane in recognition of his service to the organization. He was said to have been its most valuable member. The T.P.C., perhaps more than any other youthful influence, had brought the bookish, introverted lad out of his shell and made him more comfortable with others—those beyond his family and closest friends—than he had ever been before. Through T.P.C. discussions, he learned much about persuasion. His friendships within the club were so enduring that he would hold reunions with some former T.P.C. members for as long as they lived. The organizational and leadership skills he had to develop in connection with T.P.C. projects would prove invaluable to him in the uncertain future that lay beyond the boundaries of Boonville. When the charter and records of the club were later auctioned off to the highest bidder, Walter Williams bought the entire lot for $2.50. All in all, it was quite a bargain.

3

A Toe in the Door

 I was thirteen years old. Two lines of employment appealed to me, a clerkship in a book store or a job in a newspaper office. It was a hot sunny day. The newspaper office was on the shady side of the street. I went first to it.

—Walter Williams

In the years to come, a national magazine would describe Walter Williams as "a man who quit school at thirteen" and the *New York Times* would say of him:

Walter Williams never had a Ph.D. degree. Nor had he a bachelor's degree. He did not have even a high school diploma.[1]

These and similar stories that circulated freely throughout his life were both right and wrong. He did quit school at thirteen—though he would resume his studies, if sporadically, later on. He was indeed awarded a high school diploma, class of 1879. But, in the strict bureaucratic sense, where pedagogues measure achievement in terms of classroom subjects passed and school years completed, he did not earn it.[2]

The Boonville free public schools were not formally organized until 1868, well after the Civil War had ended, and the resolute vanguard of teachers and administrators who established the curriculum and policies were obliged to make up the rules as they went along. Walter Williams entered the system as a first grader in 1871 and remained in school for six full years. After that, he dropped out to work at a number of part-time jobs, most often for his father, helping in the pottery and other family pursuits. For portions of two subsequent winters he attended some classes in Clinton, Missouri, living with Sister Sue and her husband, who by now had become Clinton's superintendent

1. July 30, 1935. The "man who quit school at thirteen" quote was from Mary B. Mullett, "A College President Who Quit School at Thirteen," *American Magazine,* February 1931, 19.

2. Williams did not deny published reports that he never completed high school and, indeed, told friends later he had no high school education. See among others Eric G. Schroeder to the Missouri School of Journalism, March 5, 1989, Williams Papers. The adoring, unpublished biography of Williams written by his wife, Sara Lockwood Williams, though invaluable on so many points, is suspect in others, especially concerning his education: she proclaimed, for example, that Williams "graduated [from Boonville School] with highest honors."

of schools. Shortly before Walter's sixteenth birthday, however, the Boonville school made plans to hold its first graduation. The graduates-to-be, several of them, had started school when he did. Walter Williams asked to be graduated along with them. His was a remarkable request, but the authorities consented, permitting him to rejoin his old class in time to be graduated with it.[3]

And so in May of 1879, Walter Williams and five of his contemporaries became the first class ever to be graduated from Boonville High School.[4] Much was made of the ceremony, and many townspeople turned out for it. Before the six diplomas were awarded, there was a substantial program of speeches and declamations. Walter Williams, his squeaky voice under tight control, spoke on "The Instability of Human Government." By all accounts, the commencement exercises were a great success.

That he received a diploma at all is more of a tribute to the sympathetic judgment of the Boonville school administration than a coldly accurate reflection of his scholastic record. But despite the awkward gaps in his formal education, Williams was clearly an impressive teenager: he had read most of the books in the substantial collection of his cousin, James Muir—who was said to have the largest private library in the state—as well as in the Boonville Public Library. He had also plowed through many of the books owned by Sue and her husband, and he had at least some rudimentary knowledge of Latin and Greek. His interest in classical languages had been whetted by one of his Boonville schoolteachers in earlier days, Ohio-born Professor D. A. McMillan, who had permitted Walter to study with him at his room in the Boonville's City Hotel in the evenings. Then a bachelor, McMillan was glad to pass the lonely evenings in the company of an appreciative student who was willing to work hard at mastering the fundamentals of Greek grammar. An enthusiastic and gifted teacher, McMillan received no compensation for his after-hours tutoring, Williams recalled later, "except in the affectionate regard of his pupil." Well beyond that, Williams would write later, Professor McMillan "did more to help me than any other man, for he taught me to laugh at my funny looks and my funny voice."[5] The education Williams had managed was, by his own admission, "casual and superficial," but he shrewdly regarded his reading, as well as his tutorials with Professor McMillan, as "really a vestibule to larger

---

3. Williams to Mrs. D. A. McMillan, January 31, 1931, Williams Papers.

4. The other graduates are identified in school records as R. N. Morris, L. W. Edwards, L. E. Frost, Mary Morris, and Nannie Hulett.

5. Williams to Houston Harte, July 10, 1919. Harte, who later became a highly successful publisher and president of the Harte-Hanks newspaper chain, published Williams's letter in the *Central Missouri Republican* ("Dean Williams Tells of His First Job Here"), July 10, 1919.

study and wider interest."[6] Walter's leadership and public speaking skills and capacity for service to the town had been amply demonstrated through the T.P.C. He stood out, especially in a small community, where every child is the community's child. His family had high hopes for him, and so did the town. And if the school administration cut a corner or two in awarding him a high school diploma, nobody in Boonville seemed to mind.

Whenever the subject of his future had come up for discussion at home, his mother would say: "Walter will do one of two things. Either he will sit in an editorial sanctum, or he will have a bookstore."[7] He already knew a bit about printing, having hung about the office of the *Boonville Topic* long ago on Saturdays and summer holidays, thrusting paper into the sheet-fed press and performing other roustabout chores. Eleven years old at the time, he was so small that the foreman had to lift him up to the perch where he had to stand to feed the press. He received no pay, and probably expected none, but he did feel that he had made a start—not a foot through the doorway, as he would say later, but at least a toe, pointed in the direction of a career.

There were many other vocational possibilities, of course, but each was, for him at that moment, either unsatisfactory or unattainable. He was never much interested in his father's various business endeavors, and he had neither the desire nor the resources to go into farming. Politics was important to him, even then, and his family was supportive and well connected, but any thought of a political career was outrageously premature. His Presbyterian preacher, pleased with Walter's deep religious faith and speaking ability and leadership skills, encouraged him to consider a life in the ministry. But the ministry required a specific and unambiguous spiritual call that he had not received. He briefly considered following two of his brothers into careers in the law; as a boy he'd often watched his brother Billy argue a case in the Cooper County courthouse, and he was impressed with the intellectual demands posed by a legal career. But the law was a lofty profession, open only to those who could afford to complete years of expensive study in preparation for it. For Walter Williams, youngest member of aging parents in humble circumstances, a college education was out of the question. He needed a job.

Years later, Williams was fond of recalling the dilemma he faced that hot summer day when he walked down Boonville's still-unpaved Main Street to look for work, torn between seeking a job in a bookstore and one in a newspaper office, when he elected to try the newspaper first because it was situated on the

---

6. Walter Williams manuscript, 3.
7. Mullett, "A College President," 29.

shady side of the street. Indeed, some old-time Boonville residents could point to the very oak tree under which young Walter is supposed to have stood while making up his mind.[8] For whatever the reason, he climbed the stairs to the third floor of the building occupied chiefly by A. H. C. Koontz, who sold groceries and general merchandise, and presented himself to Colonel H. A. Hutchison and his partner, Francis M. Caldwell, proprietors of the *Topic*. He told them he needed work and would like to be hired. Within minutes, they made him an offer: a salary of seventy-five cents per week, payable every Saturday night. He accepted on the spot. If, indeed, he ever crossed the street in search of a counteroffer from the bookseller, there is no record of it.

His job would be that of a printer's devil—an apprentice—and despite the title it was an honorable vocation. Benjamin Franklin and Isaiah Thomas had begun their careers as printer's devils, as had many others prominent in American journalism history. The particular chores of a newspaper apprentice varied from shop to shop, but the work was invariably strenuous as well as dirty. (Early printer's apprentices were young, mischievous, and, like Isaiah Thomas and Benjamin Franklin, apt to skip town in search of something better. Because of their image as flight risks, and because their faces were often blackened by prolonged association with inks and the billowing black smoke of the casting cauldron, and perhaps for any number of other reasons as well, the apprentices in a newspaper shop were universally known throughout the trade as printer's devils.) Williams became the second devil in the *Topic* office. The other, an older man who would serve as his immediate mentor, was Humphrey Richardson, an African American who had been with the weekly newspaper for some time.

There was plenty of work for both. Walter's duties included sweeping out the shop, a more or less continuous exercise, as well as helping "Humph" Richardson in cleaning the ink-coated rollers, picking up letters of type and replacing them in their individual compartments, running errands, addressing in longhand (he no longer printed up everything he wrote, though his hand-writing remained barely legible) the subscription list, opening and sorting the day's mail, collecting bills, and soliciting advertising and subscription orders. One other task—by far the most interesting and rewarding—involved setting three sticks,[9] or thirty to forty-five lines, of poetry that always ran on page one of the *Topic*. The verse was usually selected by Hutchison, a tall, thin man

---

8. Rucker, *Walter Williams,* 27.

9. A stick, or composing stick, is a tiny tray in which individual letters of type are arranged in desired sequence before they are assembled onto a page. A "stickful" of type is about two inches' worth.

whose friends called him "Shad." Hutchison wrote poems himself, and those who had seen them thought they were pretty good. In his absence, the poetry was selected by his business partner, F. M. Caldwell, whose long, white beard made those who saw it think of him as a Hebrew prophet. He was indeed a religious man, an elder in the Presbyterian church, and the poetry he selected frequently dealt with spiritual matters.[10]

Williams found great joy in setting type, and he quickly became expert at it. His small fingers were ideal for picking the metal letters out of the tiny compartments in which they were housed, and the linear progression of it all—assembling letters into words, words into lines—connected perfectly with his budding sense of logic and order and beauty. The letters themselves are an abstraction, and as such can possess a clarity and purity all their own. Art and morality may or may not be tied together, as the British typographer Eric Gill has written, but the art of typesetting somehow seems more straightforward and freer from adulteration than most arts.[11] It is an honest craft, physically and intellectually demanding but not without its rewards for a practitioner who loves words. Williams did love words, and the underlying pleasure of typesetting stemmed from his certainty that the metal type tray would provide a stable and secure home for them, if only for a brief time. It was highly satisfying.

He finished his three sticks of poetry so swiftly that he took on other typesetting tasks as well, assembling news articles and features for the rest of the paper. Before long, Williams felt bold enough to change the copy as he set it, sharpening a sentence or clarifying a thought. This was risky business, since these improvements meant changing material written by his masters. But they were wise and tolerant men, and encouraged him to keep at it, so long as he got his facts straight and all the words spelled right. There was hell to pay if he did not, especially from Caldwell. "He impressed upon all his employees the need for accuracy, especially in spelling and in grammar," Williams would later recall. "He never forgave a printer who could not spell correctly."[12]

From typesetting the writing of others, the youthful printer's devil soon graduated to typesetting words he had written himself. The proprietors of the *Topic* allowed him to write a few news items, mostly concerning events he had happened upon while running errands. Shortly thereafter he spent more time reporting the news, less time sweeping the floor and cleaning the press. He found that he could, in fact, hand-set some articles directly into type without

---

10. Williams to Harte, July 10, 1919.
11. Eric Gill, *An Essay on Type* (London: Dent, 1960), 21.
12. Walter Williams manuscript, 6.

first writing them out in longhand. His instinctive grasp of how a news article should be organized permitted him to outline news copy at the type stand, to create it and fashion it into metal type at the same time.

His writing was rigorously critiqued by his two bosses. Caldwell was a stickler for accuracy and thoroughness, while Hutchison, the poet, emphasized style and encouraged thoughtful analysis and literary references. Both men taught him a great deal. He was an apt pupil who took criticism well. Within a few months, Hutchison awarded him responsibility for writing and editing much of the routine news of community happenings. His pay was now three dollars a week.

But for all his precociousness, he was still a lad with a streak of mischief in him that, on one occasion, at least, got the *Topic* into a nasty political squabble. The central figure was Humphrey Richardson, who, in addition to his printer's devil duties in the *Topic*'s back shop, had become a leader of some stature among the Republican Negroes of Cooper County. (Fully aware that the *Topic* staff members were impassioned Democrats, "Humph" was fond of commenting that his bosses on the paper were about the only Democrats he might ever bring himself to endorse, should they seek elective office.) Richardson and Williams had become fast friends, and the tall, sinewy black man went to great lengths to shield his smallish companion from much severe manual labor. The two engaged in prolonged conversations that often extended well past working hours, and as Walter's professional beliefs began taking shape he realized that "Humph" Richardson was an important influence on them. One day, however, the lighthearted banter that characterized their relationship misfired, triggering what turned out to be an ugly political confrontation between Republican leaders in the county and the proprietors of the *Topic*. Typesetting an article about a meeting of Cooper County Republicans, Williams found the piece a tad shorter than expected, so he added a sentence—a wicked one at that—to fill out the column: "Among the Republicans of rank at the convention," the addition stated, "Humphrey Richardson was the rankest." The local GOP hierarchy was not amused, and a delegation of angry Republicans thundered up the stairs to demand satisfaction from the owners of the *Topic*. No punches were thrown, but only because Messrs. Hutchinson and Caldwell, diplomats both when they needed to be, were able to calm things down, apologizing repeatedly for their protégé's youthful indiscretion. For his part, Humph delighted in the notoriety. "My little editor!" he cried, snatching Walter into his massive arms, as he often did, parading him around the office.[13]

---

13. Ibid., 8; Rucker, *Walter Williams*, 37.

Others in the Missouri newspaper fraternity, meanwhile, were beginning to take notice of Boonville's precocious teenager. Colonel J. West Goodwin, prominent in the state press association and publisher of the weekly *Sedalia Bazoo* (loud talk), appointed Williams his part-time correspondent from Boonville. Walter jumped at the chance for additional income and for the recognition this additional, sideline newspaper forum provided. Goodwin, whose outspoken editorials and satiric columns had made the *Bazoo* famous—it was perhaps the most widely quoted community newspaper in the state at that time—proved to be a tough editor, and Williams profited from the severe reworking his copy absorbed from Goodwin. Like most editors in the region, Colonel Goodwin was an ardent Democrat; unlike many of them, however, he prided himself on balance and fairness in his news columns. His primary contribution to the journalistic development of the green but promising Williams was to discipline him into controlling the bias that had characterized much of his writing. "Little that I wrote escaped Colonel Goodwin's blue pencil," Williams recalled. "My writing was too opinionated for the news columns of the *Bazoo,* and not well balanced enough for the editorial columns of that lively journal."[14] Equally important, in Colonel Goodwin Williams made a powerful friend, one whose support through the Missouri Press Association would serve him very well indeed in the years ahead.

There were positive developments on the social front as well, though they were less dramatic. As Williams grew into young manhood he began to lose his childish prettiness. His high-pitched voice and somewhat prissy mannerisms moderated and became less offensive. He was not so beautiful now, but considerably more attractive. Still, as a relative put it, he had much to overcome.[15] While he belonged to several clubs and kept busy with their activities and projects, he fretted that his romantic life was woefully deficient.

And this was at a time when Boonville society had never been more joyous and expansive. The old hardships following the Civil War were finally, after a generation, fading into distant memory. Exuberant young people had taken center stage, and their gaiety and activism energized the quiet river town. Future teachers and businessmen studied at the Kemper Academy, while the law offices attracted young prospects studying for the Missouri bar; dozens of teenagers, some of them bound for careers in medicine or the ministry, graced the halls of Boonville school. Lovely girls—"with slender, wasp waists," one

14. Walter Williams manuscript, 8.
15. Cosgrove, *An Old House Speaks,* 117.

Boonvillian recalled, "their hair done up in intricate fashions of braids and curls and waterfalls"[16]—formed social clubs of their own, challenging their youthful male counterparts to a nonstop succession of parties. Clubs organized picnics and excursions and boat rides in summer, skating and tobogganing and long hikes across the crunching snow in winter. This was a grand era, and Walter Williams felt he was too often only on the fringes of it.

Along with nineteen of his fellow members of the Clover Club, he developed—and probably wrote and no doubt set in type—a farcical brochure that was tucked away inside Valentines and mailed to Boonville's loveliest maidens. "Proposals Wanted," the brochure announced: "Herewith is presented a list of marriageable members of the Clover Club of Boonville with qualifications, good, bad and indifferent." The concluding entry read, in part:

Walter Williams

His carriage erect, his manner stern. Is of literary taste intermingled with a hankering for the beautiful. He has done much for the entertainment of his fellow beings, by his fathering and contriving many schemes whereby an evening's entertainment has been made to bring two-fold pleasure. His heart, in relation to the fair sex, might be termed an unknown quantity, so inactive has it seemed in that connection. Young ladies, here is the booby prize.[17]

The first girl he ever escorted anywhere was Annie Machette, dark-haired daughter of Boonville's Baptist preacher, a choice that was, literally, the luck of the draw: with the T.P.C. annual party just ahead, the club members drew names for dates and Walter drew Annie's. Shyly, he wrote her an invitation to the party and paid a lad a dime to deliver it. Her acceptance, he realized, presented a mixed blessing. On one hand, alas, he knew that Annie was already spoken for; she was the sweetheart of a young doctor-to-be, Richard Holman, whom she later would marry, and doubtless would have preferred his company to Walter's. On the positive side, however, the Baptist parsonage where she lived was situated next door to the place where the party would be held, so young Walter escaped having to hire a "glass front" buggy, the transportation of choice for sporty young T.P.C. members. "As I was making 75 cents a week at the *Topic,*" Williams recalled later, "I couldn't afford to pay for many carriages."[18] His boyhood scrapbook—he kept copious records, even then—contained a substantial collection of notes of invitation and reply. One response, from a young lady who did not sign her name, was especially candid: "Mr. Williams: Your touching little epistle just reached me. In the absence of my sister, and

16. Ibid.
17. Quoted in Sara Lockwood Williams, unpublished Walter Williams biography, 11.
18. Ibid.

also in the absence of anyone else to go with, I accept your invitation."[19] How that particular date turned out is not recorded.

At work, he was more successful. By now, his apprenticeship completed to the total satisfaction of the owners, Williams had been awarded a title, that of local editor. While not changing his duties much at all—he was already writing most of the local news anyway—the designation recognized his growth and the contribution he was making to the paper. Beyond that, he gained a measure of control of the paper's content, picking and choosing the stories he wanted to see printed. By the end of 1884, still before his twentieth birthday, he had completed nearly five years with the *Topic,* competing vigorously with its chief rival, the *Boonville Advertiser,* a weekly Francis Caldwell had begun in 1862, then later sold, and the *Central Missourier,* edited by John Haller. That November Williams wrote perhaps the biggest story the *Topic* had carried in quite a while: it was the joyous local reaction to Grover Cleveland's victory over James G. Blaine. The election had been a hard-fought one; though there were issues aplenty—the farmers and factory workers were hurting, private interests were grabbing up public lands, Blaine had been implicated in a financial scandal— the candidates instead had waged a bitter campaign of personal attacks. The election was a cliff-hanger, with a difference of only about thirty thousand votes between winner and loser in a popular vote of nearly ten million. In the Democratic stronghold that was Boonville, the election of the first Democratic president since before the Civil War was a cause for celebration. Caught up in the spirit of the event, Williams penned a windy, effusive account, cheerfully throwing whatever journalistic objectivity Colonel Goodwin had taught him into the breeze:

> On Saturday morning at 10 o'clock the courthouse bell was rung and Democrats met there to prepare for a rousing ratification on Saturday night. Captain Joseph Kinney's cannon was brought across the river and planted in Main Street. An anvil was placed at the top of river hill and another one at the corner of Main and Spring Streets. Dry goods boxes were piled high in the streets. Chinese lanterns were lighted, red fires burned, bonfires blazed, cannons roared, anvils boomed, and firecrackers, rockets, guns, etc., all over the city, mingled with joyous shouts of a thousand enthusiastic Democrats cheering in honor of the grand victory of honesty over corruption.[20]

It would be one of the last pieces he wrote for the *Topic.* The Boonville newspaper scene, livelier and far more competitive than the size of the community might indicate, was about to undergo dramatic change. Samuel W. Ravenel,

---

19. Ibid.
20. *Boonville Topic,* November 9, 1884.

part-owner of the rival *Advertiser* and the well-known and outspoken editor of it, bought the *Topic* from Francis Caldwell and Colonel Hutchison, then moved some of his key production people from his old paper to his new one. Then two of Boonville's wealthiest bankers and businessmen, Lon Vest Stephens and William Speed Stephens, bought controlling interest in the *Advertiser* and moved quickly to plug the gaping holes on the staff. Francis Caldwell, the burdens of *Topic* ownership now safely behind him and with retirement shortly ahead, was content to head up the *Advertiser*'s printing and production side. Lon V. was an imposing figure with strong political aspirations; he would become a brilliant state treasurer and, in 1896, governor of Missouri. He determined broad editorial policy, holding the *Advertiser* on its unremitting pro-Democrat course. And to edit the paper, to write the news and many of the editorials, the new owners hired Boonville's most impressive twenty-year-old, Walter Williams.

The *Advertiser*'s owners were determined to make their paper fully competitive in a tiny, but hot, newspaper market. At the outset, they doubled the size of the paper, from four pages each week to eight, prepared to lose money on an improved product for a time in hopes the additional advertising and circulation revenue income would soon catch up. It did. They also changed the typography of the paper, giving the readers a sprightly new look, and they resolved to provide Boonville with the nearest that town had ever seen to an error-free publication. Mustering up enough courage to invite trouble, the owners of the *Advertiser* boldly offered a reward of ten dollars in gold to the subscriber who found the greatest number of mistakes over a three-month period. Forty-one readers went after the prize, which ultimately went to an eagle-eyed Methodist preacher, the Reverend C. M. Hawkins, who, before receiving his call to the pulpit, had once earned his living as a typesetter. He was able to detect 172 errors—misspelled words, incorrect divisions of words hyphenated between lines, out-of-place typefaces, and the like—in the thirteen issues. This was substantially more mistakes than the confident new *Advertiser* ownership had expected, though they added, somewhat defensively, that those thirteen issues carried an estimated total of 1.8 million characters of type. Even so, the contest was regarded as a great success for the *Advertiser,* if only because Boonville's other two newspapers refused to offer their readers a comparable opportunity.[21]

The *Advertiser* was also an unusually well-printed newspaper. Francis Caldwell and two local printing craftsmen, L. J. Stahl and his son Phil, saw to that. They studied the layout and design of good newspapers elsewhere and

---

21. Rucker, *Walter Williams,* 35–40.

settled on a clean, modern, polished graphic design for the *Advertiser* that made it appear to emanate from a far larger market than it did.

But the *Advertiser*'s chief attraction was not its typography but its accurate and comprehensive reports, written with a clear, fresh style by Walter Williams. He wrote an occasional personal column as well, its tone reflecting his growing assurance of his own editorial ability and of his comfortable relationship with his readers. One such piece, called "A Look at Our Letters," read in part:

> There is in the file in our office a letter from an individual in which, after asking for the insertion of a half-column obituary, he says: "Please send me your paper. I will pay for it soon." We will occasionally forgive a deadbeat but a liar never.
>
> In the same mail came a letter from a lady who is not only an old subscriber but an appreciative one. She writes: "Enclosed find postal note for which please send the *Advertiser* to my friend (naming her). Your paper is so good that I'd like to send it to all my friends."
>
> And an old yap from North Missouri who can't tell the difference between Sunday and Santa Claus has the effrontery to send $2.00, the amount due on the paper (that part's all right) and to add: "You may stop the *Advertiser*. It has too little general news and too much about Boonville and Cooper County. And it is too derned Democratic." The yappo didn't know that was a compliment. We are certain he didn't intend it as such.[22]

Williams was determined that one and all should know that he, and he alone, was editor of the *Advertiser*. When older brother Billy, perhaps in a patronizing gesture, wrote two editorials for the paper and slipped them underneath the front door of the newspaper office, Walter promptly deposited them in the woodstove. More amused than chagrined, Billy stuck to his law practice and never questioned Walter's editorial judgment again.[23]

The slight, well-mannered young editor knew how to make his point. One episode, recalled by his boyhood pal Emile Paillou years later in *Home Town Sketches*, is illustrative:

> The paper had published an item saying that a young man, whom we will call Henry James, Jr., had been in Boonville, "hobnobbing with his many friends," Henry being the son of a farmer of substance living about five miles from Boonville.
>
> Now Henry James, Sr., had a fixed definition in his mind for "hobnobbing" and his idea was that it meant bacchanalian carousal—in other words, drunk and disorderly. So Mr. James hied himself to Boonville, and called on the editor with blood in his eye. For what had his steady, sober son been "written up" in so outrageous a manner?
>
> In vain did Mr. Williams by soft answer endeavor to turn away his wrath, as he explained that hobnobbing was a perfectly innocent procedure. No, sir! Mr. James

---

22. Ibid., 45.
23. Cosgrove, *An Old House Speaks*, 115.

came for an apology and he would have that or blood. So the editor, having no blood to spare, had to agree to straighten things out in the next issue.

Do you know Walter Williams? Ever read or hear one of his apologies? Well, this time he just had to square himself and this is how he did it. The next edition of the *Advertiser* carried in prominent position this item: "Henry James, Sr., was in Boonville this week hobnobbing with his many friends."

I could tell worse ones on Walter Williams, but it is unsafe to stick a pin into the business end of a mule for, when you come to, you are likely to be looking up into the face of a white-clad nurse at the hospital murmuring, "What happened?" He [Walter Williams] has a mulish attribute. He hits back.[24]

The young editor's temper was, in fact, a subject of some discussion among family and close friends, and he was frequently admonished to control it. Walter's boyhood idol and mentor, Professor D. A. McMillan, had once presented him with a Bible in which he had inscribed on the flyleaf: "He that is slow to anger is better than the mighty, and he that ruleth his spirit than he that taketh a city."[25]

In December 1885, the *Advertiser*'s owners decided to go all-out for a Christmas edition that would truly impress the Boonville audience as well as generate enough advertising revenue to assure the owners a Merry Christmas. For his part, Williams ambitiously sent off letters to celebrities around the country, inviting them to contribute photographs and articles. An astonishing number—including the columnist Eugene Field and the Chief Justice of the United States, Oliver Wendell Holmes—did so. Ad sales likewise were excellent, and the resulting Christmas edition ran to twenty-four pages, a record for that community. Both in terms of its editorial quality and the advertising income it produced, the Christmas edition garnered national attention as well as enthusiastic local applause; Williams had shrewdly sent copies to the newspaper trade journals as well as a number of metropolitan dailies, and congratulatory messages poured in from far and wide. In a triumphant editorial afterward, Williams wrote of the Christmas edition: "We have demonstrated the capacity of a country newspaper."

There was still another result, an unintended one, of the special edition that Christmastide. In effect it catapulted Williams into part-ownership of the paper. Francis Caldwell—no longer known as "Young Frank," he was now "Uncle Frank"—the painstaking craftsman responsible for getting those twenty-four pages of type and advertising produced, had worked at fever pitch throughout the month of December. The pressure, self-imposed, to do good work even under extraordinary circumstances drained his strength and spirit. Just after

24. Paillou, *Home Town Sketches,* 228–29.
25. Cosgrove, *An Old House Speaks,* 116.

the Christmas edition came off the press, he decided to retire. Uncle Frank
sold his stock to Williams.

His would be a minority holding, and details of the number of shares and
their sales price—or how they would be paid for—were not forthcoming. On
January 8, 1886, Williams published this discrete notice on the *Advertiser*'s
editorial page:

> The interest in the *Advertiser* heretofore owned by F. M. Caldwell has been
> purchased by Walter Williams, Mr. Caldwell retiring. The Advertiser Publishing
> Co. will hereafter consist of L. M. Stahl, Phil W. Stahl, and Walter Williams. The
> last named continues as the editor of the *Advertiser,* and there will be no change in
> the business management or editorial policy of the paper.[26]

But as Williams had now become a copublisher as well as man of property, he
had also mired himself deeper and deeper into what was becoming an ugly—
and at times highly personal—newspaper war. Newspaper competition for
circulation, for advertising revenue, and for editorial and political leadership
was hardly new. As early as 1840 in New York, for example, Park Benjamin of
the *New York Signal* declared a "Moral War" against James Gordon Bennett's
Herald, alleging indecency, blasphemy, libel, and blackmail. The following
year, when the mercurial Horace Greeley began his *New York Tribune* as a
"respectable" cheap paper, his competitors refused to do business with anyone
patronizing the *Tribune.* Boonville, Missouri, was not New York, certainly, but
in some ways it was even more competitive: three newspapers were struggling
against each other for survival in a community of fewer than five thousand
souls where there were precious few subscribers and advertisers, and no
Boonville paper could long sustain serious losses of either. The situation could
be characterized much the same way a cynical Henry Kissinger would later
describe the ferocity of politics inside some universities. Academic infighting
was so intense, Dr. Kissinger snorted, because the stakes involved were so
small. Increasingly, Walter Williams found himself defending the *Advertiser*
against editorial assaults from the *Topic* or the *Central Missourier:*

> Whatever the editor of the *Advertiser* may do, he never intentionally slanders or
> lies about anyone. He never allows the columns of this paper to be disgraced by
> language fit only for bar-room brawlers or blackguards. He never prints vulgar
> or obscene reading matter. He never, with intent to injure, steals the property of
> another and then boasts about it. He does not beg endorsements of his course and
> then decline to publish in full such endorsements because they contain a good
> word spoken for a neighbor. He does not publish atheistic and infidel reading

---

26. Rucker, *Walter Williams,* 46. Lon V. Stephens did not explain his reason for getting out
of the newspaper business just then, but perhaps he sensed the rancorous battle then beginning
would do his political aspirations no good.

matter to oblige his friends and please the public. He does not servilely imitate a contemporary or toady to anyone. The *Advertiser* endeavors to be at all times decent, truthful and fair. When it accidentally errs, as all papers must occasionally through misinformation, it always in a manly, honorable fashion corrects such errors. It takes care of itself, asks no one's sympathy and pleads no baby act. It would do well for the very respectable gentlemen who edit the *Topic,* if they could, with truth, say as much. Evidently they think that blackguardism in a newspaper is journalistic courtesy; that harsh epithets are sound arguments and that filthy abuse wins friends. They are welcome to such opinion.[27]

Though it was less of a threat than the *Topic,* the *Central Missourier* also assailed the *Advertiser* on occasion, attacks that inevitably provoked counterattacks. In January of 1886, as an example, Williams joined a number of other local churchgoers in an attempt to convince a prominent evangelist, Sam Jones, to conduct a week-long revival meeting in Boonville. The *Central Missourier* immediately editorialized against the plan, arguing that if any evangelizing needed doing then the local preachers could do it better. In angry response, Williams wrote:

> The *Central Missourier* throws one of its characteristic sneers at us every issue since we began our efforts toward securing Sam Jones in Boonville for a week. We did not expect the *Missourier's* support, financial or moral, and we do not need it, yet we would think since it has been trying to preach us a sermon on "patronizing home institutions," that it should not at the same time be trying to injure the city further than it has already done.[28]

The rivalry between the *Topic* and the *Advertiser* grew increasingly bitter. Though he gave as good as he got, Williams sickened of it. He envied the fellowship and clannishness of other professions: "Let a minister be guilty of a wrong-doing and his fellows shield him to the utmost so the cloth may have no stain of evil," he would write later, in a piece expressly not for a local audience in Boonville. "A lawyer's misdeeds must be so rank as to smell to heaven before he is disbarred. A physician's malpractice is seldom told of by his brother-doctor's tongue." On the other hand, there are "newspaper wars, disgraceful personal encounters, spiteful editorials, green with jealously and bitter with gall, that are all too frequent."[29] And, in the clannish small town of Boonville, there were few secrets and even fewer places of refuge. A rival editor attacked in print would likely encounter the author of the attack shortly thereafter, perhaps strolling near the courthouse on Main and High Streets, and with a

---

27. Quoted in Rucker, *Walter Williams,* 48.
28. Ibid., 49.
29. Walter Williams, "Relations of National and State Associations," a speech delivered to the Missouri Press Association June 12, 1888, and later published in the *Missouri Press Association Convention Proceedings* (Columbia, 1888), 21.

dozen or more fascinated townspeople watching expectantly. Boonville's noisy and public newspaper competition affected Walter Williams's outlook on not only his job but also the future. He would hate newspaper wars, large and small, as long as he lived.

On January 22, 1885, his mother died. Walter was nearly twenty-one years old by now, still living at home, still adoring the woman he would later describe as "a brave and gentle spirit whose influence unto good is yet a fragrant memory in the community." As a child she had come to Boonville, her family one of the first to dwell there. Petite, soft-spoken, almost frail, she still seemed more Virginia gentry than prairie pioneer. But Mary Jane Littlepage Williams had known how to cope, and in her own quiet, warmhearted way she did much to transform the rough-hewn frontier settlement into a town of substance and, for the most part, civility. The cluster of crude dwellings along the Missouri River had given way to city blocks lined with handsome homes, and hers was among the loveliest of them all. There were more than a dozen churches in Boonville now, enough to accommodate most denominations, and on Sundays most of them were filled with worshipers. Thespian Hall was the envy of the region. Boonville's municipal water works had gone on line in 1883, the same year of the town's first telephones. Plans were well along for the development of Harley Park, a charming and beautiful place, and for the paving with brick of Main Street, and Mary Jane Littlepage Williams, at sixty-three, had lived to see it all. She had raised two daughters, and knew they had married well. And she had raised four sons. One was well along in a modest but respectable career as an insurance salesman and state employee, another was United States Commissioner to Alaska. A third son was a distinguished attorney, arguably the best of his profession in Missouri. The fourth son, the youngest, was not yet out of the nest. But he, Walter Williams, had already been chosen editor of the leading local newspaper and was known throughout the state as a journalist of extraordinary promise. In an account of her death and funeral, a piece written by her grief-stricken youngest son, the *Advertiser* eulogized her as "one whose virtues were recognized by all who knew her, and whose death left a vacancy in society, in the church and among the most worthy of our matrons, that cannot be filled. Pure in every thought, she never did an intentional wrong. Sincere in her attachments, she was a true friend, always ready to contribute to the happiness of others, and there are hundreds who will unite with the writer of these lines in bearing testimony to the many admirable traits of her character."[30]

---

30. *Boonville Advertiser,* January 22, 1885, quoted in Cosgrove, *An Old House Speaks,* 114.

Just before his twenty-first birthday, Williams journeyed from Boonville to Columbia to attend his first meeting of an organization destined to be profoundly important to him in the years to come, the Missouri Press Association. Founded in 1867 as a trade federation by which newspaper publishers could protect their interests by presenting a united front to the legislature and other potentially intimidating powers, the Missouri Press Association would become one of the most effective organizations of its type in the country, wielding a collective influence on state matters that often proved decisive. When Williams entered the fold in 1885, the organization was, as Clinton H. Denman of Sikeston put it, "in the formative period, the get-acquainted period, the know-each-other period, and during [the organization's initial] 18 years Missouri editors came to realize that they could associate with each other on friendly terms."[31]

The following year, Williams was invited to address the state press association at its annual convention, and the idealistic young editor weighed in with serious words and high purpose. In a speech entitled "The Profession of Journalism from a Business, Moral and Social Standpoint," Williams told his older colleagues:

> There is room enough and to spare in the ranks of newspaper workers for talented young men whose hearts are throbbing with warm affections, and in whom the desire to be useful and noble transcends all low ambitions . . . The editor of a paper need not be a society man or a kid-gloved dude, but he should be well-posted on the social movements . . . of the entire territory over which his paper circulates.

And on the responsibilities of the editor, he warned,

> Let me write the editorials of the republic and I care not who makes the laws. If those editorials are conservative, thoughtful and scholarly, so will be public opinion; if they are tinged with the red of anarchism, rapine and lawlessness will result.[32]

The speech was well received, and at that same convention Williams was elected third vice president of the Missouri Press Association, placing him directly in the line of succession headed straight for the presidency of the organization. It was, in a way, an ordination.

The office also carried with it the opportunity for an expenses-paid trip to Denver, where he was a Missouri delegate to the convention of the National Editorial Association, a trade association comprised chiefly of smaller community newspapers. At a banquet there he was called upon to propose a toast.

31. William H. Taft, *Missouri Newspapers and the Missouri Press Association: 125 Years of Service* (Columbia: Missouri Press Association, 1992), 7.
32. Walter Williams, "Relations of National and State Associations."

It was an impromptu gesture, and there is no known record of what he said, but perhaps he told the convention a little anecdote he wrote later in a piece about his Colorado adventures:

> . . . I wore upon my breast a broad badge, with the name of my state blazing forth in great primer type. Coming down from Arapahoe street in Denver, I passed a group of rough miners on a corner. Said one to the other, gazing intently at the ribbon: "Why, that kid is from Missouri!" The second replied in a surprised, disgusted tone of voice: "Yes, and the damned fool is proud of it."[33]

Whatever he said, it must have impressed. The *Denver Post* praised "the young genius from Missouri, whose remarks elicited rounds of applause and hearty laughter," and the NEA delegates elected him assistant national secretary.

Two years later, his ascension to the press association presidency nearing and his reputation as an orator already assured, Williams addressed the convention again, this time on "The Supreme Mission of the Editor. Or, Education for Upliftment." With evangelistic fervor, he portrayed the editor as "one not here to gather gold, to seek the pottage, but to raise, as best he can, his people to higher life." In 1889, he indeed did become president of the Missouri Press Association, the youngest person ever to hold that position. He was twenty-five: "too young to be called Colonel," noted the *St. Louis Republic* in a congratulatory editorial, "too dignified and distinguished to be called Walter, he may properly be styled the infant president."[34]

It would seem to have been the moment for the infant president to start dreaming big dreams. But that epiphany had happened long ago, almost certainly two years before on his trip to Denver. To most in the newspaper trade the NEA was, in fact, little more than a loose, amiable confederation of country editors, but to Williams it exemplified a grand and glorious idea nevertheless. The Denver experience crystallized his thoughts and defined his vision. He was profoundly moved, as he would write a few weeks later, to see "the Northern Yankee and the Southern fire-eater, the black Republican and the Unterrified Democrat, the Mugwump and the Missourian live peaceably together"—journalists bonding together for the common good, becoming

> partakers of their advancement and sharers in their prosperity. We profit by their failures and grow wiser by their successes. The profession of journalism becomes ennobled . . . United, progressive, honorable, enterprising in the best sense, what a grand, inspiring thing the newspaper profession is!
> . . . To guide aright these glittering lances, to cultivate the finest chivalry, to imbue with the noblest spirit, to enlighten, to enlarge, to make broader and better and more vigorous, is the aim of the [press] associations—state and national.

---

33. Ibid.
34. Quoted in Rucker, *Walter Williams,* 50.

Missouri must not lag behind in this forward movement. Where the nation gathers she must be. Her delegates must be present to learn of others and to tell of the imperial State from whence they came.

This, then, is the relation that should exist between these bodies, state and national, the one the outgrowth of the other, neither interfering with the other's province, both united to advance the interests of the newspaper profession. Dead issues may be thus discarded, sectional strife avoided, partisan feeling allayed. We will then be hasteners on of that millennial period, when to quote the poet's words:

"Our war-drums throb no longer,
And the battle flags are furled,
In the parliament of man.
The federation of the World."[35]

A journalistic federation of the world. An end to editors assaulting other editors—"malicious, degraded, licentious, divided, waging war upon its brightest representatives," as he wrote about it, newspaper war that abased the nobility of the journalism profession. "How weak and contemptible does it become," he cried, "when a Hearst attacks a Pulitzer in New York?" Or, as he might have added but didn't, when a *Topic* attacks an *Advertiser* in Boonville, Missouri. The journalistic federation of the world. It had a nice ring to it.

---

35. Williams, *Proceedings.*

4

Transitions

I cannot claim to be much of a horticulturist, but I know a peach when I see one.

—Walter Williams

While twenty-three-year-old Walter Williams may well have been contemplating a journalistic federation of the world, he prudently realized the need to start with something a bit smaller and nearer at hand: his home state, for example. In Missouri, as everywhere, he was certain the newspaper stood in need of understanding and elevation. He saw the challenge to the press as personal and urgent, and he attacked it head-on. Throughout his one-year term as president of the Missouri Press Association, and editing the *Boonville Advertiser* all the while, he doggedly crisscrossed the state, inspecting newspaper offices, conferring with community leaders, preaching the gospel of community journalism in speech after speech to civic and church and scholastic gatherings, exhorting his brother editors to do better, urging their readers to appreciate the task local editors faced and the dedication he believed their jobs required. "It should scarcely be necessary to say that the lips and life of the editor should be clean," he declared in a typical civic club speech. "His supreme mission is, I believe, to be a teacher. He is close akin to the philosopher, poet, priest. How important is his life, which is going to project itself through the printed page into so many other lives! It should be large-souled, manly, blameless. For the sake of journalism and more, for the sake of the struggling world, for which journalism is both staff and guide, let the Press stand for the noblest in thought and deed!"[1]

Williams's oratory, high-pitched but genuine and persuasive, won him plaudits from far and wide during 1889, the year of his press association presidency. Perhaps more far-reaching in importance than his civic club evangelism, however, were the private visits to newspaper plants throughout the state. In town after town he met newspaper staff members and heard their concerns, praised a well-printed front page or an attractive ad layout or an eye-catching headline or a new piece of typesetting equipment. He learned all he could.

---

1. Published in the *Proceedings of the Missouri Press Association,* 1889, 42.

Later, over a quiet dinner with the publisher, he listened with care and talked knowingly about the community and the local newspaper's role in it. Before the evening was through, Williams typically had made the local publisher a friend for life. "Mr. Williams is an excellent gentleman, possesses splendid social qualifications, and causes cheerfulness to reign supreme wherever he is about," the editor of the *Monroe City News* wrote after one such visit in 1889. "He is . . . in every way a credit to his profession."[2]

While bonding with his fellow journalists, Williams was also impressing Missouri's powerful politicians. Many of them he knew already; largely through his distinguished brother Billy and other members of his active and unwaveringly Democratic family, he had become personally acquainted with the governor and all living past governors, senators, congressmen, justices of the Missouri Supreme Court and most officials in state government as well as a fair number of county politicians and municipal office holders across Missouri.

Especially taken with young Williams was David R. Francis, dynamic former mayor of St. Louis, now settling into the governor's mansion at Jefferson City. With his elegant handlebar mustache, penetrating eyes, easy charm and smooth, big-city ways, Francis had managed in 1888 to recruit enough country voters to join his Democratic party power base in St. Louis and edge out the Republican, Prohibition, and Union Labor candidates for the governorship. When he took the oath of office in 1889 he was only thirty-eight years of age. Later he would become Grover Cleveland's secretary of the interior and then president of the Louisiana Purchase Exposition Corporation. In 1916 President Woodrow Wilson would appoint him ambassador to Russia, where he served during the turbulent years of World War I and the Russian Revolution. On one vivid occasion in Moscow he single-handedly held off at gunpoint a Bolshevik mob on the steps of the American Embassy.[3] In 1889, meanwhile, Francis was proving to be a highly effective governor: under his leadership the Australian, or secret, ballot became the norm for Missouri elections, affording voters a degree of confidentiality they had not enjoyed previously. He established a single statewide commission to buy textbooks for Missouri pupils, saving the strapped school districts an estimated 61 percent in book purchases alone. He lowered state taxes, found money to shore up the beleaguered and chronically underfunded University of Missouri at Columbia, and substantially reduced the state's bonded indebtedness. His was a remarkable performance, and little wonder that Walter Williams was mesmerized by it.

---

2. Quoted in Rucker, *Walter Williams,* 46.
3. Duane Meyer, *The Heritage of Missouri* (St. Louis: State Publishing Co., 1963), 433.

As Williams was winding up his year as press association president, Francis summoned him to the Governor's Mansion and offered him a position in state government. The starry-eyed young editor, his dream of a journalistic federation of the world momentarily forgotten, accepted.

Williams was to become the bookkeeper in the Missouri State Penitentiary at Jefferson City. It was hardly an exalted position, though the job paid eighteen hundred dollars a year, far more money for far less work than the editorship of the *Advertiser.* This would be his first employment outside journalism, and leaving the newspaper business was not easy. "I have had—and have now—no higher ambition in life than to be a newspaper man in the highest sense of the term," he wrote in a farewell editorial for the *Advertiser.* "Whatever the future may have for me in sort of good or ill, naught can dim my remembrance of, or interest in, that which in Boonville and Cooper County is so dear, and of which the *Advertiser* forms so large a part." Effusive editorials from around the state praised Williams's shining, if brief, newspaper career and bemoaned the loss to Missouri journalism, though one editor chided him in print for "going off after lucre."[4]

Perhaps the money was appealing. More likely, Williams perceived the move to the state capital as a glorious opportunity to launch a career in the public sector, possibly to become, in time, another David R. Francis. Or perhaps, as he told friends before leaving Boonville, he was attracted by the prospect of shorter hours; he could easily dispense with the bookkeeping responsibilities in the course of a normal workday, maybe less, and have enough time and energy left over to write thoughtful articles for freelancing to important newspapers and national magazines. The ambitious pieces he had in mind required far more research and contemplation and literary polish than he could muster while still immersed in the rigors of day-to-day journalism. Or maybe, after a laborious year in which he combined his newspaper editorship with the presidency of the state press association, he was simply exhausted and thus receptive to an offer for what appeared to be a cushy state job. Whatever the reason, however, the bookkeeper's position did not pan out as he had hoped. Able to adjust neither to state government nor to living in Jefferson City, he was miserable throughout his stay there, and in less than three months he was gone.

Some newspapers reported that he had been fired. "He [Williams] was very fine on composing reports but was inefficient on figures, which is a common failing with newspaper men," wrote a *Jefferson City Daily Democrat-Tribune*

---

4. *Boonville Advertiser,* June 14, 1889; *Columbia Herald,* July 7, 1889.

columnist. "Mr. Williams held the position for about two months when Warden Morrison told the young man he was not fit for a bookkeeper and gave him the conge then and there."[5] Other papers reported much the same version.

The *Boonville Advertiser* laid the blame squarely at the feet of heavy-footed partisan politics. In loyal defense of its former editor, the *Advertiser* charged that "Mr. Williams was removed by Warden Morrison at the instigation of and in response to requests of certain Boonville 'bosses,' who are bitterly opposed to Francis, the *Advertiser,* and Mr. Williams . . . The removal was no surprise to those acquainted with the methods of the Boonville gang and their tools and henchmen at the state capital and elsewhere."[6]

Williams himself hotly denied he had been sacked. In an angry, defensive letter to a friend, he wrote:

> I was not an applicant to the place and only accepted it when urged to do so by Gov. Francis . . . Immediately upon my acceptance a fight was commenced upon me by Col. Elliott and his crowd here and State Treasurer Noland was against me because of some articles in the *Advertiser* last year and John Sebree, who is a tool of Elliott's as well as a disappointed office seeker. It was first stated that I was not competent and that the books were not properly kept . . . [penitentiary inspectors] all looked over the books and found these charges to be absolutely untrue. No one believed the charges but they were circulated by this anti-Francis gang to poison the mind of Warden Morrison. This fight was kept up in various ways until, in July . . . while Gov. Francis was away, the warden told me I would be relieved in 30 days. I immediately informed him of all the facts, stated why my removal came and from what quarters—telling pointedly and fully the whole story. By his tacit admissions the truth of what I had said was proven. When Gov. Francis returned I laid the matter before him. He interviewed the warden, who expressed repentance and promised to retain me at the Governor's request. In doing so [Warden] Morrison lied as I left in August, without a word from him as to my remaining longer, Gov. Francis being away at the time.
>
> Possibly if the Governor had not had such confidence in the warden's statements he might have interested himself more effectively in my behalf, but he was misled by Morrison and made to believe it was all right.[7]

To others, Williams confided that the prison warden and other state officials objected to his freelance magazine pieces, complaining that they wanted censorship authority over everything he wrote.[8]

Brother Billy fired off a letter to his friend, the governor: "Walter has been so much outraged and so much hurt by what he considered the gross injustice

---

5. Quoted in Rucker, *Walter Williams,* 49.

6. Ibid., 50.

7. Walter Williams to Bob (no last name located), September 28, 1889, Williams Papers.

8. Sara Lockwood Williams, unpublished Walter Williams biography.

of it, as well as the reasons assigned, and not the least the manner in which it was done," he wrote on August 28.[9]

Anxious to avoid further alienating powerful publishers in the Missouri Press Association, Francis hastily wrote a laudatory letter of recommendation for Walter Williams to use as needed. With it he included a conciliatory personal note which said, in part:

> Mr. [Warden] Morrison told me on my return . . . that you had severed your connection with the Prison voluntarily and with the best of feeling toward him and all its officers. When I left the capital it was understood with Mr. Morrison that you were not to be removed at the expiration of 30 days, and Morrison has told me since that you could have remained as long as you desired. I do not know how the impression made by the papers as to the cause of your leaving can be corrected unless through the columns of the *Advertiser,* which would be justified in publishing that you did not leave the employ of the state involuntarily, but resigned because your duties were not congenial to your tastes. You might also state that I not only did not instigate the severance of your connection with the Prison but regretted your going and tried to induce you to remain.[10]

Much was made of this at the time in the Missouri press. One of the state's most brilliant young journalists—indeed, the immediate past president of the Missouri Press Association—had ventured into low-level state government and had been publicly embarrassed. Some, including a wounded Walter Williams himself, felt he had been victimized by hardball bureaucratic and political infighting, quite possibly a carryover from the bitter campaign in which his brother Louis narrowly lost his bid to become Cooper County sheriff. That had been a long time ago, but political wounds in Cooper County rarely healed quickly. However, there may have been a far simpler explanation. As a niece would later write, Walter Williams hadn't been much good at his state job chiefly because he had not been put on this earth to be a bookkeeper.[11]

Out of work for the first time since he had been fifteen years old, Williams instinctively turned to his friends in the newspaper business for damage control, consolation, and guidance. He bailed out of Jefferson City three days before he was obliged to leave his state job and caught a train to St. Louis, where he joined the Missouri delegation of newspaper publishers bound for Detroit and the annual convention of the National Editorial Association. The *Cleveland Plain Dealer* offered him a job, probably during the NEA convention, but he declined—fearful, as an intimate would write later, that the leap from a country

---

9. William Muir Williams to David R. Francis, August 28, 1889, Williams Papers.
10. Francis to Walter Williams, September 13, 1889, Williams Papers.
11. Cosgrove, *An Old House Speaks,* 116.

weekly to a metropolitan daily was too much.[12] So, perhaps, was the move from Missouri, where he was unusually well connected, to Ohio, where he would be a virtual unknown. His former employer, Lon V. Stephens, an astute banker now living in St. Louis and the court-appointed receiver for the financially troubled Fifth National Bank, offered to hire him as his private secretary. But this would be only temporary while Lon V. was sorting out the bank's affairs. Too, Williams realized that Stephens had his eye on the governor's mansion— he would get there a few years later—and for the moment Walter Williams had had his fill of Missouri politics. The *St. Louis Republic* offered him a temporary position as a correspondent. He would be hired to tour the Northwest and send back a series of articles based on his travels. This, too, he declined; this was no time to be gone from Missouri for a prolonged period. Throughout September and much of October, he remained in Boonville and fretted, unable to find the perfect opportunity, hoping he would recognize it if and when it came. On November 8, 1889, it came.

Columbia, in Boone County, about twenty-five miles east of Boonville, had been a town for barely twenty years back in 1843 when James Leachman Stephens, an ambitious young entrepreneur, decided to make his fortune there. It was his second attempt; in his first, he had been hired off his nearby farm to be a sales clerk in Columbia at five dollars a month, but was soon perceived to be incompetent and summarily dismissed. A few years later, with hard-won commercial experience in Indiana now under his belt, he tried Columbia again, this time as owner of his own small dry-goods store. Unlike his competitors, he insisted on a cash-and-carry trade. "Credit," he was fond of saying, "is false in principle and ruinous in practice." Thus spared the problem of unpaid debts and the cost of collecting them, he could offer his customers lower prices. The business flourished. Before long heavily laden delivery wagons from the Stephens store were rolling each business day from Columbia to the settlements along the Missouri River, supplying many of the homes in between. Before he closed the doors of his rapidly expanding mercantile in the evenings he assembled his sales clerks for a time of instruction and prayer, often admonishing them not to criticize their competitors even though they might be sorely tempted to do so. He was, as the distinguished Missouri historian Floyd C. Shoemaker put it, "a hard-shelled Baptist and a hard-shelled businessman."[13] Within a few years James L. Stephens would be recognized

---

12. Sara Lockwood Williams, unpublished Walter Williams biography.
13. Carrol Jean Mills, "E. W. Stephens: Preparer of the Way," 10. This master's thesis, written in 1970 by a graduate student in the School of Journalism at the University of Missouri, has been drawn upon extensively in this chapter.

as the largest single taxpayer in Boone County. During his lifetime he also made cash donations of more than one hundred thousand dollars, including gifts to every church in Columbia. He also contributed a personal endowment of twenty thousand dollars to the Baptist Female College, saving it from almost certain bankruptcy, and raised so much additional money for the school that a grateful Baptist Convention renamed the place Stephens College.[14] He was an imposing man—"erect, suave, courtly, dignified without ostentation," a federal judge who knew him well recalled, "a great citizen, and great benefactor." In his declining years he turned over more and more of his financial interests to his son, Edwin William Stephens, who was cut from the same bolt of cloth. Indeed, as a friend said of E. W., "there is something of the tiger of his father in him."[15]

Now forty years old, E. W. Stephens was a wealthy and industrious successor to the family fortune and, arguably, Columbia's leading businessman. He had been well educated, one of only ten young men in 1867 to earn a bachelor's degree from the fledgling University of Missouri, this while he was still a teenager. Though he might have been expected to take over his father's retailing businesses, he preferred to make his own mark in printing and publishing instead. Rather than impose a career upon his son, the elder Stephens wisely acquiesced, then arranged a job for him with the *Missouri Statesman.* "My father put me in the newspaper business for two reasons," Stephens would explain later. "First, he believed that a newspaper man could have more influence than any other person in the community. And second, he thought it was a job for a lazy man. He was right on both counts."[16] The *Statesman* was an ardent pro-Democratic weekly in Columbia and a spinoff from the old *Missouri Intelligencer* at Franklin. E. W. Stephens, far more industrious than his father perceived, worked hard, demonstrated a talent for journalism, and learned his trade quickly. At the age of twenty-one and with his father's resources, he bought an interest in the *Boone County Journal.* The *Journal* reflected a die-hard pro-Confederacy editorial policy while the *Statesman* was pro-Union; Stephens's deeply entrenched racist opinions, proclaimed in embarrassing detail through his vigorous editorials, would not moderate for many years. By 1872, with the *Journal's* image still tarnished in a community where old racial divisions took a long time to heal, Stephens shrewdly decided to try burying the past. He bought complete control of the paper and changed its

---

14. The school went on to attract national prominence as a women's college and continues to flourish today.

15. Quoted in Mills, "E. W. Stephens," 15.

16. From an interview with *Missouri Magazine* on Stephens's seventy-eighth birthday, published January 27, 1927. Quoted in Mills, "E. W. Stephens," 24.

name to the *Columbia Herald.* The reborn *Herald* was well financed, nicely packaged, far less outspoken and thus less controversial. An energetic and effective editor, Stephens took a leaf from his father's forceful promotional efforts and pushed hard for readers from throughout the region. "I claim the distinction of having originated the idea of country correspondence," he once observed, in a rare moment of self-congratulation. "There was very little local news in the 'seventies. I wrote the first local personals and the first country correspondence that I ever saw anywhere, for in the old days you had to die or get married to get your name in the paper, as most everything was political news. So I selected some country correspondents and gave them their orders."[17] He deployed thirteen part-time news reporters, one for each of the tiny outlying communities in the Columbia trading area. He paid by the word for their homely reports of community comings and goings, then watched with satisfaction as new subscribers by the dozens signed on, thrusting the *Herald*'s circulation past the one thousand mark.

Stephens also moved aggressively into job printing, bidding for printing contracts from far and wide. By the late autumn of 1889, when Walter Williams came on board, the E. W. Stephens Publishing House had become Columbia's largest and most ambitious commercial enterprise, employing nearly a hundred persons. Books as well as community papers rolled off its presses, along with a myriad of job printing orders from customers in every state and U.S. territory. Stephens also landed lucrative official state contracts to print court reports or statutes for Missouri, New Mexico, Iowa, Arkansas, Tennessee, Arizona, and Utah.

Stephens drove himself hard. He was at his desk by seven each morning and rarely left before nine at night. "The newspaper business is the business of a young person with the power of locomotion," he would tell an interviewer later. "It requires versatility, aptitude, and energy to be the editor of a country newspaper. He must be much more versatile than an editor in the city."[18] Thus when his associate editor on the *Herald,* H. W. Isbell, left in 1889, Stephens went after the brightest and most energetic young man he could find—who was willing to work for twenty-five dollars a week. He turned to his young friend Walter Williams, whom he had just succeeded as president of the Missouri Press Association.

The job offer afforded Williams a joyous reentry to journalism after his nightmarish misadventure in state politics. His pay was less—thirteen hundred

17. *St. Louis Post-Dispatch,* January 20, 1929.
18. *Missourian Magazine,* January 27, 1927.

dollars a year, as opposed to the eighteen-hundred-dollar salary he was making at the penitentiary—but in all other respects the *Columbia Herald* presented him with the opportunity of his dreams. The newspaper plant, a spacious two-story brick building on the southwest corner of Eighth and Walnut Streets, across from the Boone County Courthouse, housed not only the newspaper but also the considerable resources of the Stephens job printing and publishing operation. Thus was Williams guaranteed immediate and reliable access to superb presses, a magnificent selection of typefaces, borders, dingbats, and other composition devices, and a splendid crew of production and pressroom craftsmen. This was a printing plant far better equipped and staffed than any country editor could expect, and it provided Williams the wherewithal to produce a weekly newspaper of extraordinary attractiveness. Whatever he needed, he usually got, whether it was a distinctive new typeface, a better grade of paper stock, or more columns available for printing news and features. The first telephone ever to be connected in Columbia was installed in the *Herald* office. And with Stephens's blessing, Williams resolved to use the plentiful assets at his command to make the *Herald* the finest country weekly in America.

His overriding first priority was to build upon Stephens's solid reputation for covering the news. Routine news from the courthouse, schools, city and country government, clubs, and civic organizations was reported accurately and in detail. "Spot" news reports—coverage of accidents, fires, and the like—were lively and readable. Beyond these, the meat and potatoes of newspaper journalism, Williams developed a rich diet of seasonal and human-interest articles that helped define the community's, and the paper's, personality. But news was the franchise, and Williams was determined to package it well. He devoted most of the front page to local news, mixing in some state and national news for balance, and for those *Herald* readers who did not subscribe to a metropolitan daily. Inside the paper, Williams departmentalized much of the other news and features copy into easy-to-find sections: agricultural interest, women's news, a summary of the week's state and national reports, personal items, county correspondence, a few lines of poetry, editorials. One especially popular feature was "Missouri Public Opinion," a compilation of editorials reprinted from other newspapers in the state. Another was "From the East Window," a personal column that reflected Williams's interpretation of the news.

While many editors, then and later, would limit their concern with graphic design only to the front page, largely ignoring the appearance of the inside pages, Williams carefully sketched a layout for each page of the *Herald.* He was especially meticulous with advertisements. He threw out some advertising that might be offensive, ads for patent medications of dubious value, and took pains to place the other ads as attractively as he could. Indeed, the *Herald* was credited with pioneering a pyramid layout—anchoring large ads at the bottom, stacking smaller ads on top in a way that every ad touched a news or feature story. This placement, which would become almost universal throughout the newspaper field, greatly enhanced advertising readership. The pyramid arrangement also generated goodwill from local businessmen, whose smaller ads were no longer buried on a page under layers of dominant larger advertisements. The *Herald* also was an early pacesetter in the production and use of halftone engravings, providing readers and advertisers with more and better photographs than even some of the metropolitan dailies could offer.

Soon after Williams took over as editor, he and Stephens agreed to undertake a long-range study of additional layout and to design strategic possibilities. Eventually, after examining hundreds of newspapers from across the country and consulting with big-city typographical experts, they would transform the *Herald* from its traditional blanket-sheet format to a twenty-page tabloid, printed on high-grade paper that afforded a country weekly the look of a slick magazine. "It is now the first country newspaper in Missouri to change to the present, still more convenient and handsome magazine form," Williams boasted in an editorial. "To make this change has required the construction and purchase of the latest improved machinery."[19] Walter Williams was a happy man.

But these ebullient, productive early days in Columbia were not quite perfect. For one thing, an irate reader of the *Herald* became so incensed at an editorial Williams wrote that he threatened to shoot the young journalist on sight. Williams bought a pistol and kept it in the top drawer of his editorial desk, although a colleague would remark that "he wouldn't know which end of the pistol to take hold of."[20] Soon the man's anger toward Williams cooled and the two became friends, though the pistol remained in the editor's desk for some time. Williams's other concern, about which he could do nothing, was for his father's rapidly declining health.

For Marcus Williams the end came just before the Christmas of 1890. He was seventy-four.

His pottery and woodworking shop and his other commercial ventures long behind him, Marcus had lived quietly in the Big House on Morgan Street, less the master of it now than the guest of his second son, William Muir Williams, and the prosperous attorney's lively, loving family. To his grandchildren,

---

19. *Columbia Herald,* May 13, 1898.
20. Cosgrove, *An Old House Speaks,* 118.

Marcus Williams seemed to be a very old man, withdrawn and perpetually tired, interested chiefly in tending his elegant fern bed next to the back fence of the family property. He was always on the lookout for new varieties to add to the long, narrow fern garden, and often roamed the surrounding countryside, pulled in the phaeton by a grandson's little pony named Jack Stark, in hopes of adding to his collection. He was also an avid student of the Bible and could quote entire chapters from it. During his last, long illness he was attended by a black servant, known to the grandchildren only as Uncle Alfred, who stayed at his bedside night and day.

Marcus Williams had been a pioneer settler of Boonville, the son of the town's first mayor, an enthusiastic, if unevenly successful, businessman and a builder of some of the town's most cherished institutions. But the *Boonville Advertiser,* in an affectionate obituary, preferred to focus instead on his gentle qualities, remembering him as

> . . . a kind and considerate neighbor, ever ready to console the sorrowing or to rejoice with those who rejoiced; a man of very fine intelligence, keeping intimately acquainted with the current happenings of the world; a daily reader of the Bible . . . and one who had the satisfaction of seeing his children attain to social and professional promise and loved by the communities in which they cast their several lots.[21]

Walter Williams eulogized his father as "belonging to the pioneer stock, hardy, hopeful, strenuous, adventurers in a land of larger opportunity."[22] Marcus Williams had driven a wagon all the way from Virginia to the Midwestern plains in search of a great fortune. Years earlier, he must have realized that he would never make it himself. But perhaps, before he died peacefully in his sleep that Saturday evening of December 22, 1890, he sensed that the children he fathered might succeed in ways other people could only have dreamed about.

When Walter Williams moved to Columbia, he took a room at a small residential hotel called the Power House. The hotel was in fact owned by a family named Poor, who understandably elected to give the place another name. Something more than a boardinghouse, the Power was a popular venue for Columbia's congenial, gregarious partygoers; numerous entertainment suppers and elaborate tea dances were held in its comfortable dining room, with both of the Poor's energetic and charming daughters often acting as hostesses. Several of Columbia's bachelors, young professionals like Walter Williams, lived at

---

21. *Boonville Advertiser,* December 24, 1890, quoted in Rucker, *Walter Williams,* 66.
22. Walter Williams manuscript, 2.

the Power, and many townspeople often dined there. Williams's social life took wings that incredible year of 1889—a year in which he had led the state press association, abandoned journalism to become, briefly and tragically, a state bureaucrat, moved away from the town where he had lived all his life, grieved over the declining health of his father, and reentered the newspaper field by landing a plum of an editorship. It was also the year he met Hulda Harned.

His first glimpse of her came at an evening party, and throughout the night he could think of little else. The next morning, he paced the office of a friend and confidant, saying again and again: "Miss Harned is certainly a wonderful young lady!" "Walter," his friend smiled, "you're struck. You're struck."[23]

Not, as his close friends knew, for the first time. As his old editor J. West Goodwin of the *Sedalia Bazoo* wrote after attending a newspaper convention with Williams at Boston:

> Walter Williams of the Columbia *Herald* saw a pretty girl at the Boston State House. She was exquisitely beautiful, a positive brunette with piercing eyes that no doubt are now haunting the youth in the jungles of Boone County. Walter was captivated. It looked as though Missouri was about to lose a good editor and Massachusetts secure a poor husband. He subsequently learned that the lady was married and the mother of twin babies. Walter is a changed youth.[24]

Hulda, however, was different. "Walter Williams was susceptible to all that was lovely and feminine and charming," a relative would write later, "but his heart was really touched with his first glimpse of Hulda Harned, with her brown eyes and dimples, her sweet manner and voice, indices of her lovely character."[25] The only daughter in a prosperous farm family, Hulda had studied art and literature at Hardin College, a small school in the central Missouri town of Mexico, and had won a medal there for her accomplishments as a musician. She had returned to the family farmstead to live with her parents, Mr. and Mrs. George Harned, and her three brothers. The farm was situated outside Vermont, a tiny community not far away—it was in Cooper County, a few miles from Boonville—but a hard place to reach. The train did not go there directly, but only via an inconvenient, tortured routing by one train to Mexico, Missouri, in the opposite direction, then a transfer to a different train back toward Cooper County. This last leg required a tense journey across a rickety spur line known locally as "Calamity Branch" because of its history of derailments. By carriage, Vermont was accessible only from a dirt road often rendered sodden by drenching rains or blocked by snow. But Williams

23. Cosgrove, *An Old House Speaks,* 121.
24. Sara Lockwood Williams, unpublished Walter Williams biography.
25. Cosgrove, *An Old House Speaks,* 122.

persisted, "driving down a muddy road," as he would write, his horse-and-buggy journey consuming nearly a full day in each direction. Williams's difficult yet frequent passages through that part of mid-Missouri did not go unnoticed. "Walter Williams of the Columbia *Herald* is at present busily engaged," observed the gossipy *Rocheport Commercial,* "in chasing a personal item of the Hulda Harned nature."[26]

They became engaged within weeks, but the wedding would not occur for more than two years, during which time Williams feverishly saved what money he could toward the building of a home on the lot he had picked out on Hitt Street. Every day of their prolonged engagement, when Walter and Hulda were not together, each wrote a letter to the other. (The postal clerk where Hulda got her mail eventually sent her a bill for what he called extra service. She settled the account by sending him a box of her wedding cake.)

On Thursday, June 30, 1892, "a beautiful and cloudless day," recalled a niece,[27] Walter and Hulda were married at two in the afternoon at what was described as a simple and unpretentious ceremony at the Harned home. "The parlors and halls of the substantial farm home were all handsomely decorated and made a scene of beauty," the *Tipton Times* account of the wedding exclaimed, "while a bevy of young lady friends of the bride flitted here and there with happy faces and gave additional charm to the occasion." The Reverend A. E. Rogers of the Mexico Baptist Church performed the ceremony. He was assisted by Walter's brother-in-law, the Reverend Horace B. Banks, then pastor of the Presbyterian church in Odessa. The next morning the entire wedding party adjourned to the Big House in Boonville, where brother Billy and his wife had laid on an elaborate reception. It was a grand occasion. The Big House on Morgan Street, the home where Walter Williams had been born, was newly renovated, decorated to the hilt, and had never looked better.

For his part, Walter Williams felt he was fortunate to have gotten there in the first place. Earlier on his wedding day, as he was waiting to change trains in Mexico, three of his friends nabbed him and held him down while the outbound train was leaving the terminal. When they finally released him the train was beginning to build up speed. By running hard he was able to just catch the last car in time to swing onto the steps.[28]

After the reception and dinner and the harrowing train ride across the Calamity Branch spur line back to Columbia, Williams and his bride finally arrived in Columbia, there to be met by a horse and carriage he had arranged

---

26. Ibid.
27. Ibid., 123.
28. Ibid.

to take them to the rented red brick house they were to occupy for a time while their new home was being built. But the horse inexplicably refused to budge and the nervous bridegroom, after repeated movements of the reins, soon found himself entangled in them. Hulda, who'd spent her life on a farm, giggled but said nothing. "I was just dying to take the reins away from Walter and drive the horse myself," she admitted later.[29] It had been a full day.

The wedding was fully reported upon in the Missouri press. One paper, Columbia's other weekly, the *Statesman,* even carried an editorial on the subject:

> To hear him [Walter Williams] talk, the conclusion was immediately drawn that he was a happy bachelor and as such chose to remain. In fact his boon companions were chosen from the toughest and hardest old "bachs" that could be found in the city. Of the many beauteous maidens with which Columbia is blest, he fought shy, and none, try as hard as she might, was able to touch a responsive chord in his, what was thought to be callous heart . . . But little did his friends, save a few suspicious characters, dream of his long walks with the time-tried and fire-tested sinners mentioned above and when he would semi-monthly quietly steal away for a few days it was generally agreed that he had gone "to see his brother."
>
> But the light has broken forth and the truth with it, and . . . Walter Williams, the bachelor, will be no more, but in his place will appear Walter Williams, the Benedict.[30]

The Saturday night after his wedding, E. W. Stephens hosted a huge reception to introduce Hulda Harned Williams to Columbia society. It was a grand gesture, eloquent testament to Stephens's continuing pride in his youthful editor for whom he had already done so much. Walter Williams owed a debt of staggering proportions to his friend and boss. It was E. W. Stephens who had conferred the editorship of an already prestigious newspaper upon Walter Williams and had given him free rein and ample resources to elevate the paper to national excellence. Stephens's sponsorship proved to be the only channel Williams would need to gain instant acceptance in Columbia's business community as well as its cautious, if active, social circles. Stephens's statewide connections were formidable; where a politically immature Walter Williams of Boonville might have been summarily dismissed from a middle-level state job, a Walter Williams now known to represent the E. W. Stephens editorial interests in Columbia was a man to be taken seriously.

For his part, Williams was expected to deliver the goods, and he did. Under his gifted editorial hand, each issue of the *Herald* seemed newsier and

---

29. Ibid., 124.
30. *Columbia Statesman,* June 29, 1892, quoted in Rucker, *Walter Williams,* 67.

more polished than the one before. And by dispatching copies of the paper to publishers across the country and singing its praises at one press convention after another, Williams shrewdly called attention from the entire newspaper industry to the kind of journalism then being practiced in Columbia, Missouri. Three years after he had taken it over, the *Herald* was being described in the trade press as "America's model weekly," and in 1895 the *Newspaper Blue Book* rated it as the best country weekly in the United States.

The precocious little editor and the tall, courtly publisher became a splendid team, two very different kinds of men who often dreamed and acted as one. "It was at this point that some difficulty arises in distinguishing between the thoughts, ideas, and accomplishments of the two," wrote one scholar who had studied the lives of both men. "They were espousing the same causes, lending each other moral support, voicing similar opinions."[31] And if Walter Williams was gaining the greater visibility, it was largely because Stephens left to him the responsibility of developing their combined ideas through to closure. Stephens seemed to care not at all that his protégé gained such notoriety, even as editor of the newspaper he himself had launched and in the nurturing environment he had created for him. Rather, it was said, Stephens seemed to have intended it to happen just that way. He rejoiced at Williams's achievements.

In his own reserved fashion Stephens was fully as idealistic as any man, and thus he appreciated totally that the *Columbia Herald* now carried the reputation of being a hometown weekly the nation's press could respect and admire. Perhaps he realized that for Walter Williams those heady successes with the *Herald* were only the beginning.

---

31. Mills, "E. W. Stephens," 97.

5

The Most Popular Man in Columbia

The position of country editor will compare favorably with that held by any prince or potentate. He has a larger audience than all the preachers in his town. He has more influence than the banker or the lawyer. He has lots of fun, and if he loves his profession as all good editors do, nothing could prompt him from it.

—Walter Williams, 1897

The sponsorship of E. W. Stephens guaranteed Walter Williams immediate access to the upper levels of Columbia's highly stratified society. For some in that sometimes distant community where newcomers could be subjected to years of patronizing delay before gaining full acceptance, he had come up too fast. "Who is this little upstart who has come to town with his shirttail full of type?" demanded one the town's wealthiest party-givers at a downtown luncheon, in a voice that others seated around her could hear. The woman was Mrs. Emma Price Willis, daughter of Columbia's leading banker, Colonel R. B. Price, and Williams soon learned of what she had said. The following Sunday he confidently sought her out at Columbia's Presbyterian church, introduced himself as a newcomer to the community, and asked her one or two questions about the congregation. Perhaps to her surprise, she found him a lively conversationalist who would not, as others often did, automatically agree with her peremptory opinions on civic and church matters. Before long, the two had become fast friends, for she seemed to relish her spirited debates with him. Others in the First Presbyterian Church would later entertain themselves by provoking heated discussions between the two so they could observe the verbal fireworks. Mrs. Willis took her religion seriously, however, and would stop going to church whenever she disapproved of some church policy or of what she regarded as lack of discretion in a young minister's sermon. After one such walkout, more severe and prolonged than the rest, anxious members of the congregation sent a delegation to her home with a plea that she come back again. She told the committee that she would return only when Walter Williams would be there. Williams, who had been out of town and had missed several Sunday services, sent word to her that he would escort her to church on the next cool Sunday.[1]

Where the First Presbyterian Church was concerned, Mrs. Willis was only one of Walter Williams's success stories. By 1894 he had been named one of the elders in the congregational governing body, and more and more had assumed positions of responsibility and leadership in church affairs. He was also a frequent contributor to state and national Presbyterian publications. His most dramatic achievement at the church, however, had its beginnings in 1895, when he took over a tiny Sunday school group called the Bible class. Though only six pupils were attending the class when Williams first started teaching it, he nevertheless developed his lessons carefully, engaging the class in a free-wheeling discussion in which all could participate. Word of the class spread, especially among college students, and attendance picked up. Soon the weekly lessons necessarily took on a different character. There was less discussion— there were too many people now for that—and instead Williams began giving thoughtful, powerful lectures based on his interpretation of the Scriptures. By the dozens young men and women trooped into the First Presbyterian Church to hear this gifted, self-educated teacher, barely thirty years old, demonstrate his understanding of the Bible and proclaim his faith in it. Often they were visitors from other congregations, dashing over for the Bible class at First Presbyterian, then prudently rejoining their families at their home churches for the regular worship services. There were so many now in the class that Williams found himself making a special effort to get them acquainted with each other. "I don't want to have to say to old St. Peter when I get up yonder, 'who is that fellow?' " he repeatedly told his class. " 'I ought to know him. He was a member of our Bible class in Columbia, but I never knew his name.' "

By 1902, when Williams had been teaching the class for seven years, the class numbered in the hundreds. Williams's lectures were supplemented by a monthly newsletter written and distributed by class members, many of whom were University of Missouri students. Called *The Class Paper,* it sold for ten cents a year and reported news of attendance, offerings collected, previews of forthcoming lessons, and inspirational messages specifically elicited from prominent figures ranging from John Wanamaker to Booker T. Washington to William Jennings Bryan. The Bible class had long since outgrown the tiny classroom where Williams had begun with it. His was now acknowledged to be the largest single Sunday school class in Missouri, and the *St. Louis Republic* sent a reporter to Columbia to write about it and Walter Williams. "Last year the membership became so large that it was necessary to remove from the Sunday

---

1. Sara Lockwood Williams, unpublished Walter Williams biography.

School room to the main church auditorium in order to seat the assemblage that thronged to hear him talk," the article said of Williams. "A three-hundred mark was set as a goal, and the attendance overreached that number before the close of last year's term. Last Sunday 384 people crowded in to hear the story of 'Joseph and His Brethren.' "[2]

Some of Williams's Sunday school lectures became guest sermons, dusted off and recycled when he was invited, as he often was, to occupy an out-of-town pulpit. One of his most popular, especially with young people, was an address Williams entitled "The Gospel According to You":

> It is a mistaken notion that there are but four gospels, for there are five. Matthew wrote of Jesus as a king; Mark wrote of him as a servant; Luke wrote of him as a man; and John wrote of him as the very Christ. But the gospel with which mankind today is most concerned is the gospel according to you.[3]

Even the president, Theodore Roosevelt, was notified about the amazing Sunday school class at the First Presbyterian Church in Columbia, Missouri, and its charismatic teacher. "Mr. Williams is a close Bible student and a powerful speaker," Roosevelt wrote, knowingly, in a letter to *The Class Paper.* "And, personally, undoubtedly the most popular man in Columbia."[4]

Williams's success as a speaker did not come easily, for he had much to overcome. Unimposing physically, he was a tiny, frail-looking man whose narrow shoulders were somewhat bent. His nose, broken by an errant baseball when he was a child, remained a tad crooked, and his lower lip protruded slightly. His hairline, even when he was in his twenties, was receding to a conspicuous degree.

Most glaringly apparent, however, was his piping, shrill voice, which, as he pushed hard to emphasize a point, would rise to an uncontrollable pitch. Journalists who wrote favorably about the content of his speeches found themselves criticizing his delivery. "He had a peculiar, squeaky voice but was a very entertaining off-hand speaker," wrote one Colorado newspaperman about a speech Williams made to the National Editorial Association. A West Virginia writer, reporting on that same convention speech, described Williams as "a young man who, in spite of a disagreeable defect in voice, provoked hearty applause by an eloquence that grew rapidly in power and influence."[5]

While these embarrassing voice problems would have stopped a lesser man in his tracks, Williams was determined not to give in to them. To compensate

---

2. *St. Louis Republic,* November 2, 1902.
3. Rucker, *Walter Williams,* 80.
4. *St. Louis Post-Dispatch,* September 28, 1902.
5. Quoted in Rucker, *Walter Williams,* 82.

for disagreeable tone and unreliable pitch quality, he worked hard at the other aspects of public speaking. He pored over books on oratory, watched and listened to every competent guest speaker he could, trained himself to speak slowly and pause often. Hour after hour he rehearsed, disciplining himself to hold back the tempo of his sentences even when he ached to rush ahead, always striving for perfect combinations of cadence and phrasing. Most of all, he made sure he had something to say. He kept meticulous notes, filling tablet after tablet with quotes from the likes of Longfellow and Lowell, of John Greenleaf Whittier and James Whitcomb Riley, of Shakespeare and Joseph Pulitzer, anecdotes and illustrations and verse and epigrams for all occasions. He also kept a secret file on state legislators and other important personages in Missouri, chronicling what he was able to find out about their backgrounds and hobbies and other interests, surprising, and flattering, them from the lecture platform by mentioning little-known items about them in his talk. He spent his evenings writing and revising the text for a talk. The finished text was then, as the *Paris* (Mo.) *Herald* reported on one Walter Williams speech, "a medley of description, philosophy, religion, humor, and poetry and was enjoyed to the fullest." "Walter told an anecdote gravely, dropped in the point innocently, almost indifferently and in a casual way, and pretended surprise when the audiences burst into laughter," an admiring colleague wrote of the technique he had developed. "Only if you were close enough to see his twinkling eyes could you guess his enjoyment." Williams believed, or convinced his audience he believed, every word he spoke. An audience was moved, he wrote, "not by the pale gray logic of the lecturer, but the rich red sentiment of the genial friend. Stir the emotion," he said, "touch the heart, and the brain will follow."[6]

Once he connected with his audience, he could sell whatever text he had prepared, even one dripping with purple prose:

> . . . we will learn to know, also, that Missouri is not bounded by the limits of our print-shop, or the United States within the borders of Missouri, that the yellow Tiber, the castled Rhine and the beautiful blue Danube sink into insignificance beside the mighty Mississippi and the muddy Missouri; that ours is the greatest country the sun ever shone on. Upon all this pendant globe no fairer, richer realm unfolds itself to tempt the angels down; that our thousand lakes, like jewels studding the earth, far surpass in witching beauty Como or Killarney. That ours are the loveliest ladies and the manliest men. That the roars of Niagara, the curious canyons of Colorado, the billowy verdure of our prairies and the matchless richness of our valleys, the exhaustless treasurers of our mines and the boundless

---

6. Sara Lockwood Williams, unpublished Walter Williams biography. Rucker, *Walter Williams,* 83. Helen Brookshire Adams, "Walter Williams: Spokesman for Journalism and Spokesman for the University of Missouri," Ph.D. diss., University of Missouri, 1969, 71.

capabilities of our climate from Maine to California—are unequalled in any nation. Here we have a republic with soils and climates as varied as the tastes of man, and capacities for production as unlimited as the needs of man. As someone has said, yielding everything cereal, vegetable, animal, textile, mineral, agricultural, horticultural, geological, zoological, homological, piscatorial and ornithological, ovine, bovine, capricorn, equine, and assinine (the last including most of our alleged statesmen, whether from Kansas or Indiana) . . . [7]

"Modern critics," sniffed one scholar after an extensive study of his oratory, "would advise Williams to limit his topics, to tighten his organization, to support his ideas with specifics, and to use concrete terms . . . Even though his weaknesses seemed to outweigh his rhetorical strengths, Williams was considered an effective speaker by those who heard him."[8] As indeed he was. Walter Williams could inform, entertain, persuade. He could make his audience laugh, cry, soar on the wings of a new idea, grieve over a loss, resolve to try to do better. At times, such was his skill that he seemed able to accomplish them all in a single speech. Civic club luncheon talks, formal lectures, Sunday school lessons, sermons, commencement addresses—Williams did them all, usually in exemplary and memorable fashion, leaving his audience applauding for more.

There was still the voice defect. But even that, too, would one day disappear as if by magic. The most popular man in Columbia was leading a charmed life.

A journalist from St. Louis wrote that Democratic party leaders were urging him to run for Congress. Another delegation called upon him, brandishing a petition signed by hundreds of registered Democrats imploring him to run for the state legislature. Williams declined both overtures, singing the praises of community journalism and reaffirming his satisfaction in being a country editor. When Missouri's powerful Senate leader, Champ Clark, suggested that Williams plot his course for the Governor's Mansion in Jefferson City, Williams was said to have quipped, "Friendships are preferable to governorships."[9] Approached again by still another delegation of Democrats, Williams felt it necessary to make public his intentions, and in a somber editorial for the *Herald* he wrote:

My duty does not lie in the direction of office-seeking or office-holding. In the profession of journalism there can be no half-hearted service if one is to attain the largest usefulness. Journalism is a serious mistress and cannot be made the handmaiden of politics. The editor, to do his full duty to the public, must not

7. Ibid., 83.
8. Ibid., 94.
9. Cosgrove, *An Old House Speaks,* 125.

be engaged in any vocation that will distract his thoughts, color his editorials or occupy his time. He must be free from entangling alliances that politics establishes.[10]

But the kind of political attention he attracted raised his stock still higher in Columbia, where he had found himself instantly propelled onto the A list for top-of-the-line social occasions. Soon after he had won her over, Emma Price Williams got him invited to a lavish dinner party at the home of her father. The event was in honor of a Missouri congressman who was being considered for the presidency of the University of Missouri. The congressman, it was said later, had already made up his mind not to accept the position if it were offered to him. But the dinner proved to be so gracious as to make the university presidency suddenly irresistible. Emboldened by mint juleps— Colonel Price's personal recipe, brought with him when he had moved to Missouri from Virginia—and the euphoria of the occasion, the congressman, by now slightly unsteady on his feet, announced in a loud, boozy voice that he was ready to accept the offer. It never came.[11] Perhaps the congressman's public conversion was manifest at a point a mint julep or two beyond what the other guests thought appropriate. But if the congressman was swayed by the grandeur of the occasion, so, in a different way, was Walter Williams. This was his first big, opulent dinner party in a private home wherein thirty or forty of the town's most prominent citizens were assembled for a night of food and drink and fellowship and, in effect, to evaluate the fitness of an outsider to occupy a leadership role in the town. The occasion made a great impression on him. Perhaps he now realized that, for all he had presumed about the influence of a newspaper's editorial page, the real power inside a community was so often wielded when the elites assembled at social gatherings such as this. Many more such princely evenings lay ahead—and Williams, now demonstrably a member of Columbia's inner circle, would be part of them.

Life at the Williams home on Hitt Street went on in storybook fashion. Those who visited the little white frame house were struck by the affection and joy they found there. And by two rituals. One was the merry greeting that accompanied his homecoming every evening. "Hello, folks!" Williams would exclaim, as he opened the front door. No matter where she was or what she was doing, Hulda Harned Williams would reply in the same words. The

---

10. Quoted in Rucker, *Walter Williams,* 91.
11. Sara Lockwood Williams, unpublished Walter Williams biography. The convivial congressman's name was not provided.

other custom was repeated every payday. Williams presented Hulda with her household allowance—an uncommonly generous one, relatives recalled, given the family's limited means. And Hulda never tired of replying, "Oh, Walter! I never can spend all that!"[12]

If their friends and neighbors regarded these and other peculiarities of the Williams household as exaggerated and banal, there is no evidence of it. Indeed, relatives and friends recall that the townspeople perceived the Williams home as a place of genuine love and stability, and some even found it a refuge. One young man and woman eloped from their homes nearby and, upon returning to Columbia afterward, were denied access by their own families. The bride's parents were prepared to welcome her, but not her husband. The groom's father and mother said he could move back in with them, but not if his bride were with him. Walter and Hulda took in the newlyweds, announcing to the community that both bride and groom could stay with the Williams family on Hitt Street for as long as they liked. A few days later, when the outraged parents had cooled down, both sets of parents accepted their newlyweds and both fathers, together, went to Williams to thank him. Friends and relatives recall other occasions where those struck by tragedy found shelter and haven and kindnesses with the Williamses. "It was just like throwing open the doors of Heaven to me!" recalled one whom Walter and Hulda had taken in after his own disapproving parents threw him out.[13]

On August 1, 1893, their first child was born. They named him Walter Winston Williams, but friends and family called him Walter, Jr. He was a handsome child and, as one relative described him, "seems to have the fine mentality of his father and to have acquired similar interests."[14]

Overjoyed with his new role as a father, Williams devoted much of his free time to Walter, Jr., talking to him—earnestly, as if he were an adult, one relative recalled—and reading to him by the hour. When he had exhausted all the childrens' books available, he created stories especially for the lad. One of these tales, which Walter, Jr., wanted to hear again and again, Williams entitled "How the Cap'n Saved the Day." When other children in the neighborhood asked to hear it as well, Williams decided, on a whim, to submit the piece to the *Saturday Evening Post*. The *Post* bought the manuscript, illustrated it with two sketches, then featured it in the November 5, 1898, issue. "How the Cap'n Saved the Day" was a dramatic piece about a child whose boldness and

---

12. Cosgrove, *An Old House Speaks,* 124.
13. Ibid., 122.
14. Sara Lockwood Williams, unpublished Walter Williams biography.

heroism rescued his fellow soldiers, then surrounded and greatly outnumbered, from a hostile army. The central character was someone with whom a small boy might readily identify:

> He was such a little fellow. The lily which bloomed in the corner of the yard was taller and scarcely more slender than he. His head, even when he wore his high-heeled shoes, did not reach up to the great iron knocker that hung on the front door. The calendar said the Cap'n was five years old, but nobody believed the calendar, least of all those who saw the small figure for the first time . . . [15]

So far as is known, this was Walter Williams's first and last attempt to write fiction for the slick national magazines that were so popular during that era. He submitted just the one piece. The leading family magazine in the country bought that manuscript and featured the story on its cover. His payment, not disclosed, would have been substantial. He decided to quit fiction writing while he was ahead.

His daughter, Helen Harned Williams, was born in 1896, and a second son, Edwin Moss Williams, was born in 1898. The family was a very close one, as relatives recall, and Williams spent as much time with the children as he could, especially on Sunday afternoons, when the entire brood could be spotted tramping through the fields outside Columbia and alongside the banks of Hinkson Creek. These outings typically concluded with a storytelling session, led by Walter Williams. At one point the three Williams children were organized, almost certainly by their father, into a family club, with each member pledging "to be kind to all living creatures, not kill birds, and not use a checkrein or blinders on a horse." It was not exactly the T.P.C. from Boonville days, when Walter Williams had been a teenager, but there were parallels. Far more than most, Williams sensed it was his mission to organize all that was around him, to give structure and focus and guidance, to compile a record of activity and preserve that record for the future. The closer he was to a group, the more leadership he wanted to give it. His own children, closest to him of all, would never lack direction from their father.

In the spring of 1896, Williams made up his mind to temporarily forgo his self-imposed eschewal of politics and run for the Columbia Board of Education. He was elected, and would serve for six years. In 1898 his peers on the board chose him to be chairman, a position he took seriously. Not content merely to preside at board meetings, Williams became an energetic lobbyist for the public schools; during his time on the board he helped put through tax increases

---

15. *Saturday Evening Post,* November 5, 1898, 1.

to build a new high school, improve teachers' salaries, get telephones installed in school buildings, and shore up janitorial and repair service.

And despite his own spotty high school record—or maybe because of it—Williams took an activist role in academic affairs. It was his resolution, adopted by the board during Williams's first year as a member, that required principals to report on books and periodicals dealing with teaching that their faculty members had read during the year. Another Williams initiative established a policy that no new teachers would be hired without a degree from the University of Missouri or an accredited Normal school or at least four successful years of practical classroom experience in another town. He lobbied for a directive, which later became official policy, requiring teachers to complete additional education courses to keep them fresh and current in the classes they taught throughout their careers.

In a bit of backseat driving that latter-day schoolteachers might have found outrageously intrusive, Williams even imposed on the schoolteachers of Columbia his own policy of how the name of the state should be pronounced. While many who lived there, especially in the southern and bootheel regions, called their state "Mizzourah," others called it "Mizzouree." Williams himself used "Mizzouree," and insisted that all teachers in the Columbia school system instruct their pupils to do the same.

Williams's vigorous leadership won him the attention of the State Association of School Boards, and in 1899 he served for a year as its president.[16]

The *Columbia Herald* continued to uphold its reputation as "The Model American Weekly." Williams's editorial leadership sustained the paper at a high level, while E. W. Stephens's astute performance as publisher kept the operation prosperous. The superintendent of the huge printing plant was Stephens's brother-in-law, James Moss. Williams regarded Moss as an artistic genius and, indeed, admired him so much he had named his second son in Moss's honor. They, and the others in the big Stephens printing plant, evolved a comfortable, harmonious routine that only rarely, for a business as volatile as newspapers, malfunctioned.

One such breakdown—so atypical that staff members would talk about it for years—found Walter Williams using language he would never have used in the *Herald.* The paper's makeup man—the production worker who assembles the trays of headlines and body type onto the forms that will become pages on the press—was a skilled craftsman by the name of Evans. In the rush of putting together one edition, however, Evans mixed up two headlines. As a

---

16. Rucker, *Walter Williams,* 75–77.

result, the *Herald* ran "Making Love," which was intended to go over the marriage licenses, over the record of births. Charles G. Ross, who would later win a Pulitzer prize as a Washington correspondent for the *St. Louis Post-Dispatch* but was then a student intern at the *Herald,* recalled what happened next: "With the sly or scandalized comments of *Herald* readers in his ears, Williams summoned the stricken Evans before him and in the curious falsetto that was then his normal voice, and with impressive spacing of words, made one remark:

'Mr. Evans—you—have—simply—played—Hell!' "[17]

Williams's reputation as an editor, helped along by his standing in the National Editorial Association, prompted job offers from afar. One of these was especially tempting. From his Miramar Ranch headquarters in California, the powerful press lord E. W. Scripps sent a trusted lieutenant, "Doc" Woods, to Kansas City to launch the *World,* an ambitious challenge to the entrenched *Kansas City Evening Star.* Woods offered the editorship of the *World* to Walter Williams. The job would pay one hundred dollars a week, or four times what Williams was earning in Columbia. Williams declined the offer, telling associates at the time he wanted control of editorial policy, a stipulation that Woods, himself under tight control by the hard-driving Scripps, could not offer.[18] Perhaps Williams also sensed, sooner than Scripps did, the staggering difficulty any newspaper would face in attempting to dislodge the *Evening Star,* a forceful, crusading newspaper founded by William Rockhill Nelson in 1880 and destined to dominate the Kansas City market for generations to come. Walter Williams had been in one newspaper war before, back in Boonville, and he wanted no part of another.

He did face competition, of a far milder sort, in Columbia, of course. Aside from the *Statesman,* other weeklies popped up from time to time, only to be disappointed in their attempts to wrest editorial and advertising and circulation leadership from E. W. Stephens, Walter Williams, and the *Herald.* But the Columbia market was becoming increasingly attractive.

The turn of the century found Columbia with a population of more than five thousand. Francis Pike, popular longtime newspaperman and unofficial town historian, later wrote that around that time Columbia

> boasted two music stores, two department stores, two finely equipped colleges for girls (Stephens and Christian) and the University of Missouri, with an enrollment of about 2,000 students. It had four hotels, six churches—better than the churches in

17. Sara Lockwood Williams, unpublished Walter Williams biography.
18. Ibid. Also, Alfred M. Lee, *The Daily Newspaper in America* (New York: Macmillan, 1937), 213.

larger cities—several churches for "colored people," three meat markets, seventeen grocery stores, three hardware stores, eighteen practicing attorneys, one full-time and three part-time men on the police force . . . three shoe stores, a large electric light and water system, three large clothing stores, a "new and cómmodious" city hall, twenty-three practicing physicians, five doctors in dentistry, a healthy climate and beautiful scenery . . . an excellent telephone system with connections to nearly all points of importance in the country, a splendid high school, three large lumber yards, two book stores, three saloons, three billiard halls, two cafes and three restaurants, and enough boarding houses for everybody. Six large livery barns . . . a bowling alley, two bakeries, two railway trunk lines, three drayage companies, a large brick manufacturer . . . a handle factory, a wagon factory, and one of the largest flouring mills in the state.[19]

And as of September 12, 1901, Columbia would boast its own daily newspaper.

The *Daily Tribune* was founded by Charles Munro Strong, freshly graduated from the University of Missouri, an eager young man with a yen to stay in Columbia and few dollars to spare on what appeared to be an unpromising gamble. His partner and mentor was a veteran printer named Charles G. Duncan. It was said that Duncan had memorized the complete works of Shakespeare. A few days later they were joined by Barrett O'Hara, another recent graduate of the university. The three operated out of the third floor of Stone's Music Hall at 15 South Ninth Street.[20] Chronically undercapitalized and poorly edited, the *Daily Tribune* would not pose much of a threat to the *Herald* until late in 1905, when a smart and aggressive journalist and lawyer named Ed Watson took over the paper. From that moment on the *Daily Tribune* would become quite a competitor indeed.

Meanwhile, Walter Williams remained comfortably on top of his job. Editing America's Model Weekly had become, if not routine, at least a smooth and efficient exercise. Even with his parental responsibilities and extensive Sunday school and public speaking responsibilities, he had time on his hands.

He devoted more and more attention to professional activities, notably the state press association and the National Editorial Association. He attended NEA conventions almost every year, and at the Chicago convention in 1893 he was elected national president—at thirty, the youngest person ever to hold that office. While the post was largely honorary, it was a remarkable acknowledgment of the esteem he commanded among his fellow country editors.

---

19. Leland Francis Pike, *Ed Watson: Country Editor* (Marceline, Mo.: Walsworth Publishing Co., 1982), 20.

20. Ibid., 163.

With E. W. Stephens, he began in 1894 a monthly journal for the press association, the *Missouri Editor.* Newsy and folksy, the *Missouri Editor* reported on ownership changes, developments in printing equipment, new staff appointments around the state, editorials vigorously defending legal advertising (official notices paid for by local and state government, an important source of revenue for country papers), and business tips, such as when it specifically named some national advertisers who had failed to pay their accounts. Shady advertisers were exposed: "H. Benjamin & Co. of St. Louis are sending out propositions offering 6 cents per inch gross, payable in trade, for advertising. Any paper that accepts them ought to starve—and most of them will." And, "Have no dealings with the Grey Eagle Gold Mining Company, Denver, unless they pay cash in advance."[21] After a few issues, Williams and Stephens decided to raise the subscription price to fifty cents per year. "If this publication isn't worth fifty cents," Williams editorialized, "it isn't worth anything." He also used the *Editor* to promulgate his own standards of professionalism. "The ideal country paper should be the keeper of the conscience of the town in which it is published," he wrote, adding that personal bias in the news columns was no longer acceptable: "It requires a high journalistic sense to divest a paper of prejudice, for editors are human, but no paper will get there until it eliminates every vestige of it."[22]

The *Missouri Editor,* four smallish pages each month, was tightly edited and proved a useful forum for the state press. Journalists from outside Missouri also subscribed, enough to prompt Stephens and Williams to change the publication's name to the *Country Editor* and expand its coverage for a wider audience. Even then, the publication operated in the red. A few hundred editors constituted an influential readership but a small and unprofitable market for advertisers. Early in 1898 Stephens told the Missouri Press Association that the publication was costing him money. The members voted to subsidize the *Editor* and adopt it as the association's official journal, but Stephens and Williams had tired of it and, without rancor, announced to sympathetic colleagues their intentions to quit publishing the *Editor.* Some publishers in northern Missouri took it over, but they too abandoned it a short time later, and the publication died. The *Editor* had served a useful purpose, however, and variations of the old *Missouri Editor* began appearing under the sponsorship of press associations in other states. It had been good for Walter Williams as well, reaffirming friendships he had developed during his presidency of the association, and reinforcing his leadership role with the state's press. As with his speeches, the

21. Mills, "E. W. Stephens," 119.
22. Taft, *Missouri Newspapers,* 8–9.

Editor had given him a platform from which he could stake out the journalistic high ground. To a gratifying degree, he was known to be a spokesman for tough professional standards and strong ethical values in journalism. It was not a bad reputation to have.

Williams took on two other part-time editing assignments as well. In 1895, the national convention of the Presbyterian Church ratified his appointment as editor of the *St. Louis Presbyterian,* the monthly paper serving parishioners in the region. Soon after that, the church decided to sell off the paper to private ownership, and a modest stock company, managed by Walter Williams, took over the paper. The paper was not profitable, but neither was it particularly demanding; mostly he published news releases from national and state head-quarters, supplementing them with news items from correspondents represent-ing local congregations. But Williams's editorship was especially appreciated by the church hierarchy. He was appointed a delegate to numerous church conferences, invited often to deliver guest sermons at churches throughout the state, and increasingly recognized for his service and leadership. In 1899 he was elected moderator of the state governance organization, the Missouri Presbytery.[23]

The other part-time work, which lasted four years, was as absentee editor of the *Jefferson City Tribune.* E. W. Stephens bought the *Tribune* in 1898, probably with the idea of eventually expanding his holdings to develop a chain of newspapers.[24] He gave some of the stock to his son, Hugh, and then, as incentives for the additional work involved, gave some shares to James H. Moss, the *Herald*'s production foreman, and to Walter Williams. Stephens and Williams ran the *Tribune* from Columbia, for the most part; Stephens kept track of the business side and Williams dictated editorials and news assignments via telephone. Stephens eventually found the arrangement too much of an additional burden and sold off his entire interest to his son. When Stephens bowed out of the *Tribune* in 1903, Williams did also. Stephens, as Williams soon learned, had other plans for himself—and for his protégé.

Just after the turn of the century, Williams embarked upon what would become his most ambitious editorial project. In 1904 the World's Fair was to be in St. Louis, and the Missouri legislature was keenly aware of the opportunities this presented for showcasing the state to tens of thousands of visitors to what was called the Louisiana Purchase Exposition. The legislators

---

23. Sara Lockwood Williams, unpublished Walter Williams biography.
24. Mills, "E. W. Stephens," 124.

appropriated $1 million for a Missouri exhibit at the fair—officially it was called the Louisiana Purchase Exposition—and part of that sum was earmarked for an official encyclopedia of the state. Walter Williams was chosen by the World's Fair Commission to edit the volume, which he described as "the State's autobiography."

Entitled *The State of Missouri,* it was an ambitious compilation, twenty-three chapters and nearly six hundred pages in all, covering Missouri's history, governance, geology, business and industry, agriculture, mining and minerals, people, and communities. The state's ten largest cities were profiled, and there were sketches tracing developments in each of Missouri's 114 counties. In planning the volume, Williams crisscrossed the state, enlisting qualified writers for each locality and topic. Several of the chapters were written by the most accomplished professors at the University of Missouri: Isidor Loeb in politics and law, F. B. Mumford in agriculture, G. E. Ladd in mining and metallurgy, B. M. Duggar in botany. Eighty thousand copies were printed—the contract was awarded to the E. W. Stephens Company of Columbia—and distributed to private purchasers and libraries throughout the land.

Years later, Missouri's distinguished historian, Floyd C. Shoemaker, would describe *The State of Missouri* as "one of the most unusual books ever published on an American commonwealth. It was the most widely distributed, the most complete, and the most reliable of modern Missouri gazetteers and was the only book awarded a grand prize by the Louisiana Purchase Exposition. It is still a standard reference work."[25]

Williams himself was proud of the finished product, writing in his editor's foreword of his "confident expectation that it [*The State of Missouri*] will result in large and lasting good in acquainting the world with the possibilities of Missouri to the end that these possibilities may be realized to the fullest measure." And in the opening chapter, which he had written himself, he glorified his home state—which, he cautioned, should be pronounced Mis-zoo-ry—as the Old Testament had described Canaan: "A good land, a land of brooks of water, of fountains and depths that spring out of valleys and hills; a land of wheat and barley and vines; a land wherein thou shalt eat bread without scarceness; thou shalt not lack anything in it." But the book's dedication was pure Walter Williams: "To those who are Missourians and to those who should be."[26]

Missourians' pride in their home state had, in fact, taken a serious hit some years earlier. In 1870 St. Louis had been the fourth-largest city in the country,

25. Quoted in Sara Lockwood Williams, unpublished Walter Williams biography.
26. Walter Williams, ed., *The State of Missouri* (Columbia: E. W. Stephens Co., 1904).

one place ahead of Chicago (though later scholarship suggests that the 1870 census figures for St. Louis had been fraudulently inflated to ensure that the city could claim a larger population than rival Chicago). But only a decade later Chicago's booming economy and attendant population surge had clearly outstripped St. Louis, leading one Missouri historian to describe the city's mood as one of "great gloom," with the entire state now bewildered and in the throes of a collective "inferiority complex."[27] St. Louis's spirits would be further dampened a few years later: when preparations were underway to hold a Columbian Exposition in 1892, to commemorate the four hundredth anniversary of Columbus's great discovery, St. Louis put in an impassioned bid to be host city, only to lose out to Chicago. Not to be outdone, and spurred on by editorial writers at the *St. Louis Globe* and the *Post-Dispatch,* Missourians decided in 1898 to begin planning for a world's fair of their own, this one to commemorate the centennial of the Louisiana Purchase. It was clear from the start that the planning committee was determined to make the St. Louis exposition larger and more spectacular than the Chicago world's fair had been.

Indeed, the Louisiana Purchase Exposition would develop into the biggest, grandest, most elaborate, and best-produced exposition that had ever been provided by any city. Nearly twelve hundred acres in Forest Park, near downtown, provided a splendid setting. Fifteen sizable exposition buildings were erected and positioned on the fairgrounds in a pattern scheme more or less suggesting an enormous fan. The structures reflected wildly different architectural concepts—"an astonishing pattern of elaborate and universal chaos," as one art critic described it. The emphasis was on U.S. progress, of course— railroad and locomotive development, state-of-the-art industry and agricultural technology, something new contributed from every state (except Delaware). An even hundred motorcars were on display, including one that had made the trip from New York to St. Louis "on its own power." But there also was much to be shown from overseas, in the most energetic and extensive foreign exhibitions yet attempted by any American fair. Some sixty-two nations were represented, "with living specimens of the world's peoples from Pygmies to Patagonians," as one historian noted.[28]

Thomas Jefferson's Louisiana Purchase, consummated with France for $15 million only a century before, had added 827,987 square miles and what would become fifteen new states to the nation, virtually doubling its size.

---

27. Meyer, *Heritage of Missouri,* 501. The charge that St. Louis influenced the 1870 census is argued persuasively in James Neal Primm's *Lion in the Valley* (Boulder, Colo.: Pruett, 1981).

28. Edwin C. McReynolds, *Missouri: A History of the Crossroads State* (Norman: University of Oklahoma Press, 1962), 312 ff. Meyer, *Heritage of Missouri,* 503.

When Jefferson had been warned at the time that the Constitution did not authorize the acquisition of land, he shrewdly countered by pointing out that it did permit the making of treaties. His decision, which he had described as "stretching the Constitution until it cracked," would be well and truly commemorated in St. Louis a hundred years later. More than one hundred thousand new visitors a day, nearly twenty million in all, would attend the Louisiana Purchase Exhibition between April 30 and December 1, 1904. And if St. Louis would remain destined forever to trail Chicago in population, it had nevertheless presented in 1904 an exposition by which all ensuing world's fairs would be judged.

The head of the executive committee for the Louisiana Purchase Exposition was former Governor David R. Francis. Although Francis's appointment of Williams to a state job had turned out badly, the two men had remained friends. Just after the turn of the century, Francis called upon Williams again, this time to be publicity director of the Louisiana Purchase Exposition. This position would work out very well indeed.

Here, as had so often been the case, E. W. Stephens positioned Walter Williams directly in the spotlight. One historian explained it this way:

> One of the high planes in the evolution of the new journalism in Missouri was reached in 1902. E. W. Stephens came down from Columbia and laid before the press and publicity committee of the St. Louis World's Fair a plan for foreign press propaganda. Mr. Stephens's own experience and that of Walter Williams in developing the organization and increasing the efficiency of first the Missouri Press Association and later the National Editorial Association had impressed them with the possibilities of what might be done by direct effort with the press of other countries in the interest of the World's Fair. The plan of E. W. Stephens was adopted without hesitation.[29]

Stephens's promotional campaign called for face-to-face promotion of the fair around the globe. Upon his recommendation, the World's Fair executive committee dispatched Williams on a world tour in which he was to contact newspaper publishers directly, urging them to encourage their countries to participate in the Louisiana Purchase Exposition. It would not be an easy sell. Francis himself, only recently returned from an extensive promotional tour of Europe, had met with ranking officials of many countries but had failed to secure as much cooperation as he had expected. The key, Francis and Stephens were convinced, would be to cultivate foreign press support for the world's fair in hopes that national commitments would follow. Williams was given

---

29. Walter B. Stevens, "The New Journalism in Missouri," *Missouri Historical Review* 19:1 (October 1924): 105.

an impressive title, Commissioner to the Foreign Press, and, with Stephens's blessing, a six-month leave of absence from the *Herald.* He was told to sell the fair anywhere in the world he could. James H. Moss, the production foreman at the *Herald,* went along as photographer. Their journey would ultimately last nine months, rather than six, and cover some twenty-five thousand miles. By their own accounts, Williams and Moss visited more than one thousand newspaper offices in twenty-seven nations on four continents.

Williams sent back an article, illustrated with Moss's photographs, for each week's issue of the *Herald.* The pieces, many of which were carried by other papers as well, were informative and folksy, almost like letters home from adventurous friends. Williams often described himself and Moss as simply "your Missouri pilgrims." The *Herald*'s headlines read like a travelogue: "Switzerland, the Colorado of Europe," "Jerusalem, City of the Great King," "Seven Hills of Rome and Other Things," "Three Days in Darkest Africa," "Venice: Where Gondolas Take the Place of Cabs," "A Scamper Through Scotland."[30]

Williams and Moss were zestful travelers. As Frank Rucker, a distinguished publisher and friend of Williams, would write later of the pair, "In Ireland they kissed the Blarney Stone, in Egypt they rode on camels to the Sphinx and the Pyramids. They visited the great cathedrals of Europe and worshipped there and in the village churches . . ."[31] The dispatches Williams sent home not only gave an overview of a given city but also suggested something of its mood. From London, for example, Williams wrote about what was to be the coronation of King Edward VII:

> We had just inspected the seats from which we were to have the privilege, at a
> guinea each, of seeing the [royal] procession pass. A newsboy thrust an "extra"
> edition of the *Westminster Gazette* into our hands and we read: "Dangerous Illness
> of the King." It was as though a blow had struck the great sentient city in the face.
> We walked down the Pall Mall, across Trafalgar Square and through the Strand.
> It needed not the printed words of the newspaper, nor the bulletins sprinkled
> in the windows, to tell that something terrible and unexpected had taken place.
> That could be read in the appearance of the crowd, could be felt in the very
> atmosphere. London, at 11 o'clock gay and jubilant, became in the noon hour
> sober, silent, sad.[32]

In country after country, meanwhile, Williams was plugging the fair. Sometimes his message got garbled, as in one city in Spain where the local editor wrote:

---

30. Quoted In Rucker, *Walter Williams,* 90.
31. Ibid.
32. Quoted in ibid.

Señor Williams of St. Louis was in the office today and reported that he had
just purchased seven million square miles of land from France, which he named
Louisiana, and in honor of that event has decided to hold a fiesta, to which the
entire world is invited.[33]

On the whole, though, the sales pitch registered effectively, and the entire
trip was a smashing success. In one nation after another, Williams nailed down
expressions of support and assurances of participation. "No representative who
has gone to Europe or another country has so ably promoted the exposition or
done more intelligent, productive work," David Francis would say later. "Mr.
Williams has served the people of the entire state of Missouri."[34]

The success of the mission was assured early in 1902, when the International Congress of Press Associations convened in Berne, Switzerland. Walter
Williams, thirty-seven, a country editor from Columbia, Missouri, asked permission to address this large, influential gathering, and in his speech invited the
congress to hold its 1904 meeting in St. Louis during the Louisiana Purchase
Exposition. To his astonishment, the invitation was accepted. The presence
of hundreds of foreign journalists, and thus reams of publicity throughout the
world, was guaranteed. The Missouri pilgrims would make many more sales
calls after that, and Williams would find some extra time to study and write
and do research in the Holy Land, this for his Bible class back at the First
Presbyterian Church. But after the acceptance of the International Congress of
Press Associations, anything more was mere icing on the cake. Williams had
been asked to drum up support among the world's press for the exposition,
and this, demonstrably, he had done. He returned home in triumph, honored in
St. Louis with a banquet and a glowing tribute from his hero, David R. Francis.
It was a splendid moment. But in gracious remarks at the dinner that night,
Williams modestly deflected the credit. "The four Americans most heard of
in Europe are President [Theodore] Roosevelt, [financier] Pierpont Morgan,
David R. Francis, and the Missouri mule," he said. "When I became lonesome
I hunted an American consul's office to gaze on the President's proclamation
concerning the World's Fair and a picture of Ex-Governor Francis, or I walked
the streets to hear the bray of a mule drawing a streetcar."[35]

The expedition reaffirmed Williams's belief that journalistic professionalism could cut through whatever political and cultural barriers nations might
erect. "One touch of printer's ink makes the whole world kin," he would
exclaim to the Missouri Press Association in a speech about his voyage

---

33. Quoted in Mills, "E. W. Stephens," 118.
34. Rucker, *Walter Williams,* 99.
35. Ibid., 99.

of discovery. "There is a fraternity among newspaper workers everywhere, a free masonry which binds together German and French and British and American, toiling with pen and pencil and press, with type and typewriter . . . The American editor has a foreign brother."[36]

The exposition itself lived up to all that Williams had promised his brother editors around the world. As visitors streamed into the fairgrounds, Williams spent so much time in St. Louis that he moved his family there, taking an apartment not far away from his office at the Missouri building on the exposition site. Williams and his assistants worked night and day, handling press inquiries, writing press releases, arranging interviews with celebrities. He ghosted some articles to be published under the bylines of Francis and other leaders, and wrote other articles, including one for *Century Illustrated Monthly,* one of the nation's best magazines.

As measured by attendance, the international press gathering, held between May 19 and 21, 1904, was an extraordinary success. More than five thousand journalists, representing thirty-seven nations and each state in the Union, were on hand. They were officially welcomed by John Hay, President Roosevelt's secretary of state. Presiding was Sir Hugh Gilzean-Reid, publisher of England's prestigious *Manchester Guardian.* (Afterwards Williams would whisk Sir Hugh off to Columbia, where he would be awarded an honorary degree from the University of Missouri. "His head was as big as a barrel," Williams confided to a friend later. "But he pulled from his pocket a Scots cap, such as students at St. Andrews University wore, put it on, keeping it on with difficulty, and replied to the citation in a Scots accent that captured everyone."[37] When the ceremonies were concluded, Williams took Sir Hugh to the lavish estate of E. W. Stephens, where he was served mint juleps. The British press lord was so taken with the drink, which was new to him, that he asked another visitor there, Professor J. C. Whitten of the horticulture department, to send mint plants to him so that he might introduce the drink back in his home country.)

The press convention program itself was not terribly substantial—"more a social and sightseeing reunion than a meeting for serious discussion," later wrote William H. Taft, a shrewd observer of Missouri journalism, "and [mostly] members visited 'the biggest show on earth.' " But there were some solemn, and even moving, addresses delivered. Several speakers, notably the delegate from Russia, deplored the lack of press freedom in their native lands. These talks, and the extensive U.S. press coverage they received, prompted some

36. Quoted in ibid., 100.
37. Ibid.

thoughtful observers to declare the press convention one of the exposition's crowning achievements.[38] That assessment may or may not have been accurate, but by any standard the exposition was a personal triumph for Walter Williams. Not only was his book, *The State of Missouri,* singled out for a special award, but Williams himself was elected secretary of the world press gathering, with friendly votes coming from his NEA colleagues and from the visiting editors he had met on his global promotional journey as well.

It was during this St. Louis convention that the journalists voted to change the name of the association from the International Congress of Press Associations to something a little more ambitious: The World Press Parliament. How much Walter Williams had to do with the name change is not known, but certainly he approved. His first choice would have been to have the organization entitled the Press Congress of the World—which, in a few years and under his deft leadership, it would be.

The World Press Parliament also heard speakers sound a plea for some form of professional training for journalists. One rousing speaker, Crosby S. Noyes, publisher of the *Washington Star,* proclaimed it high time that courses in journalism be offered by colleges and universities. He added that "the student of journalism should be taught, and as well in the public schools as anywhere, to write with directness, precision, and force . . . in words comprehended by everyone, high or low."[39]

Education for journalism. Walter Williams had some ideas about that, too.

---

38. Taft, *Missouri Newspapers,* 167. Stevens, "New Journalism in Missouri."
39. Taft, *Missouri Newspapers,* 166.

6

A Door Opens, Then Closes

Journalism—country journalism—has become a profession.
The time has passed when one-horse lawyers or school teachers
can hope to sustain themselves or the town paper by writing for it.

—E. W. Stephens, 1880

Newspaper reporting was forever changed by the Civil War. That epic struggle, as Thomas Jefferson had written much earlier about a different conflict, "between rivers and mountains which must have shaken the earth itself to its center,"[1] made news a priceless commodity. Even the fragmentary and improbable dispatch from a harried correspondent in the field would be read with desperate intensity. The war was not only the all-important national story; it was also a poignant local story of urgent and direct concern to families everywhere. The telegraph, though not always accessible to the press—military transmission took top priority—placed a premium on immediacy in getting the news back to the home office. Until then reporters had often preferred to develop their articles in lofty, literary fashion that crept toward a climax. But dramatically changed circumstances compelled reporters to disclose their most important facts—to answer the classic questions (Who? What? When? Where? Why?)—at the very beginning of the piece. Lesser details might follow, but if only that single fact-filled opening paragraph got through on the telegraph, the reporter knew, the home office had at least the salient points, enough for a page-one bulletin at press time. Journalists by the dozens traveled with the Union and Confederate armies, crowding against each other in desperate competition for what telegraph service might be available. In the aggregate, they sent back more reportage than the country had ever seen before. The *New York Herald* alone spent half a million dollars in correspondents' salaries, telegraph tolls, and charter fees for horses, wagons, special trains, and steamboats.[2]

With their persistent demands for access and information, the journalists more often than not found themselves in an angry, adversarial relationship with the top brass. William Tecumseh Sherman, the huffy, hard-charging Union

---

1. Quoted in Louis L. Snyder and Richard B. Morris, eds., *A Treasury of Great Reporting* (Simon and Schuster, 1949), 120.
2. Bernard A. Weisberger, *The American Newspaperman* (Chicago, 1961), 118.

general, endured more troubles with the press than most. His outbursts against newspapermen were frequent, bitter, and, at times, understandable. As, for example, when the *Cincinnati Commercial* carried a piece calling him "stark mad" and mistakenly alleging that he had been relieved of his command. Sherman would have tarred all reporters with the same brush:

> They come into camp, poke about among the lazy shirks and pick up their camp rumors and publish them as facts, and the avidity with which these rumors are swallowed by the public makes even some of our officers bow to them. I will not. They are a pest and shall not approach me and I will treat them as spies, which in truth they are.[3]

Reporters covering the Confederate troops tended to be more sympathetic to their army's cause, but could be dismally inept in writing about it. Produced and transmitted under wretched conditions, their dispatches too often were fraught with errors. Indeed, a classic headline once appeared in the *Memphis Appeal:* IMPORTANT—IF TRUE.[4] Where Sherman had been outraged, General Robert E. Lee was merely dismayed. News reporting was coming of age, but news reporters, too many of them, were not. And yet for all his frailties, the reporter was now thrust into unaccustomed prominence. To an extraordinary degree, the reporter, the one with a firsthand account from the scene, was emerging as the central figure in American journalism.

The press had a different focus now. Back in the 1830s, when newspapers first began to break away from narrow partisanship in quest of the mass audience, publishers tended to be promoters bent on making profits. For these cold-eyed individuals, staffing was easy; there was almost always a bright young person around with a literary flair and an eagerness to become a newspaper reporter or editor. A few publishers of this period were splendid teachers as well, and they were able to train their staffs to perform outstanding work. Many journalists would share the view of an early press historian, Frederic Hudson, who proclaimed that the office of a newspaper "is the one true college for newspaper students. Professor James Gordon Bennett and Professor Horace Greeley would turn out more genuine journalists in one year than the Harvards, the Yales, and the Dartmouths could produce in a generation."[5]

But only a privileged few would ever work for Bennett's *New York Herald* or Greeley's *Tribune,* and as events grew more complex, the uneven quality

---

3. Quoted in Jean Folkerts and Dwight L. Teeter, Jr., *Voices of a Nation* (Macmillan, 1994), 198.

4. The most comprehensive studies of Civil War journalism are J. Cutler Andrews, *The North Reports the Civil War* (Pittsburgh, 1955), followed by his *The South Reports the Civil War* (Princeton University Press, 1970).

5. Frederic Hudson, *Journalism in the United States, 1690–1872* (Harper, 1873), 713.

of news reporting became embarrassingly apparent. The Civil War coverage, sometimes brilliant,[6] more often inaccurate and incomplete, massively underscored this point. General Lee's experience with reporters assigned to his headquarters convinced him that formal education in the journalism field was long overdue. After the war, when he was named president of Washington College, Lee decided to offer full-tuition scholarships to selected students on the condition that each "would labor one hour a day in his profession of journalism" and spend considerable time, in addition to the normal liberal arts curriculum, studying with an outstanding editor, much as a would-be lawyer of the period would study in the office library of a good attorney. It was his hope, Bobby Lee said at the time, that an infusion of dedicated yet well-educated young journalists might assist in the rebuilding of that strife-torn region; perhaps they would improve Southern newspapers beyond the dismal level at which they had performed during the war. But if the idea was a good one, the location for implementing it was not. Washington College was situated in the lovely but isolated town of Lexington in the mountains of western Virginia. Whatever else it might have been, Lexington was no hotbed of newspaperdom. Little interest in improving the newspaper business was manifest there, either by Washington College students or the local editor. Only six of the fifty scholarships Lee offered the prospective journalists were actually claimed, and so far as is known none of those six students ever became much of a journalist. Lee's plan had merit, however, and had been well publicized; other institutions of higher learning around the country soon began, in one way or another, to explore ways in which systematic instruction in journalism might be offered.

David Russell McAnally joined the faculty of the University of Missouri in 1877. He was thirty years old at the time and already had a little newspaper work under his belt as well as five years of high school teaching experience and two years as dean of tiny Arcadia College. At Missouri the gifted, self-educated young McAnally had been hired to teach undergraduates something about English literature: he taught classes in Shakespeare, Milton, Chaucer, Bacon, the history of drama. He was an ebullient classroom lecturer, comfortable with his students, inevitably well prepared for each class meeting. Some of his lectures were so meticulously researched and authoritative that a publisher invited him to flesh them out into book form. One such compilation, his

---

6. Many Civil War correspondents were courageous and more than a few were brilliant. Some, such as Henry Villard of the *New York Herald,* Henry J. Raymond of the *New York Times,* and B. S. Osbon of the *New York World,* to cite only three, were both.

Philosophy of English Poetry, would become a popular college text. The debonair McAnally was also something of a campus character, much discussed by students: he was a diligent reader, especially of the Bible, and an energetic intellectual stimulated by all things cultural. Of all the arts, music was his favorite; he was said to have spent at least one hour a day at the keyboard of the pipe organ at his home. He was also inordinately fond of flowers and grew them in great profusion, keeping the two large hothouses in his gardens filled with blossoms. Each morning he carried bouquets of flowers to the office, and on days when he worked at home he would often send flowers to the office by messenger for his colleagues to enjoy. He was adored by students, though not always by his faculty colleagues, and appreciated by the university administrators, who eventually conferred upon him a full professorship and the chairmanship of the English department. During his third year on the Missouri faculty, and almost as an afterthought, David R. McAnally also became the first college professor ever to teach a course in journalism.

He created a new course and entitled it the History of Journalism. The university catalogue described it as "lectures with practical explanations of daily newspaper life. The *Spectator,* the London *Times,* the New York *Herald."* There was no textbook, although at least one trade book, *Hints to Young Editors,* had been published as early as 1872. Instead, McAnally used his class sessions to analyze various newspapers, to investigate trends in content, to challenge editorial decisions, to explain how newsrooms operated and why articles were developed the way they were. While this was the first course known to have used the word "journalism" in its title, it was not McAnally's only foray into the journalism field. The previous year he had required his students to employ journalistic methods in his course called Political Economy: the class was "Taught by means of lectures," in the college catalogue's somber explanation, "of which the students are required to make copious notes, to be worked up into essays, theses, and similar expositions. The habit of reporting the lectures is found beneficial in the highest degree, since it contributes to accuracy in thought and statement, and furnishes no small amount of exercises in practical composition."[7] One of his goals, McAnally said, was simply to expose his students to good examples of vigorous and clear English in a contemporary way that the study of ancient literature could not.

---

7. Sara Lockwood Williams, *Twenty Years of Education for Journalism* (E. W. Stephens, 1922), 13. *Hints to Young Editors* is referred to in an unpublished manuscript, "Pioneer Thoughts on Journalism," written by Dr. William H. Taft, former professor at the University of Missouri School of Journalism, and dated March 22, 1982.

For all his creativity and personal popularity, however, McAnally found his teaching of journalism a tough sell. Some elitist students grumbled about using newspapers as models. Professorial colleagues debunked the idea of McAnally's de facto acknowledgment that journalism might have standing in higher education. Surprisingly, many newspaper editors did also. "Only the faith of intensity," a University of Missouri president would later recall of McAnally, "could have made possible the establishment of a journalism class on a college campus."[8] But this was the sort of faith that dwelled in David Russell McAnally, a dapper, cheerful, exceedingly courteous man with a handlebar mustache, a flower in his lapel, a walking stick, which also served as a pointer in the classroom, clutched in his hand, and a song in his heart.

McAnally was descended from an old-line Virginia family—his maternal grandmother was Patrick Henry's sister—and he grew up in a genteel, devout, Southern Methodist household. His father, David Rice McAnally, was a Methodist minister who shifted to newspaper work and later achieved considerable distinction as editor of the thoughtful, widely circulated *St. Louis Christian Advocate.* The father tutored young David McAnally in journalism—as, indeed, in a great many other things as well; David Russell McAnally, the University of Missouri's learned chair of the English department, and journalism's first professor, had attended elementary and high schools only sporadically. He never went to college.

Bored by vicarious journalism—or academic politics, perhaps—McAnally left the university in 1885, returning to St. Louis and a job on the *Globe-Democrat.* He had worked for that newspaper earlier in his career and, in all, would be associated with it for more than twenty years. An editorial writer during much of that time, McAnally contributed cultural pieces as well. His music reviews were considered especially good. After hours he wrote a number of songs, at least one operetta, and, though he never married, a book entitled *Love, Courtship and Marriage* and another, *How Men Make Love and Get Married.* A modest and retiring man, McAnally rarely attended public functions; apart from church services and artistic performances, he preferred to remain alone with his books and his flower gardens. His reputation as a scholar brought him dozens of invitations, which he may or may not have welcomed, to deliver public lectures. Some of these, such as one dealing with word origins,

---

8. Dr. J. C. Jones, former president of the University of Missouri, as quoted in *The McAnally Missourian,* a special issue of the *Columbia Missourian,* published at a School of Journalism banquet honoring the memory of McAnally, February 20, 1930, and found in the Western Historical Manuscript Collection, Columbia, Mo.

were so popular they were reprinted and sold as monographs.[9] The University of Missouri continued to invite him back each year to teach short courses and to serve on the editorial board of various literary and official publications. And for all his shyness, McAnally was a charismatic public speaker who inspired audiences wherever he went, infusing them with his own zest for learning and culture. "No gentleman of his age has greater educational prominence in Missouri," wrote Colonel William F. Switzler in his *History of Boone County*.[10] Four colleges would later award him honorary degrees.

Yet McAnally would always be regarded as something of a dilettante, never fully accepted by his associates. On the campus, some of his brother faculty members distrusted his enthusiasm for journalism. And for all his erudition (and popularity with students), said faculty members again and again of McAnally, *the man did not hold a college degree.* Yet when he returned to newspaper work, his editors would refer to him as "the professor," and frequently point out that although he did well enough as an editorial writer, he could not be taken seriously as a "real journalist" because he had never pounded the streets as a news reporter, much less paid his dues as a city editor or managing editor.[11] At times, David McAnally must have regarded himself as a colossal misfit, a lonely man torn between the academy and the harsh professional world outside, never fully comfortable in either place.

He had many admirers but few intimate friends. His devotion to his father was especially touching. The two were close throughout the father's life, and after his death David spent Sunday afternoons by his father's grave. Friends thought that McAnally's own grasp on life was never quite the same after his father's death. McAnally himself would die in 1909 of cerebroapoplexy. He was sixty-one. In his obituary he was described as "a gentleman and a scholar of the old school." The University of Missouri established the McAnally Medal, for excellence in composition, in his honor, but in a few years the memories of McAnally grew dimmer. On occasion he would be recalled as a brilliant visionary too far ahead of his time, "an almost forgotten educator and journalist," a famous dean at Missouri would say of McAnally later.[12] His course in the History of Journalism was abandoned when he left the Missouri faculty. But if others had forgotten McAnally and what he attempted to do at the university, E. W. Stephens and Walter Williams had not. To them, McAnally was more than a brilliant teacher and academic innovator; he was a respected

9. Ibid.

10. *Columbia Missourian,* February 14, 1956.

11. William H. Taft, "Establishing the School of Journalism," *Missouri Historical Review* 84 (October 1989): 63.

12. Earl English, quoted in the *Columbia Missourian,* April 30, 1954.

academic who had convincingly demonstrated that a course in journalism could be taught at the university level. It was a start.

Even before McAnally, there had been isolated calls for colleges and universities to offer courses in journalism. The *Boone County Journal* (forerunner to the *Herald*) in its second issue in 1869 fired off an editorial entitled "A School of Journalism":

> . . . why should we not have a school for editors? At least instruct the student in the true theory of editorial duty. Precisely how such a school should be conducted it would be very difficult to say . . . But there is manifestly not only room, but a real demand for it. We have an abundance of good newspaper writers, but a paucity of skillful editors.[13]

That same year a prominent St. Louis journalist named Norman J. Colman proposed that "a course of study" in journalism be offered by the university. Colman had considerable political as well as journalistic influence. He had published several agricultural papers, and *Colman's Rural World* was a leading farm journal in the region. Colman would later become Missouri's lieutenant governor and, in 1889, the nation's first secretary of agriculture. His interest in higher education had won him an appointment to the University of Missouri's Board of Curators, where he would become, in historian Floyd Shoemaker's words, "the guiding hand behind University politics for nearly half a century." Colman lobbied hard among his fellow curators for the establishment of a journalism program at the University of Missouri.[14] His advice, though not always followed, was listened to attentively. One of Colman's speeches was said to have galvanized the Missouri Press Association into a call for action:

> Like all other professions, the Editorial has grave and responsible duties devolving upon it—but unlike others, certain prescribed qualifications have not been required before entering upon the discharge of professional duty. No attendance in the lecture hall, or particular course of study, or training has been exacted . . . The Teacher, the Physician, the Lawyer, and the Divine must each undergo a thorough preparatory course before being permitted to enter on his chosen career. Schools and colleges must be attended, lectures listened to, and thorough examinations undergone before a license will be granted . . . An *esprit de corps* is thus cultivated, which is lasting and attended with the most beneficial results. But any particular training, or course of study, or lectures, or schools, or colleges, to prepare young men for the most important of all professions—the Editorial—has never been heard of. That institutions of this kind could be established, and would be attended with the most beneficial results can scarcely be doubted. Each member of the

---

13. Quoted in Mills, "E. W. Stephens."
14. Taft, "Establishing the School of Journalism," 63.

profession has now to learn for himself all that is to be known of the duties
devolving upon him.[15]

At Colman's urging, and reinforced by pressure from the powerful Missouri
Press Association, the College of Arts and Science at the University of Missouri
in 1873 organized and presented a series of lectures on journalism, prompting
some historians to describe the series as the first ever systematic attempt at
journalism education at the university level.[16] The lectures were supposed to
generate a groundswell of public support for further coursework in journalism,
but they did not. At least, not immediately.

After McAnally's departure from the Missouri faculty in 1885 there would
be no more purely journalistic courses offered for more than a decade. Still,
classes dealing peripherally with news writing were taught in the English
department on occasion.[17]

A Missouri alumnus who had become a prominent New York banker,
Leonidas M. Lawson, returned to the campus in 1879 for a speech in which he
urged the University of Missouri to launch a series of studies in journalism:

> May we not see the increasing volume and influence of newspaper and periodical
> literature soon place the profession of journalism within the sphere of university
> training? We are inspired with the hope that the beneficence of the State will
> soon supplement the wisdom and abilities of the faculty and the intelligence
> of the curators in making this place the famed seat of polite learning, to attract
> such multitudes as in former times flowed to Bologna and Paris and Oxford and
> Salamanca.[18]

This brought a sharp response from John A. Dillon of St. Louis, a noted
journalist of his day, in a letter to James S. Rollins, the Boone County legislator
whose politicking nearly half a century before had led to the founding of the
University of Missouri:

> I do not agree with you about the possibility of a professorship of journalism
> at the University. Only a journalist could qualify as a professor, and it is the
> fixed conviction of every one of us that we are like the poets, "born, not made";
> moreover, every journalist holds that when he was born, the seed gave out.
> Seriously, there is a racial instinct of animosity between the daily paper editor and
> the college professor; it is dying out in the east where journalism is in the hands of

---

15. Taft, *Missouri Newspapers,* 126.

16. Floyd Shoemaker's unpublished manuscript, "History of the Missouri Press Association,"
160–61; also Taft, "Establishing the School of Journalism."

17. Sara Lockwood Williams, *Twenty Years of Education for Journalism,* 18. The classes
were taught by Professor E. A. Allen in 1891, Professors G. A. Wauchope and E. W. Bowen in
1892–1893, and from 1893–1900 by Professors H. M. Belden and H. C. Penn.

18. Ibid.

college men; in the west the papers are still in the era of Horace Greeley: "of all horned cattle, deliver me from a college graduate."[19]

Increasingly, however, the notion began to take hold among Missouri editors that journalism could be taught and, indeed, should be taught at the state university. Sentiment for creating a journalism school was expressed at virtually every meeting of the Missouri Press Association during the 1890s. In January 1895, Missouri State Senator Charles E. Yeater of Sedalia introduced a bill in the legislature calling upon the University of Missouri to establish a chair of journalism and empower the university to grant the degree of bachelor of journalism. No funds were mentioned in his bill, the assumption, a fatal one, being that the university could absorb the costs of the journalism program within its current budget. The bill was defeated.[20]

Through editorials and signed columns, Walter Williams frequently stressed the need for a school of journalism. In one such essay, a detailed and well-reasoned argument addressed to his fellow journalists in *The Country Editor,* Williams made his case:

> The careful reader of the newspapers cannot fail to notice the errors that appear therein. Not errors of fact, but errors due to ignorance of history, geography, political economy, grammar, and other branches of learning. These mistakes are not confined to any one class or condition of journals. They are found in country and city publications, in the writings of the reporter, the telegraph editor and the editor-in-chief. One purpose of a school of journalism would be to direct the thought and studies of the student along the lines that would be useful to him in avoiding such errors.
>
> The practical side of journalism should also be taught in such a school. The student should learn there all about type, subscription books, advertising records. He should be instructed in headline writing, editorial composition and the preparation of advertisements. He might be given certain events to write up and then have pointed out wherein his write-up could be improved. Stereotyping, press feeding, typesetting machines and all the mechanical equipment of a printing office could be explained. In a few months in such a school, conducted by an experienced newspaper man, the student would be better fitted for active newspaper work than he could possibly be by the fragmentary knowledge gained elsewhere. He would not have to practice on the public as all our green reporters and editors do today.
>
> The law of libel could be explained and made clear in the school. Occasional lectures by the leading members of each profession would help give the student a knowledge of those things about which he must write. The newspaper man would thus learn a little of everything besides his own special work and be better trained,

---

19. Ibid., 15.
20. Ibid.; also Taft, "Establishing the School of Journalism," 68.

broader, and a more thoroughly disciplined writer in consequence. These are but hints at the many things that such a school could profitably teach.

The objection that newspaper work can only be successfully learned in a newspaper office is not a fair one. It is not expected that the school of journalism should turn out full-fledged editors. It is only intended that they should be better equipped for their work. Schools of law are not criticized because they do not turn out ready-made lawyers, or schools of medicine because their graduates must study beside the sick bed to become experienced doctors. Is there anything more mysterious about journalism than about law or medicine that young people may not prepare themselves for it? If it is insisted that journalism is not a profession, but a trade, it may be pointed out that there are schools of tailoring, watchmaking, embalming and everything else that requires skill and intelligence. Agricultural colleges teach farming but do not graduate farmers. Dental schools instruct in dentistry but do not turn out dentists. Business colleges and normal schools train but do not create business men or teachers. There is scarcely a single line of human activity in which there is not a school for preparation. Only in journalism is the beginner turned loose upon an unsuspecting public without the slightest knowledge of his duties or work.

Some newspaper men oppose such a school. Their arguments really find basis in the fact that they have succeeded admirably without this training. This, however, should be no argument at all. Would they not have accomplished more, at less sacrifice of time and grey matter had they been properly trained at the outset? Certainly they would. To claim the opposite is to assert that they were gifted with some peculiar, heaven-born capacity denied to other men and limited altogether to editors.

We cannot believe that any one who will weigh carefully the reasons for and against a school of journalism will decide against it. To declare newspaper men need no education along the line of their work is to put a premium on ignorance and to assert that the less an editor knows the better fitted he is for his duties. We hardly think newspaper men are ready for such a creed.[21]

In this as he had in so much else, Walter Williams took his lead from E. W. Stephens. As early as 1884, Stephens became known as the Missouri Press Association's leading advocate of a school of journalism. Again and again in his press association speeches, Stephens pushed his fellow editors to demand that formal instruction in journalism be offered at the college level, preferably at his alma mater, the University of Missouri. In 1891, as Stephens was serving a term as president of the National Editorial Association, he took his campaign to the national level. His presidential address that year at the annual convention in St. Paul, Minnesota, before an audience of delegates from forty-five states, was a sturdy call for universities to begin programs in education for journalism:

---

21. Walter Williams, editorial in *The Country Editor,* February 1897.

If there is a vocation in existence whose members may reap advantage from organization, it is the vocation of journalism. Entering his profession without any specific training in the schools, relying purely upon observation within the prescribed limits of his workshop, deprived by the peculiar competitions and frictions of his business of even the benefits of personal association with those of his own profession—dependent, in fact, upon his own personal experience—the newspaper man is the most isolated and lonesome of men . . .

The newspaper is now the acknowledged literature of the world. It is growing with a rapidity that is bewildering . . . It is the greatest of all educators, and its pupils are confined to no class or condition of life. It is a teacher who never takes a vacation, and one who never has to be sought . . .

A vocation involving such responsibility, endowed with such dignity, is in the highest sense a profession, demanding specific training and qualification, and to this end I believe the time is not distant when there will be schools of journalism just as there are of medicine, or law, or theology. It is not more just to the journalist that he should be compelled to acquire full preparation for his business in his printing office than it would be to the lawyer that he would obtain all his knowledge in the courtroom, or to the physician or minister that they should be dependent for their equipment upon the hospital or the pulpit. While journalism demands a broad culture and great experience, like all other professions, it requires a specific and rational training.[22]

Stephens's pleas did not impress all of his fellow journalists. Snorted the *St. Louis Globe-Democrat:* "The country printing office is really our only school of journalism . . . There is no other place where preparatory general training for the duties of the profession can be obtained, where a young man can learn to be an all-round journalist." The *Kansas City Star* warned in an editorial that while "this branch of literary manufacture [a journalism school] may be pushed in Columbia, the establishment will never receive an order from any newspaper office for one complete journalist ready to work." Some of his friends in the press association, Stephens would admit later, laughed at his ideas.[23] But such opposition prompted the stubborn Columbia publisher to redouble his efforts. The following year, he told the press association that the journalist of the future should not only be formally educated in a journalism school, but, in fact, licensed:

While I have the greatest respect for and the greatest confidence in newspaper men all over this state, still there are men in this state who are positively unfit for the place they fill, and we need this school [of journalism] for our own protection; and I believe the time will come in the history of journalism when no man will be allowed to publish a newspaper who has not a license to publish it and who has not a moral character fitted for the profession. Now, gentlemen, I believe in ten years

---

22. Quoted in Mills, "E. W. Stephens," 106.

23. *Missouri Editor,* February 1895. Taft, "Establishing the School of Journalism," 69. Mills, "E. W. Stephens," 118.

it will do more to elevate the young men of this state than anything that has ever been set on foot.[24]

While lacking Walter Williams's oratorical brilliance, Stephens nevertheless shared—and, indeed, nurtured—Williams's soaring idealism. Stephens's integrity, as a hard-headed, principled, and highly successful businessman who played by the rules and served his community and state in the most affirmative way, was unquestioned, and his achievements were formidable. He had built a vast printing and publishing business, won state and national office in the journalism field, been a founder of worthy enterprises such as the State Historical Society, and personally helped guarantee the success of Stephens College. He would live until 1930, but long before then he was publicly deferred to as "the grand old man of Missouri." And yet for all his earnest, dogged approach to life and business, E. W. Stephens never was interested in personal aggrandizement—or much impressed with it, either. "Great men are no different from others," the tall, erect Stephens remarked to a reporter near the end of his life. "They are only more well known . . . There are many men who have in them the qualities that make for greatness but they are not 'great' in the world's eye because they have never been written about. They do their best in an unassuming way and never give a thought to fame."[25]

E. W. Stephens lived to see many, but not all, of his dreams come true. His scheme for the official licensing of journalists—a frightening prospect, fraught with grave First Amendment implications—would not be taken seriously. His crusade to establish a school of journalism would eventually succeed. And though he had done much to make it happen, Stephens would receive little credit for it. Floyd C. Shoemaker, distinguished Missouri state historian, characterized E. W. Stephens as a John the Baptist: "a voice crying in the wilderness, prepare ye the way . . ."[26] A Messiah, as Shoemaker reverentially described him, was on the way.

In February 1898, Stephens appeared to have made his long-awaited breakthrough. At the urging of the Missouri Press Association, the Board of Curators of the University of Missouri adopted a resolution calling for establishment of a chair of journalism on the campus. A three-man committee was appointed to formulate a curriculum in journalism and announce the prospective courses in the next edition of the university's official catalogue. Stephens, who was a

24. *Proceedings of the Missouri Press Association, 1896;* quoted in Mills, "E. W. Stephens," 108.
25. Quoted in Mills, "E. W. Stephens," 110.
26. Shoemaker, "History of the Missouri Press Association."

curator, was named to the committee, along with Richard Henry Jesse, then president of the university, and H. J. Walters, dean of the College of Agriculture. The curriculum they proposed, and published in the 1898–1899 catalogue, outlined these classes:

—*Art and History of Newspaper Making:* The history of printing and the evolution of the newspaper. Typography, presswork, and engraving.

—*Newspaper Making:* Business management, cost and revenue, advertising, editorials, reporting, clipping from exchanges, method of criticism.

—*Newspaper Practice:* Exercises in editing copy, handling telegraph service, condensation, interviewing, gathering news.

—*Current Topics:* Constitutional law, political science, history of the United States, and of Missouri. Economic questions, the libel law, and other laws pertaining to newspapers. Live issues in the United States and foreign countries. A study of the best newspaper models and lectures by men engaged in the profession.

The announcement added that a thorough knowledge of English would be helpful, as would some understanding of literature, and prescribed a lengthy series of liberal arts courses the journalism student should complete in addition to professional classes.[27]

But despite what the catalogue of 1898—and 1899 and 1900—promised, the chair of journalism would not be funded and the classes were not taught. The curators' resolution of 1898 had stipulated that the courses would be offered "as soon as the finances of the University will permit." But the state legislature, still unconvinced that a journalism program was either necessary or even desirable, refused to appropriate the funds for hiring the chair of journalism. Faced with some internal opposition to the plan, the university president and the curators were reluctant to divert existing resources, already slim, away from other departments in order to set up a new chair in an untried academic enterprise. The chair of journalism would not be filled. Neither the university nor the legislature ever said so directly. Instead, they left those who had championed the journalism idea thinking for months they had won, when in fact they had not.

Despite the humiliation imposed on his friend and boss, Walter Williams did not give up. That spring of 1898 he told the Missouri Press Association:

> The editor is an educator, for good or for ill. He is a teacher, whether he will or not. The supreme mission of the journalist is to lead the people into a higher life.[28]

27. Sara Lockwood Williams, *Twenty Years of Education for Journalism,* 17.
28. *Proceedings of the Missouri Press Association,* 1898, 21.

But Williams knew that convention speeches—even his own, like his editorials—often amounted to little more than high-flown, ineffective rhetoric. The real power often was wielded subtly, discretely, and from within. Such were the lessons in political pragmatism he had learned early in his time at Columbia, at quiet meetings and dinner parties when the community's movers and shakers talked things over and got things done. Williams had been arguing his case for a school of journalism loudly and publicly, attempting to mobilize popular support through the lecture platform and the editorial page. However, outside pressure, even from respected journalists, had not worked; the curators and the president of the university had found it relatively easy to resist. A different strategy was now indicated. This time, Williams resolved, he would work from the inside.

Walter Williams. (State Historical Society of Missouri)

Hulda Harned Williams in 1892. (Western Historical Manuscript Collection, University of Missouri–Columbia)

Sara Lockwood, while on the School of Journalism faculty and before her marriage to Walter Williams. She was the first woman ever to hold a full-time job as a journalism teacher. (State Historical Society of Missouri)

A news reporting class at the School of Journalism, probably in 1910. The professor (standing) is Charles G. Ross. (Western Historical Manuscript Collection, University of Missouri–Columbia)

Charles G. Ross, during his tenure as press secretary to President Harry S. Truman, c. 1948. Ross died at his desk in the White House in 1950. (State Historical Society of Missouri)

The "Big House" in Boonville where Walter Williams was born in 1864. The wing at the right was added later, when Walter's brother, Judge William Williams, and his family lived there. (State Historical Society of Missouri)

Neff Hall in 1928. This building, funded by a gift from an early alumnus of the School of Journalism, was the first ever designed, built, and equipped for teaching journalism. (State Historical Society of Missouri)

This portrait, of Williams at his desk in 1909 at Switzler Hall—an early home of the School of Journalism—was painted by John Sites Ankeney, an assistant professor of illustrative art who sometimes taught an advertising design class in the School of Journalism. (State Historical Society of Missouri)

Williams and Sara in Germany, 1931. Though Williams often used a walking cane while abroad, he never would do so in Columbia, lest his neighbors think him affected or, worse yet, decrepit. (Western Historical Manuscript Collection, University of Missouri–Columbia)

*Sara Lockwood, during her days as a newspaper reporter. This photo was probably
shot while she was on the staff of the* Philadelphia Public Ledger *around the end of
World War I. (Western Historical Manuscript Collection, University of
Missouri–Columbia)*

The first house Walter and Hulda Williams lived in, on Waugh Street in Columbia, after their marriage in 1892. (Western Historical Manuscript Collection, University of Missouri–Columbia)

The house at 102 South Glenwood Street in Columbia, where Williams lived during much of his later life. The expansive back garden contained many shrubs and plants collected during his world travels. (Western Historical Manuscript Collection, University of Missouri–Columbia)

Williams placing a wreath upon the site of the first printing office in the Western Hemisphere, established in Mexico City in 1534. Williams was a visiting lecturer at the University of Mexico in 1926, when this photo presumably was taken. (State Historical Society of Missouri)

Famous speakers such as Oswald Garrison Villard (front row at right) assured the success of Journalism Week. Then arguably the best-known journalist in the nation, Villard keynoted the first annual Journalism Week in 1911. With him are Williams (front row left) and, in the back, journalism professor Charles G. Ross; Isidor Loeb, a former dean and acting president of the University of Missouri; journalism professor Frank Lee Martin; and another Journalism Week speaker, B. B. Herbert, editor of the National Printer-Journalist *in Chicago. (State Historical Society of Missouri)*

7

Breakthrough

President Jesse combed the country for possible candidates, even at the instructor level. An important, though unofficial, part of such an interview was the entertainment of the candidate by members of the faculty. Dinners would be followed by evenings "beside the Anheuser-Busch" and reminiscent of the Germany most our faculty had known. There is nothing like loosening up his reflexes to tell you what a fellow is really like. Next day and before an appointment was offered Mr. Williams would make his contacts with some of his trusted faculty members. "Well, what did you fellows think of him?" If we turned thumbs down there was little chance that the candidate would be offered a place on the faculty.

—Winterton T. Curtis, Professor of Zoology, 1901

For Walter Williams, being "inside" of the particular power structure that mattered most to him meant only one thing: a seat on the Board of Curators of the University of Missouri. There was no pathway toward the creation, and funding, of a school of journalism that did not lead straight through the curators.

Created in 1839 as an unofficial steering committee to establish and govern the University of Missouri, the Board of Curators later came under control of the state government. Individual curators were confirmed by the legislature or, when the legislature was not in session, appointed by the governor. Because of the difficulties in obtaining a quorum for the meetings—travel was difficult and there was no financial incentive to attend—Columbia and Boone County were typically overrepresented on the board. Seldom would more than ten of the fifteen curators be present for any meeting; usually eight of those ten, the six appointed by the governor and the two elected by the legislature, were local people from Columbia and its immediate environs. While any appointment to the Board of Curators was an important honor, an appointment from Boone County carried with it more than ordinary clout. The curators tended to be affable, well-connected individuals with strong personalities, men who were at times deeply caught up in partisan politics. Outwardly, however, they appeared to have been cut from similar cloth: by law, each curator was required to be a "free, white, male citizen who had lived in Missouri for at least two years."[1]

E. W. Stephens had spent a number of years as a curator, following his graduation from the university in 1867, and, despite his persistent, and possibly tiresome, campaigning for the creation of a school of journalism, was well liked by his fellow members of the board. Indeed, when the curators had caved in, or so it had appeared, to legislative pressure in 1898 and voted to create (but not fund) a chair of journalism, they offered the position to him. But Stephens, who had a business to run and was disinclined to grovel for monies to develop an untested and controversial academic program, turned down the offer.[2] Realizing he was being told, in effect, by the curators and the legislature to put up or shut up, Stephens backed away. He passed the baton to Walter Williams, who was eager for it, and the timing was perfect. Walter's old friend and former boss from Boonville newspaper days, Lon V. Stephens, was now governor. Anxious to place his political allies in key positions, Lon V. happily rewarded his friend, former neighbor, and fellow Democrat with a spot on the university's governing board. Almost as an afterthought, the governor asked Williams if he had any recommendations for two other vacant spots on the curators. Williams did indeed. He suggested the name of J. F. Gemelich of Boonville, a longtime friend of the Williams family. And for the other vacancy, Williams nominated D. A. McMillan.[3] Then living in Mexico, Missouri, Professor McMillan had been Walter Williams's beloved tutor in Boonville, the man who perhaps more than any other had instilled in his receptive young pupil a love for learning. Governor Stephens promptly appointed both men. Thus when Williams began his initial six-year term, effective on May 23, 1899, he brought his own power base with him.

As he did with everything else, Williams plowed into his assignment on the Board of Curators with enthusiasm and intensity. Blessed with a flexible, relatively undemanding work schedule—the *Columbia Herald* by now seemed almost to run itself—and situated only a few minutes' walk from the campus, Williams soon found himself devoting more and more time to university

---

1. Frank F. Stephens, *A History of the University of Missouri* (University of Missouri Press, 1962), 18.

2. Ibid., 382.

3. Sara Lockwood Williams, unpublished Walter Williams biography.

business. Far from resenting such close attention by a member of the Board of Curators, the University's ambitious and overworked president, Richard Henry Jesse, welcomed it.

Inaugurated in 1891, Jesse was, at thirty-eight, the youngest president the University of Missouri had ever had.[4] Jesse had been born in Lancaster County, Virginia, in 1853, and attended local public schools and Hanover Academy before entering the University of Virginia. He dropped out of his undergraduate studies to teach French and mathematics at Hanover and at Washington Academy in Maryland. When the University of Louisiana (later Louisiana State University) reopened after the Civil War, in 1878, Jesse, though technically still an undergraduate, was appointed dean of the academic department and professor of Greek, Latin, and English. Six years later, when Paul Tulane reorganized the moribund university in New Orleans that was soon to bear his name, Jesse was hired there as professor of Latin. Seven years after that he left Tulane to become president of the University of Missouri.

An intense, reserved, yet courtly man who could be, as a young professor noted, "rather pompous on occasion,"[5] Jesse wore a neatly trimmed black beard and was given to wing collars and frock coats. His thick Virginia accent became even more noticeable when he was tired or, uncharacteristically, relaxed. Such unguarded moments were rare, for Jesse had set lofty goals for his presidency and drove himself hard to meet them. Determined to raise standards throughout the university, he enlarged the faculty and upgraded its quality. His widespread recruiting searches and intensive interviewing resulted in some remarkable hires. From throughout the country, one rising star after another joined the Missouri faculty. Many would soon establish scholarly reputations for themselves, then leave for better positions elsewhere. Jesse regretted the resignations but accepted them as the price he paid for seeking top talent. He wanted scholars so productive that other institutions would want them also. There was no problem on that score. Among the dozens he recruited and eventually lost were Frank Thilly in philosophy, to be hired away by Princeton; Harlow Shapley in astronomy, who would become director of the Harvard Observatory and later president of Washington University; Howard Ayers in biology, later to be chosen president of the University of Cincinnati, and Frederick H. Seares, a brilliant astronomer who would be tapped to direct the

---

4. This background on Richard Jesse is drawn largely from James and Vera Olson, *The University of Missouri* (University of Missouri Press, 1988), 23 ff, and Stephens, *A History of the University of Missouri,* 326, 384.

5. Winterton T. Curtis, "Missouri: Mother of the West," unpublished manuscript describing his early years at the University of Missouri, Williams Papers.

new Mount Wilson Solar Observatory in California. "They were so good," one professor would write of these and other departed colleagues later, "we could not keep them." Despite the discouraging losses of friends and colleagues, the faculty applauded Jesse's dogged pursuit of superior scholars: "It gave us a sense of partnership," one professor wrote. "Just see what those who left us did and where they went before they were through."[6]

Jesse tightened admission standards for entering freshmen and pushed his faculty to develop programs of graduate study to handle the added demands of an expanding campus where, just after the turn of the century, enrollment moved past the one thousand mark. He strengthened the library's holdings and campaigned hard for a separate library building while at the same time successfully raising money for the medical school's teaching hospital. Jesse also cultivated alumni, organizing local clubs of Missouri graduates throughout the state. He pressed for, and got, national recognition for the university by obtaining a Phi Beta Kappa chapter—then, as now, awarded only to a relatively few campuses—and an institutional membership in the prestigious Association of American Universities. He crusaded for better student housing, especially for female students. All of this, he accomplished with limited resources and virtually no staff help. He answered thousands of letters by hand; during the early years of his presidency he did not even have a secretary. In 1898, when the curators insisted Jesse take a short leave, it was his first vacation in seven years.[7] So he was grateful for Walter Williams, who soon became his friend and confidant, administrative partner as well as aide and, not infrequently, personal cheerleader. Ground down by long hours and the unremitting shortage of funds, Jesse's spirits often required the kind of affirmation and gentle boosting that Walter Williams instinctively could provide. "What I wouldn't give if we only had a green campus at the Uni-vah-sity of Missouri as they have at Illinois," Jesse was heard to drawl at a dinner party, bemoaning a maintenance budget so meager that he could not keep the grounds properly watered. "But President Jesse," Walter Williams replied, "you should remember that what the University of Missouri lacks in its campus is made up for by its president."[8]

Only months after Williams took his seat on the Board of Curators, Jesse created an Executive Committee of the Board and installed Williams as its chairman. Williams was manifestly the most conscientious and hard-working member of the board, a shrewd administrator who could be counted upon to deliver not only his own vote on crucial issues but those of his close friends on

6. Ibid.; also Olson and Olson, *The University of Missouri,* 36.
7. Olson and Olson, *The University of Missouri,* 36.
8. Curtis, "Missouri."

the board as well. Jesse relied more and more upon the diminutive editor and trusted him completely. For his part, Williams savored his deepening association with the academy. He admired Richard Jesse, was intensely loyal to him, and he delighted—as perhaps only one who had never finished high school could—in the management of a university. Soon he was personally handling dozens of day-to-day matters, including a share of Jesse's official correspondence. Many of the unremarkable items meant for the curators would be swiftly disposed of by Williams himself, permitting him to streamline the agenda before each meeting of the full board. Jesse made use of Williams's business skills not only to solve routine administrative problems but also increasingly to help him shape university policy and lobby the legislature for funding. "He was more effective in gaining support for his ideas and plans than anyone I have ever known," an appreciative faculty member wrote of Williams. "He was cunning and clever, but never dishonest or unfair."[9] Years later, a historian would call Williams's chairmanship of the executive committee "of paramount importance . . . the Curators' reports and especially the statements of needs of the University showed far more evidence of long-range planning than ever before; perhaps it would be fairer to say that for the first time such planning seemed practical and worthwhile."[10]

Williams shared Jesse's goals, especially his most important one, recruiting outstanding young professors in all available fields. The agriculture faculty, important to Missouri for political as well as economic reasons, was singled out for special attention and soon became one of the strongest in the nation.[11] Jesse was always on the lookout for promising young scientists. From Johns Hopkins University he heard of an exceptional prospect in zoology, Winterton Curtis, then just finishing his doctoral dissertation, and invited him to visit the Missouri campus. Curtis would describe the experience, typical, as he learned, of many of his colleagues:

> The Wabash branch from Centralia to Columbia was, even then, something to discourage a newcomer. George [Lefevre, professor of biology] had warned me concerning this and written that the country about Columbia was not like that surrounding Centralia, so I took the branch in stride and watched for the landscape to change from prairie to hills. We call them "hills," but as one of my friends remarked that first year, "These are not *hills*. A hill is a place you go up and come down. These are places where you go down and come up." George met me at the station with its crowd of people, mostly black, who were there to see the train

---

9. Quoted in Rucker, *Walter Williams,* 76.
10. Jonas Viles, *Centennial History of the University of Missouri* (E. W. Stephens Publishing Co., 1939), 137.
11. Olson and Olson, *The University of Missouri,* 45.

come in. We drove in a hack over dusty and unpaved streets, where I saw stepping
stones for the first time, taking a turn around the campus to reach his home on
Ninth Street . . .

At dinner that night I was thrilled to meet Professor Frank Thilly, who had
translated the edition of Paulsen's "History of Philosophy," which I had devoured
at Williams College and reread again and again.

The next morning I was introduced to President Jesse and to Walter Williams,
then a Curator . . . As I talked with the President and Mr. Williams, at length
and in the absence of Professor Lefevre, I realized that they were making me
do most of the talking. After they had continued this process for a good hour,
asking about my work and interests, President Jesse said to me, in the somewhat
pompous manner he assumed on occasion, "Of course, Doc-tah Curtis, we do not
expect to judge your scholastic attainments on the basis of this brief interview. We
have information on that from o-thah sources." Then came my introduction to the
Williams humor, for Mr. Williams interjected, "Yes, Dr. Curtis, President Jesse
merely wanted to talk with you for an hour and to entertain you at his house for
dinner in order that he may inspect your table manners."[12]

"The reception I received," Curtis recalled, "was more than friendly. Never
in all my life did I have so much good time packed into so few days." He was
offered the job, and accepted on the spot. Unlike many who were recruited
with him, Curtis would stay on at Missouri, rise steadily through the ranks,
become dean of the College of Arts and Sciences, and live to see a campus
building named after him.

Attracting the likes of a Winterton Curtis to the rustic environment of
central Missouri was not easy, but plainly necessary. "Missouri raises the best
mules in the United States," exclaimed a bewildered member of the legislature
in a speech deploring the appointment of Yankees to the university faculty.
"Why can't she raise university professors?"[13] Certain alumni shared this view,
enough to protest the hiring of professors "from a distance when alumni of
equal or superior qualifications are available." One disgruntled Missourian
who had failed to receive an offer to join the faculty wrote a threatening
letter to Williams, demanding that the hiring of outsiders "has got to stop or I
will get up a movement that will kick the President, Curators and Faculty so
unceremoniously out of court that they will never know what struck them." In
cold fury, Williams wrote back:

Demands are scarcely given the consideration that suggestions receive. Nor are
requests best accompanied by brutal threats to "kick out" the curators who do not
agree with your view. While it may be true, my dear sir, that the board is not all
competent to fill scientific chairs . . . it is unquestionably true that the Constitution
of Missouri has placed this duty upon the curators and that they must endeavor to

12. Curtis, "Missouri."
13. Ibid.

do the best they can under all circumstances . . . I shudder at the thought of the consequence which must befall the University of Missouri should you become disabled by death, disgust or otherwise from giving us the guidance of your inerrant wisdom. Your letters are refreshing. They afford in their coolness a welcome contrast to the summer heat. Aside from this, they are delightful in their evidence of the misinformation they contain and delicious in their self-appreciation.[14]

As his boyhood pal Emile Paillou had written many years before about a teenaged editor in Boonville, "Walter Williams has a mulish attitude. He hits back."[15] Williams's stinging letter silenced the critic and blunted the attack on the university's national searches for outstanding faculty.

Though he normally followed Jesse's lead, Williams occasionally spoke out on matters of personal concern. As, for example, when he learned about some hard-working faculty members who were putting in a seven-day week. In a crisp note to Jesse, Williams wrote:

I am credibly informed that a number of the University professors are in the habit of devoting practically all of Sunday to work in their offices on the campus. I am told that in some instances they have students to assist them. Of course, this is a somewhat delicate question with which to deal but it occurs to me that the practice of Sunday work in a state institution does not help toward proper respect for law.[16]

Jesse was unwilling or unable to keep faculty out of their offices on Sunday; as he cheerfully admitted, he was likewise powerless to respond to those townspeople who complained about faculty and students who were seen to be playing golf on the university's links on the Sabbath.[17]

On more substantive matters, however, Williams made sure the executive committee lent solid support to the president as he dealt with a wide range of controversial issues. Among them:

—*Free speech on the campus.* Noisy protests erupted from student Republicans (and their parents) when the staff of the *Savitar*—the yearbook—invited William Jennings Bryan to lecture in the university auditorium. Jesse defended the right of the students to hear Bryan and, with executive committee backing, invited student Republicans to bring in their own speaker.

—*Student conduct.* Overruling a faculty committee recommendation that would go lightly on students caught cheating on exams, Jesse insisted on tougher punishment. The executive committee supported him, as it also did when Jesse cracked down on fraternity hazing.

14. Quoted in Rucker, *Walter Williams,* 131.
15. Paillou, *Home Town Sketches,* 11.
16. Rucker, *Walter Williams,* 127.
17. Ibid., 128.

—The alcohol question. Adolphus Busch, the St. Louis beer baron and a longtime supporter of the university, publicly offered Jesse five thousand dollars to help with construction of the teaching hospital. Angry protestors from the Anti-Saloon League demanded the gift be refused. But Jesse quietly accepted the money, held onto it until the situation cooled down, then used the Busch funds to build an addition to the hospital clinic. And when parents and townspeople objected to boozy parties on the campus, Jesse mollified them with a stern letter, almost certainly written by Walter Williams, to local liquor dealers threatening arrest and prosecution of those who sold alcohol to underage students.

—Intercollegiate athletics. The win-at-all-cost philosophy arrived early on college campuses, including Missouri. "Two of your baseball nine are evidently professional," wrote an indignant president of the University of Kansas to Jesse. "A catcher received five dollars a game and a pitcher the same money. Both entered your school at the opening of the baseball season and left immediately after the game with K. U." Jesse turned the matter over to Williams and the executive committee. They brought in a new professor of physical culture and director of the gymnasium, Clark W. Hetherington, who improved the facilities and cleaned up the university's sports teams by eliminating the play-for-pay athletes. Soon afterward Hetherington organized the Missouri Valley athletic conference and worked hard to ensure that all its member universities abided by the rules. Hetherington's simon-pure athletes did not win Missouri many championships, especially in football, but they were popular with the curators, faculty, administration, and students—if not always with alumni.[18]

Jesse emerged from these and other crises with a distinguished reputation for professional integrity and effectiveness as a problem solver. Yet he never lost sight of his foremost objective: to raise the quality of work done by the faculty and students. In this he succeeded admirably and, indeed, was commended for elevating the whole field of education in Missouri.[19] His was shaping up as a remarkable presidency, and much of the credit, he realized, was due to the unflinching support he got from the Board of Curators and, especially, his friend who headed the executive committee. He owed Walter Williams, and Richard Henry Jesse paid his debts.

In 1905, when Walter Williams was forty-one years of age, he became president of the *Herald* and a substantial stockholder in it. The new corporation,

---

18. Ibid., 128–30; Stephens, *A History of the University of Missouri,* 365; Olson and Olson, *The University of Missouri,* 41.

19. Stephens, *A History of the University of Missouri,* 384.

with capital stock listed at ten thousand dollars, was created when E. W. Stephens decided the time had come for him to concentrate on his expanding publishing business. Handling the affairs of both the newspaper and the printing operation was too much for him, he wrote in a *Herald* editorial:

> The present intention of the writer is to apply himself to the publishing and other business, and he hardly thinks he will return to the editorial work, much as he enjoys it . . . It is a gratification to know that the paper is turned over to younger and fresher hands when it is at a high tide, when its circulation and its advertising patronage are greater than at any period in its history. [20]

James L. Stephens, Jr., E. W.'s son, would be vice president of the *Herald* corporation, with Carl Crow, the bookkeeper, as secretary and business manager. E. W. himself remained as a stockholder as well, though the extent of each person's holdings was not reported. At the same time, Stephens separately incorporated his E. W. Stephens Publishing Company, with capital stock listed at forty thousand dollars.

While insisting that he would "continue to retain a substantial and active business relation to the *Herald,*" Stephens had in fact opted out of the newspaper business. The *Herald,* he felt, had gone about as far as it could under the circumstances, and Stephens was not interested in maintaining the status quo, albeit a status quo that was pleasant and profitable. His alternatives, as he saw them, were to buy up properties in other towns to create a chain of newspapers, or to convert the *Herald* into a daily. There was a third option, and that was to focus on the work he did best, building a printing business of substantial proportions. The E. W. Stephens Publishing Company was already the largest private payroll and perhaps the best-known business in the community. Street locations in Columbia frequently were defined by their proximity to the Stephens printing plant at Eighth and Walnut, a downtown landmark seemingly as identifiable as the Boone County courthouse. Columbia residents were audibly reminded of the plant's presence each evening: after enacting a local curfew for youngsters the city council had arranged with Stephens for his publishing plant whistle, the loudest in town, to be blown every night at nine o'clock. Respected throughout Missouri, Stephens was chosen to head any number of blue-ribbon government commissions, including one early in the new century to oversee building the new state capitol building in Jefferson City. Friends and business associates encouraged Stephens to run for governor. His family, somewhat more persuasive, urged him to take things easier instead. So as he put some distance between himself and the *Herald,*

---

20. *Columbia Herald,* April 14, 1905.

Stephens began spending a bit more time at his palatial home and in planning a little vacation trip, a voyage around the world.[21]

And Walter Williams was now president of the company that published America's Model Weekly.

Despite his growing curator responsibilities, Williams continued to spend a great deal of time with his family. He and Hulda especially protected their coveted Sunday afternoon walks, especially alongside Hinkson Creek. While picnicking on the grassy creekbanks, they would watch other strollers, many of them students at the university. More than a few were members of his Sunday school class. (Gone for "a Hink," or "Hinking it," as the students described these leisurely promenades, were outings that more often occurred on moonlit evenings, perhaps, than on Sunday afternoons.) The summer of 1905 was a happy time, possibly the most pleasant he ever spent.

Only a few weeks later, however, he would be fighting for his life.

The typhus that raged through much of the country struck Williams in late August. His was a classic case, causing severe headache and pain in his back and arms and legs. Prolonged nausea led to appetite loss and dehydration. Never robust, Williams deteriorated rapidly and for days lay near death. "I regret to hear that Walter Williams is still so very ill," wrote James C. Breckenridge, a prominent lumber mill owner in St. Louis, to a friend. "Trust that he may be spared to us for many more years of usefulness."[22] After three weeks, Williams's raging typhoid fever reached its worst, controlled—just—by the cool, damp sponges Hulda applied around the clock. By mid-September, after nearly a month, the fever finally went away.

When he was recovered, his voice had changed.

No longer impaired by "the curious falsetto that was then his normal voice,"[23] as his *Herald* reporter, Charles G. Ross, would later describe it, Williams now could speak consistently in mellow, deep, inviting tones. It was nothing short of a miracle, and the change was widely noticed by those who heard his speeches. "The delivery of Mr. Williams was a surprise to all," wrote the *Columbia Tribune* following a speech Williams made to an audience of six hundred on the subject of "Jesus: The First Gentleman." "Since his

---

21. Mills, "E. W. Stephens," 120, 125. Pike, *Ed Watson,* 86.

22. James C. Breckenridge to F. A. Sampson, September 8, 1905, Sampson Papers, Western Historical Manuscript Collection.

23. Charles G. Ross, "Sun's Rays Through His East Window Inspired Williams's First Paper," *Editor and Publisher,* September 24, 1921.

change of voice, he has undoubted oratorical abilities." Mary Paxton Keeley, a plainspoken young news reporter who would one day become honored as "The First Lady of Missouri Journalism," said flatly, "Typhoid fever made Walter Williams. He had a pipsqueak voice until he got sick, and he had a beautiful voice afterward."[24]

In truth, there is little medical evidence to support any assertion that a major illness could effect a voice change in a postadolescent male. Any time after the age of twenty or so is very late for the typical pubertal voice change to occur, especially in a married man who, by 1905, had already fathered three children and presumably possessed an adult amount of androgen and all that goes with it. The vocal chords are much like guitar strings: make them thicker or place them under less tension and a lower voice pitch results.[25]

For whatever the reason, however, Walter Williams had a pleasanter and far more resonant voice after his fearsome struggle with typhoid fever than he had previously. His marathon efforts over the years to compensate for an uncertain, falsetto delivery had already paid off: through pauses and cadence and other rhetorical devices, fortified by painstakingly written texts and intense rehearsals, Williams had worked around his squeaky delivery and made himself a very fine public speaker. Now, miraculously blessed as he was with a golden voice, he would be even better.

If there was a downside to this changed condition, it was that Williams would for a long time live in dread that this godsend, this wondrous new vocal instrument, might suddenly leave him. For years following his 1905 illness he would resist going to a dentist, refuse to have his tonsils removed, refuse again when a physician recommended a nasal resection to correct a slight breathing problem—all out of fear that such treatments might affect his voice and bring back the shrillness he had despised for so much of his life.

Typhoid fever struck another prominent Columbian that year. Ernest Mitchell, owner of the *Columbia Daily Tribune,* contracted the disease in the fall, and on November 29, 1905, he died of it. The bereaved family sought a buyer for their struggling paper and soon located one, Edwin Moss Watson, a man who would become a powerful force in local and state journalism for the next thirty years.

The son of a physician, Ed Watson had grown up in comfortable circumstances in Columbia. But he chose to work his way through the University of

24. *Columbia Tribune,* February 19, 1906. Interview with the author, July 15, 1964.

25. The author is grateful to his son-in-law, Mark T. Worthington, M.D., for assistance in researching this point.

Missouri, setting type by hand in the printing plant owned by E. W. Stephens, and was graduated with honors in 1890. He learned to write news as well as advertising copy on the *Columbia Herald* and took a liking to newspaper life. In all, as a schoolboy and afterward, he worked nine years on the *Herald* before moving to St. Joseph and a job on the *Ballot.* Two years after that he went to the *Fort Worth Star-Telegram,* then abruptly quit newspapers and returned home to study law. He earned his LL.B. at the university's law school and practiced law in Columbia, serving a term as city attorney. But printer's ink was in his blood, and a few years later he was firmly back in journalism, holding down a reporting job on the *St. Louis Globe-Democrat.* While on vacation, sailing with a friend in the Caribbean, Watson was told of Mitchell's death. He hurried back to Columbia, negotiated a loan of three thousand dollars, and took title to the *Daily Tribune.* In a front-page editorial written on his first day as publisher, Watson promised to make the *Tribune* "a newspaper for all the people . . . to chronicle in full the happenings in Columbia and vicinity."[26]

Watson and Walter Williams had once been coworkers, and they remained friends. But as of December 15, 1905, they would be competitors: friendly, civil, even genteel competitors, but competitors nevertheless. They would remain so as long as each man lived.

In what had already been an eventful professional career for Walter Williams, some periods would stand out as moments of genuine contentment. The end of 1905 was one of those. The most popular man in Columbia was now president of, and a substantial stockholder in, one of the finest weekly newspapers in America. He was esteemed by his fellow journalists here and abroad, and was recognized as a major force in the administration of a rising state university. He had a good marriage, a lovely wife, and three handsome children. His health, after his harrowing bout with typhoid fever, was fully restored. And with his recovery from that life-and-death struggle had come a special gift that meant so much to him, a voice that was richer, mellower, more appealing than he could have imagined. Life was good.

Of all the goals he had set for himself, only one was yet unattained. That was the founding of a school of journalism. Until now, the journalism school proposed years earlier by Williams, E. W. Stephens, and others in the Missouri Press Association had been considered unique. By the end of 1905, however, other men in other states were advocating much the same idea. "The time, I think, is opportune for the establishment of schools of journalism in the great American colleges and universities," announced Dr. James K. Patterson,

26. Pike, *Ed Watson,* 6 ff. *Columbia Tribune,* December 15, 1905.

president of the University of Kentucky, to his trustees. "To prepare young journalists to handle intelligently and profitably the great questions with which the American citizen has to deal . . . to furnish the necessary information to the general public, and to become an intelligent leader of thought, giving thought definite and consistent shape for the realization of great and noble ends."[27] The University of Kentucky, like Missouri and any number of other public colleges and universities, was strapped for funds. But others also took up the call. Most prominent among these was Joseph Pulitzer, the rich and powerful publisher of the *New York World* and the *St. Louis Post-Dispatch.* For reasons very similar to those of Walter Williams, Pulitzer, too, had resolved to establish a school of journalism. Unlike Walter Williams, however, Pulitzer was able to back up his proposal with several million dollars.

Had it not been for a cruel prank, Joseph Pulitzer would never have gone to St. Louis at all.[28] He was a teenaged adventurer who emigrated from Hungary during the last months of the Civil War. His overseas passage was paid, along with a five-hundred-dollar bounty, by an enterprising profiteer who combed Europe recruiting young men for the Union army to replace wealthy draftees who could afford to hire substitutes to do their fighting for them. Discharged when the war ended soon thereafter, Pulitzer found himself alone and miserable in New York, surrounded by thousands of penniless, jobless immigrants like himself whose English was as halting as his. In disgust he resolved to go to another city, one that was, as he put it, more Americanized. Someone told him that the best place for this was, but of course, St. Louis. It was meant as a joke, but Pulitzer took the advice as gospel, not knowing as he hitched his way by freight train toward the West that St. Louis boasted one of the largest concentrations of German immigrants in the country.

But there was no turning back, so Pulitzer stuck it out for three years, maintaining a meager existence by working at odd jobs, before he fell into a news reporting spot on Carl Schurz's *Westliche Post,* most prominent of the several German-language newspapers in St. Louis. Here, for the first time in his young life, Joseph Pulitzer met success. He was a natural reporter who possessed incredible amounts of curiosity and energy, and he pushed himself hard. In his spare hours he studied law and politics. Before long he was the best-known reporter in St. Louis. He made numerous friendships, enough to get him elected to a seat in the state legislature, and for a while he seemed

---

27. Ronald Farrar, *Mass Communication: An Introduction to the Field,* 2d ed. (Brown and Benchmark, 1996), 347.

28. This passage is drawn largely from the author's *Reluctant Servant: The Story of Charles G. Ross* (University of Missouri Press, 1969), 56 ff.

headed for a political career, possibly a brilliant one. But in 1878 he bought a newspaper, and from then on he was to be involved in journalism to the exclusion of everything else.

The newspaper was the *St. Louis Dispatch,* and it cost him twenty-five hundred dollars at a sheriff's auction. There was no visible potential to the *Dispatch,* and it was thirty thousand dollars in debt. There was only one asset of any consequence, an Associated Press membership. Three days later Pulitzer formed a partnership that resulted in the merger of the *Dispatch* with the *St. Louis Post,* a paper with some promise but hamstrung by its not having a coveted AP membership. The merger, a natural, soon began paying off in a big way. A year later Pulitzer gained complete control; within three years the annual profits were approaching one hundred thousand dollars. Driven by Pulitzer's unremitting energy and his impassioned, sensational local crusades, the *Post-Dispatch* became the leading evening newspaper in a city with a population of more than half a million.

Not yet forty, Joseph Pulitzer was at the top of his game. He was also restless and itched to try his hand in the biggest market of them all, to return in triumph to New York. It was at this point that he bought the *New York World,* a once-proud newspaper skidding downhill, both in terms of editorial quality and profits, under the aloof, absentee ownership of Jay Gould, the most notorious land pirate of all the railroad tycoons. Gould had bought the paper for political reasons, to help combat some of the negative publicity he and his fellow robber barons, as they were termed, absorbed from the other papers. But the *World* was soon losing him forty thousand dollars a year and was not helping him politically either, so he was happy to unload it.

Pulitzer's down payment on the *World* came from *Post-Dispatch* earnings, but ensuing payments were generated by the *World* itself, for the Pulitzer brand of crusading caught on quickly in New York, a city where journalism had been in steady decline since the deaths of Henry J. Raymond of the *Times,* Horace Greeley of the *Tribune,* and the elder James Gordon Bennett of the *Herald.* In four months Pulitzer doubled the *World*'s circulation of twenty thousand. By 1884 the figure hit one hundred thousand; two years later it passed a quarter of a million and was still climbing. Joseph Pulitzer was never to think much about St. Louis again.

"Gentlemen, here is the editor of my Western newspaper," Pulitzer once told his Manhattan dinner guests in introducing George S. Johns, editor of the *Post-Dispatch.* "I don't write to him more than once a year. The fact is that I don't worry about the paper at all. My chief interest is in the dividends it produces. I assure you, it is a perfect mint."[29]

---

29. Jack Alexander, "The Last Shall Be First," *Saturday Evening Post,* January 14, 1939, 22.

Pulitzer's *World* was undeniably appealing: lowbrow news columns for a vast blue-collar audience, a distinctly highbrow editorial page for the influentials. The combination guaranteed the high-strung publisher profits and power—and, eventually, bitter competition. His chief rival would be William Randolph Hearst. Destined to become the most flamboyant publisher of the era, the youthful Hearst was uniquely prepared to take on the master. Hearst was smart and energetic, adored by his mother, who gave him what seemed to be unlimited access to the family's immense wealth. Charging into New York from San Francisco in 1895, Hearst bought the nondescript *New York Journal,* poured big money into revitalizing it, then brazenly challenged Pulitzer for the editorial, circulation, and advertising leadership of New York. Having come too far to back down now, Pulitzer decided to match Hearst's sensationalism crusade for crusade, story for story. Pulitzer's decision, a fateful one, touched off a sordid newspaper war marked by lurid news practices that ultimately became known far and wide as "yellow journalism."[30] The sensationalistic, demagogic articles published in the *World* and the *Journal* would do wonders for circulation—eventually each paper went over the million mark in daily sales—but also would shock and stir the nation for years to come. An embarrassed contemporary, the distinguished Edwin L. Godkin of the *New York Post,* reflected the dismay and contempt felt by many of his fellow editors:

> Nothing so disgraceful as the behavior of two of these newspapers [the *World* and the *Journal*] has been known in the history of American journalism. Gross misrepresentation of the facts, deliberate invention of tales calculated to excite the public, and wanton recklessness in the construction of headlines which outdid even these inventions, have combined to make the issues of the most widely circulated newspapers firebrands scattered broadcast throughout the country . . . It is a crying shame that men should work such mischief simply in order to sell more papers.[31]

Yellow journalism was widely blamed for the Spanish American War. While Hearst—and, to a somewhat lesser degree, Pulitzer—exaggerated the atrocities committed by the Spanish against the independence-seeking rebels, the sufferings of the rebels were in any case horrible enough to arouse deep sympathies among Americans.[32] Nevertheless, the jingoistic yellow press did much to inflame the national mood. Hearst gladly accepted the responsibility: "How Do You Like *The Journal*'s War Now?" he asked his readers, in a

---

30. In the opinion of some leading scholars of the period, the term "yellow journalism," a scornful one, was coined to describe the cutthroat competition between Hearst and Pulitzer over publication rights to a popular cartoon feature, "The Yellow Kid," drawn by Richard F. Outcault.

31. Quoted in Kenneth Stewart and John Tebbel, *Makers of Modern Journalism* (Prentice-Hall, 1952), 111.

32. John Blum et al., *The National Experience* (Harcourt, Brace, 1968), 526.

page-one box after a series of U.S. victories early in the conflict. For his part, Joseph Pulitzer grew progressively ashamed of himself. Finally conceding sensationalism to Hearst, who was more comfortable with it anyhow, Pulitzer retreated to higher ground. Then, in what seemed like a fit of remorse, Pulitzer decided to spend some of his fortune to improve the country's newspapers. He offered Columbia University $2 million to start a school of journalism, a place where young men could study how to do journalism better.

"Almost more than any other man," a biographer would write of Pulitzer later, "he saw the ambivalence of journalism, its conflict of counting-room and ideals, the terrible pressure for circulation and success which so often eroded its honesty."[33] "My idea," Pulitzer himself explained, "is to raise the character of the profession to a higher level." Unlike Walter Williams, Pulitzer wanted no part of a trade school approach. But like Williams, Pulitzer wished to elevate the newspaperman to an enlightenment, sense of ethical responsibility, and prestige comparable to that of the physician or lawyer.

But Columbia University's administration was wary. The excesses of yellow journalism were still painfully recalled, and in the popular view, newspaper work remained something less than a respectable profession. The vigorous liberalism of Pulitzer's *World* did not endear it to the more conservative professors at Columbia. So, for precisely opposite reasons, both Columbia University and the University of Missouri were hamstrung in their efforts to begin a school of journalism. Where the University of Missouri had the desire to start a school but no funding for one, Columbia had the money available but not the inclination. So Joseph Pulitzer's offer to Columbia suffered a rare fate—a multimillion-dollar gift for higher education that was not accepted gratefully, unconditionally, and on the spot.

The Missouri Press Association enthusiastically passed a resolution commending Pulitzer's journalism school proposal, noting pointedly "our special gratification that the man who first planned and provided for the most practical scheme for the advancement of the newspaper business made his start and his first success in Missouri."[34]

In time Columbia University's trustees would indeed welcome Pulitzer's offer and commit his millions not only toward building a distinguished school of journalism but also to create awards to honor exemplary journalistic performance. But neither the Pulitzer Graduate School of Journalism nor the Pulitzer Prizes would be established, despite his coaxing, until the end of the great publisher's life.

---

33. William A. Swanberg, *Pulitzer* (Scribner's, 1967), 349.
34. Quoted by William H. Taft, "Establishing the School of Journalism," 63.

Walter Williams could not know this, however, and his vision for a school
of journalism at Missouri—one that would be the world's first—now seemed
little more than idle fancy.

While so much else was happening in 1905, the strain and the years of
overwork began to catch up with Richard Henry Jesse. Concerned friends
urged him to go easier on himself. When it became plain he would not slow
his feverish pace, the curators insisted he take a brief vacation, an absence
that stretched into a year's leave. He returned to his office in May of 1906,
but within three months all who worked with him could sense that his health
had cracked. Medical authorities in Columbia and St. Louis could find nothing
organically wrong, but concluded that his nervous system had been broken by
care and work.[35] As early as the middle of 1905 Jesse seemed to have realized
that a medical retirement lay inevitably ahead, and he began to take care of the
few remaining loose ends surrounding his presidency. One of these would be
to give Walter Williams a school of journalism.

This reward did not come directly. Instead, following a time-honored
bureaucratic tradition, Jesse simply appointed a committee to make recommendations—being certain, through his choice of committee members, what
the recommendations would be. The committee charged to explore the possibilities of establishing a journalism program at the University of Missouri had
only three members: J. Carleton Jones, A. Ross Hill, and Walter Williams.

Jones was a veteran professor of Latin and dean of the College of Arts and
Sciences. A man trusted by Jesse and the curators, Jones possessed impeccable
academic credentials and knew the campus inside and out. Later he would
fill the new, and long-overdue, position of vice president of the university.
A. Ross Hill had been recruited by Jesse from the University of Nebraska to
rescue the Normal department, or teacher's college, a task he had performed
with distinction. A native of Nova Scotia who had been educated at Dalhousie
College in Halifax, Hill was a brilliant young scholar who had ascended quickly
to the leadership of the faculty when Frank Thilly left for Princeton.[36] Both men
were close to Walter Williams and, like him, totally familiar with the innermost
workings of the university. Hill was a shrewd administrator and a master of
detail, especially where curricular affairs were concerned, and Jones wielded
forceful influence in faculty governance matters. Walter Williams, who not
only represented the curators but also was acknowledged as the driving force
on the board, gave the committee a full head of political steam.

---

35. Stephens, *A History of the University of Missouri,* 184.
36. Ibid., 385.

The committee's final report was presented to the Board of Curators on December 13, 1906, in what would be the final year of Jesse's presidency. The document was succinct, as academic committee reports go, and contained three specific recommendations:

(1) That a College or School of Journalism be established as a department of the University, co-ordinate in rank with the departments of Law, Medicine, and other Professional Schools.
(2) That the School of Journalism be provided with adequate laboratory equipment for practical journalistic training.
(3) That the course of study be at least four years in length and that the entrance requirements be at least equal to those of the Academic Department, and

That the curriculum be so organized as to insure co-operation between this school and the Academic Department including many courses now offered in Arts along such lines as English, foreign languages, history, and the social sciences, etc.; some general courses in journalism might count toward a degree in Arts; together with some strictly professional courses intended only for those who wish to secure a professional degree or certificate from the School of Journalism.[37]

Thus was the world's first school of journalism chartered and given its marching orders. Legislative approval, with accompanying funds, would quickly follow. The school was assured both academic standing and financial support.

The next step would be to find a dean who could run it.

37. Quoted in Sara Lockwood Williams, *Twenty Years of Education for Journalism,* 21.

8

"We Must Begin"

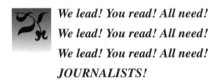

We lead! You read! All need!
We lead! You read! All need!
We lead! You read! All need!
JOURNALISTS!

—School of Journalism Departmental yell, from
University of Missouri Songs, 1929

Though he hardly would have thought so at the time, the long wait, the eight years after the curators' disingenuous vote in 1898 to establish, but not fund, a chair in journalism, in the end proved a good thing for Walter Williams. Criticism of the notion of college training for journalists, vigorous and widespread initially, had largely played itself out. By 1908, scoffing at the school of journalism idea still could be heard, but it came largely from lesser figures in the profession. Joseph Pulitzer's plan for a journalism school, though cooly received at Columbia University, had gained favorable endorsements from such respected figures within the academy as the presidents of Harvard, Michigan, and Northwestern. Some leading publishers in the United States and Europe had also publicly expressed support for the idea of a school of journalism. Thus Missouri's delay until a separate division could be established possibly prevented an abortive beginning of Missouri's educational program for young journalists.[1]

Chairs in journalism had been set up at Cornell in 1888, the University of Pennsylvania in 1893, and at Kansas in 1903.[2] But these had enjoyed only modest success, and the idea of another mere professorship of journalism, housed in an academic department and almost certain to be swallowed up by that department's larger concerns, now held little appeal for Williams. His years as a curator had convinced him of the necessity for practical applications of classroom instruction. Just as a chemistry class could not be effectively taught without a chemistry lab, so, too, did journalism teachers need a laboratory newspaper. And a laboratory newspaper, requiring close faculty supervision

---

1. Viles, *A Centennial History,* 419.
2. Ibid.

of student reporting and editing work, would be an unwieldy and expensive undertaking, one almost certainly destined to be pretty far down on an English department's list of priorities.

The curator experience had taught Williams something else as well, and that was his obligation to take the broader view. Until this point he had advocated the establishment of a school of journalism chiefly because he and E. W. Stephens wanted one and they and the Missouri Press Association thought the newspaper industry needed one. But the teaching faculty at the university had not bought into the idea. More to the point, students themselves had shown no enthusiasm for a school of journalism. Although they had delighted in David McAnally's classes a generation earlier and had responded warmly to various newspaper editors who had delivered guest lectures on the campus, substantial numbers of students had never professed a keen interest in becoming a part of a formal program of education for journalism. Indeed, back in 1898, when the curators had first authorized the chair of journalism, the student newspaper, the *Independent,* had been sharply critical of the proposal. Perhaps student opposition had been subtly encouraged by the faculty members, a number of whom were miffed because they had not been consulted. But by 1905, when Richard Jesse finally appointed the committee to explore the possibility of establishing a school of journalism, Walter Williams had done his homework, soliciting faculty and student opinions and courting support from a rich variety of sources. Not the least of these was his Sunday school class, with its hundreds of students and some faculty as members. Indeed, there is some evidence to suggest that he delayed pushing for the creation of a journalism school until student and faculty opinion was reasonably favorable. When Williams, who had chaired the journalism committee, delivered the report to the Board of Curators, he was certain of support across the campus. A short time later, the *Independent* editorially urged "a college of journalism" for the University of Missouri.[3]

On December 10, 1907, his flashes of temper more frequent and his health further deteriorated, Richard Henry Jesse notified the curators of his intention to resign the presidency, effective the following summer.[4] A committee, chaired by Walter Williams, was appointed to look for a successor. In just three weeks— a fleeting instant, as academic searches are measured—one was found. He was Albert Ross Hill, former dean of the Teachers College who had left Missouri

---

3. Ibid., 421.
4. There was a flurry of correspondence among the curators at this time; see especially the papers of two of them, P. E. Burton and J. C. Parrish, Western Historical Manuscript Collection.

only eight months before to become dean of Arts and Sciences at Cornell. Hill's progressive attitudes, his decisiveness, and his natural leadership made him a logical choice, one destined to infuse new life into the campus.[5] Hill was, manifestly, a friend and favorite of Walter Williams. There would be no need to sell Ross Hill on the need for a school of journalism; he and Walter Williams had formed two-thirds of the select committee that had recommended one to the curators in the first place. From the outset, Walter Williams would have a friend in power. So would his school of journalism.

The search for a dean of journalism, more typically, went on for more than a year. Because the new school would operate as a separate enterprise, Jesse found it made sense to consider a more professionally experienced head than would have been practicable in the case of a chair, where academic credentials would necessarily take precedence. Besides, in an untried teaching field, one closely tied to the working press, academic credentials could become far less pertinent than professional standing. Several prominent newspaper executives were approached, but all rejected the prospect as being too risky. No names were officially mentioned, although there was speculation in the press. "The Board of Curators," a Columbia newspaper reported, "offered the deanship to a distinguished Missouri journalist, who declined." Williams himself suggested to the board that one candidate, unnamed, was interested but "magazine and newspaper engagements" might make it impossible to take the job any time soon. Earlier it had been revealed that one of those under consideration was Walter B. Stevens, Washington correspondent for the *St. Louis Globe-Democrat.* Stevens, a well-known writer then earning more than four thousand dollars a year, had already declined a lush political appointment, the secretaryship of the Philippines Commission at a salary of six thousand dollars, with two thousand more for expenses. Rumors abounded. The school was too speculative to attract a first-rate person, it was said; the professional risks were too great for the money involved. The salary mentioned for deanship was four thousand dollars, which, though less than a prominent editor of the period might be paid, still was more than other Missouri deans were earning. President Hill's pay would be the same as Jesse's had been, six thousand dollars a year.[6]

In early April 1908, the outgoing and incoming presidents jointly asked their friend and the school's chief booster, Walter Williams, to take the deanship.

5. Stephens, *A History of the University of Missouri,* 386, 387.

6. Viles, *A Centennial History,* 415. *University Missourian,* September 15, 1908. P. E. Burton to Dr. J. C. Parrish, June 8, 1908, Parrish Papers. *Columbia Tribune,* April 3, 1908. Taft, *Missouri Newspapers,* 177.

Offering a man who never finished high school an academic deanship may or may not have been unprecedented, but the very organization of a full-blown school of journalism was itself something new. Perhaps Jesse and Hill sensed that a man who had proved himself as an editor and public relations expert (and lobbyist, not only for the school, but for the university itself) might be better equipped for this particular job than a scholar whose training had been purely academic.

Requesting time to think it over, Williams consulted a number of his closest friends, both in journalism and in higher education. To Professor Frank Thilly, now at Princeton, he wrote:

> I want your advice. If the Curators . . . offer me the headship of the College of Journalism, should I accept?
>
> You know the circumstances.
>
> It would not be financially advantageous. I am not a College graduate. I am on the Board. The field is new and unorganized. The risk of failure is considerable and might be larger for me. I would change from one official relation with the University to another, and the attitude of the faculty and, to some extent, of the students might affect unfavorably on my chances for success. Finally, it would bring about a recasting and reshaping of my life plans.
>
> On the other hand, the work has a large chance for good. It is in the interests of my profession. It would give opportunity to do some literary work that I cannot otherwise accomplish. There is fascination in the creation of a new school, on the broad lines existing nowhere else. I might be of service to the University, the state, and journalism. Somebody must do the work. Am I the right man?[7]

"You have a rich experience in your profession," Thilly wrote back, urging him to take the deanship. "You have ideas and ideals concerning it; you have gained through your long connection with the University an insight into the educational problems of your age; you have a wide knowledge of men and affairs in your state; you enjoy the confidence of the people; and you have a mind that can learn quickly how to solve new problems." Similar encouragement came from others he consulted, including Champ Clark, then Speaker of the House of Representatives in Washington, Judge Billy Williams, Walter's elder brother, and a number of friends in the press association. "Mr. Williams' friends hope he will accept the position," commented the *Columbia Daily Tribune,* "as they deem him peculiarly fitted for the position."[8]

Still, Williams remained on the fence. And A. Ross Hill seemed to be having second thoughts. "What would become of the University of Missouri," the president-elect wrote from Cornell to a curator, "if it were to lose [Williams's]

---

7. Quoted in Sara Lockwood Williams, unpublished Walter Williams biography.

8. Sara Lockwood Williams, unpublished Walter Williams biography. Rucker, *Walter Williams,* 141. *Columbia Tribune,* June 4, 1908.

unique and far-reaching services?"[9] Hearing of Hill's ambivalence, Williams astounded the curators by announcing that he would like to do *both*—become dean of the School of Journalism while at the same time remaining on the Board of Curators as head of the executive committee. At least until the new school took hold. Stunned, the board members acquiesced—for the time being.

It was one of the few times when Williams's normally reliable political instincts deserted him. His desire to hang on to his curator's position may well have been intended to protect the interests of the embryo journalism school, but it was perceived as something far less noble than that. Individual curators were outraged, soon demanding that Williams choose one job or the other. Others had privately resented for years the power Williams wielded over the board and thought it time to rein him in. One curator who had been absent that day wrote:

> I am very sorry I was not able to be at the Columbia meeting. I certainly would never have given my consent to the delay in the resignation of Williams. The fact is, I had written a member of our Board asking that he support my motion to demand his resignation as a member of the Board or as Dean of the School of Journalism . . .
>
> If this condition continues, I shall not care again to be on the legislative committee to secure for the University adequate appropriations from the legislature, because knowing the prejudice against Williams which existed before, I should be unwilling to encounter the added prejudice which is sure to follow the knowledge (on the part of the legislators) on his use of his position of trust to forward his individual schemes and ambitions . . .
>
> From your letter there appears to be no doubt that Williams is aiming to perpetuate through the new members his influence on the Board. It seems to be that self-respect demands that we refuse to tolerate a further continuance of this condition.[10]

Another curator wrote that he had hurriedly scheduled a meeting with Williams to "ask him to appreciate the probability of a prolonged factional fight in view of his remaining on the board and at the same time taking active charge of the school of journalism."[11]

Feeling the heat, Williams backed down, and reluctantly made his choice. He prepared to accept the deanship and resign from the curators. And to step down as president and editor of the *Columbia Herald*. The *Kansas City Star* got the story first, if unofficially, from an enterprising reporter, Lee Shippey, who had found himself seated beside Walter Williams on a train ride to Columbia.

---

9. Taft, "Establishing the School of Journalism," 63.

10. C. C. Goodale to P. E. Burton, June 8, 1908, Burton Papers, Western Historical Manuscript Collection.

11. P. E. Burton to Dr. J. C. Parrish, June 11, 1908, Parrish Papers.

In an unguarded conversation Williams told Shippey of his plans for the new school of journalism.[12] The official announcement would come in late June 1908, but three weeks before that the *Columbia Tribune* had already figured it out.

> With today's issue of the Columbia *Herald,* Redmond S. Cole assumes editorial control of the paper . . . Walter Williams retires from active editorial control, but retains an interest in the *Herald.* The announcement in the *Herald* today means that Mr. Williams has decided to accept the deanship of the department of journalism.[13]

As indeed he had. His acceptance, accompanied by his resignation from the Board of Curators, would become effective on July 1, 1908. Now he had been given not only a school of journalism but also the means and the opportunity to make it go. To a friend on the board he wrote:

> I will take up the new work for the University with misgivings as to my own fitness for it, with knowledge that it involves some personal sacrifice and with full realization that I will have the hardships and possibly meet the fate of most pioneers. But I take it up also with the firm belief that it can be the means of doing good, or serving the commonwealth most helpfully. If I did not so believe, the attractiveness and hardships of the new work—both of which appeal to me—would not have inducement sufficient to justify my acceptance. If, after fair trial, the new work, under my direction, does not, in the opinion of the president and the board, prove of value to the larger interests of the University and the State, my abandonment of connection with it will promptly come. But the work itself should continue for the certain and lasting benefit it will be to the University and to the State.[14]

The curators made it clear, as the *Tribune* reported, that the newly chosen dean "is to resign all positions he holds at present, to devote his whole time to the work of the department of journalism, and to withdraw from politics and the lecture platform." His momentary indecision now forgotten, Williams agreed to the conditions, then added one of his own: he insisted that his salary, which had been budgeted at four thousand dollars, be *reduced* to thirty-three hundred. This was as low a salary as any dean at Missouri was earning at the time. "Many University professors have been dissatisfied over the low salaries now being paid," Williams said, "and it would create dissatisfaction for a new Dean to enter upon his duties at the salary of more experienced

---

12. D. Van Quackenbush to the author, March 27, 1993. Shippey later became a correspondent from the front lines in World War I, then wrote a column for the *Los Angeles Times* for three decades.

13. *Columbia Tribune,* June 4, 1908. Eventually, the *Herald* would merge with the *Statesman,* and later the *Herald-Statesman* would become a community journalism training paper for the School of Journalism.

14. Williams to Dr. J. C. Parrish, a member of the board from Vandalia, June 29, 1908, Parrish Papers.

men." The curators happily concurred. Disparaging remarks about Williams's ambitions and his sincerity were put to rest, and the curators wished their former colleague, who had been first among equals on the board but who now worked for them, great success—roasting him, as one affectionate letter-writer recalled, "to a fare-thee-well."[15]

Williams's departure from the Board of Curators and the changes in his working relationship with Richard Henry Jesse were painful. But he could handle the pain, for he knew the direction in which he was headed. Two resolute men, incoming President A. Ross Hill and incoming Dean Walter Williams, would begin their new jobs on the same day.

Once a dean was in place, the Missouri legislature reconfirmed its approval of the School of Journalism and freed up operating funds for it.[16] In one of the last acts of his presidency, Jesse assigned the School of Journalism rooms on the second floor of Academic Hall, which, when it had been constructed in 1843, was the university's earliest building. He also authorized Williams to fill additional positions on what would become the School of Journalism's original faculty. There were two of these, each carrying a princely title. One was to be professor of the theory and practice of journalism, the other assistant professor of newspaper administration. In point of fact, Williams simply wanted the two best newspapermen available. Preferably, they would also possess solid big-city experience to complement his community journalism background. He found them both in St. Louis.

The first man he sent for was Charles G. Ross. Once his protégé on the *Herald,* Charlie Ross was now copy chief on the *St. Louis Republic,* having recently moved over from the *Post-Dispatch.* Williams offered Ross an instructorship at a nine-month salary of fifteen hundred dollars—less, no doubt, than he was earning in St. Louis. But if Ross hesitated for a moment to accept the new job, there is no evidence of it. He gave notice immediately; the school would open in September and there was no time to waste.

A native Missourian, Charlie Ross had grown up in Independence and was graduated first in his high school class, edging out his bespectacled friend, Harry S. Truman. The two had been close friends since early boyhood, sharing a general dislike for playground sports and a strong love for reading. At the University of Missouri, the tall, soft-spoken Ross had won a Phi Beta Kappa key and other academic honors while serving as Walter Williams's reporter on

15. *Columbia Tribune,* June 29, 1908. P. E. Burton to Dr. J. C. Parrish, June 28, 1908, Parrish Papers.

16. Sara Lockwood Williams, *Twenty Years of Education for Journalism,* 22.

the *Herald.* He was hired after graduation by the *St. Louis Post-Dispatch*—a glowing recommendation from Walter Williams helped in that regard—and he had learned much about metropolitan journalism from one of the toughest managing editors in the business, Oliver K. Bovard.

Ross himself contributed to the Bovard legend by becoming the victim of one of the managing editor's famous object lessons. Ross had been dispatched to the extreme southwestern corner of St. Louis for a news story about a painter who had fallen from a smokestack. The accident occurred at a point well beyond the outermost point of the streetcar line, so Ross was compelled to trudge a considerable distance in the middle of a hot, dusty day. After much exertion, he finally located the factory, gathered the information he thought he would need, and started back toward the newspaper office, arriving there late in the afternoon. Bovard looked over Ross's account of the accident, then crushed his young reporter with a single question: "How *tall* was the smokestack?"

Ross could not reply in specific terms, but said he had seen the smokestack, and that it was "quite tall."

"Tall is a relative term," Bovard said crisply. "I want you to go back and find out the exact height."

It was late that night when Ross returned to the city room on Olive Street once again, this time with the precise information, in feet and inches.[17] The lesson, etched deeply into Ross's experience, was incorporated into an emerging, rigorous professional discipline that would make him a splendid classroom teacher.

Williams's other hire was Silas Bent, who had not agreed to terms until mid-August, less than a month before classes began.[18] Then assistant city editor to Bovard on the *Post-Dispatch,* Bent was a dark-haired, spirited, good-looking young man from Kentucky whose courtly manner and flashing wit assured his popularity wherever he went. Still in his twenties in 1908, Bent had risen rapidly in journalism. After his graduation from Ogden College in 1902, he had joined the *Louisville Herald,* where in three years he was promoted to assistant city editor. He transferred to the *Louisville Times* for a few months before moving to St. Louis to join Bovard's bright young reporting staff in 1905. Soon afterward Bovard elevated him to an assistant city editor's desk, and Bent was widely regarded as a comer.[19]

Besides the teaching faculty, Williams had funds to employ a tiny support staff. Warren H. Orr and E. R. Evans, both student assistants, were hired as

---

17. Farrar, *Reluctant Servant,* 33.
18. *Columbia Tribune,* August 21, 1908.
19. Farrar, *Reluctant Servant,* 37.

circulation and advertising managers, respectively, of the laboratory news-paper, to be called the *University Missourian.* Cannie R. Quinn was hired as a stenographer.[20]

The University of Missouri's Columbia campus would enroll 2,307 students that autumn of 1908. Tighter admission standards, which Jesse had fought long and hard to enact, now required incoming freshmen to have completed fifteen high school units—a full course load, in other words, through the twelfth grade. The thirty-two-acre main campus now boasted some twenty-three buildings and a faculty of 138, nearly all of them men. Salaries of full professors ranged from $1,800 to $2,850. Deans received up to $700 more.[21]

Albert Ross Hill's administration had begun on July 1. Like Richard Jesse, Hill also had become a university president at a youthful age—he was thirty-seven at the time, a year younger than Jesse had been when he started—but in other respects the two men were more different than they were alike. Jesse was a driven man, impatient and frequently overbearing, while Hill was more relaxed and low-key, blessed with a keen analytical mind, imposing good looks, and a clubby, winning personality. Hill's crisp Canadian accent contrasted sharply with Jesse's Virginia drawl. But there would be continuity between the two administrations. Hill had long admired Jesse, appreciated the gutsy battles he had fought, and was determined to continue his predecessor's quest for quality, though with a temperament and management style that were very different. Hill's presidency would be characterized by educational reform and innovation, and he was bristling with new ideas from the start. Before classes began that autumn he made a speech to the general faculty, outlining some of his plans and aspirations. In that well-crafted address was a graceful passage welcoming the new school of journalism into the fold:

> The University of Missouri is the first in America to establish and organize a School of Journalism. I believe it is possible for this School to give dignity to the profession of journalism, to anticipate to some extent the difficulties that journalism must meet and to prepare its graduates to overcome them; to give prospective journalists a professional spirit and high ideals of service; to discover those with real talent for the work in the profession, and to discourage those who are likely to prove failures in the profession, and to give the State better newspapers and a better citizenship. I hope the faculty of the School of Journalism, upon whom rests the responsibility for all this, will prove worthy of the trust imposed in them.[22]

---

20. *Columbia Tribune,* September 14, 1908.
21. Stephens, *A History of the University of Missouri,* 388.
22. Sara Lockwood Williams, *Twenty Years of Education for Journalism,* 25.

Publicly, at least, Walter Williams was confident. "There is no doubt in my mind but that it will be a success from the first," he said, in an interview with the *Joplin Globe*. Meanwhile, he immersed himself in preparations for the critical academic year ahead. Hulda and the children went to the lakeside resort in Michigan without him.[23] There would be no vacation for Walter Williams that summer.

Williams had spent much of his July and August writing out the lectures for the one class he felt he alone must teach, the History and Principles of Journalism. In drawing up the school's curriculum, Williams had determined that History and Principles of Journalism would be the beginning course, and every student in the school would be required to complete it. In the University of Missouri catalogue description, the course was described as being "designed to present the main facts of the history of newspaper making, of journalism in various periods and conditions, the meaning and aims of journalism and its fundamental principles." But Williams knew it would have to do more than that. This class *must* set the tone for the school, must generate the spirit and energy to permeate all that would follow. From the first class meeting, Williams realized, he would have to sell his students—sell them on the task ahead, on the worth of their chosen major and, indeed, on the worth of journalism itself.

Williams's first lectures were variations on a single, impassioned theme:

Other professions deal with phases of life. The law thrives upon the quarrels of men. When peace comes there will be no need for lawyers. Medicine thrives upon the disease of mankind, and when hygiene has done its best or worst, we shall have no need for the doctor. Theology deals with man's relation to God and spiritualistic ills. When we all get as good as we should be we shall not need the preacher.

Journalism is more. It deals with the body politic. An old Roman once said, "I am a man, and whatever concerns man concerns me." Heaven has no room for lawyers; or doctors or preachers, but we will want to know what the other angels are doing, so there will be a morning and an afternoon newspaper in the New Jerusalem. Journalism is also concerned with literature. The layman thinks that literature creates and that journalism records. He who records, re-creates. Personality creates literature, and much of what is called literature is created by journalists who are dead. Speaker Tom Read said: "A statesman is a dead politician." When we study Addison, Steele, and Swift we study what they did as journalists. Kipling's "Plain Tales from the Hills" is work that he did on an English newspaper. The very use of the word "story" is significant. We speak of all as stories, but this does not mean that it is fiction, but that it is more than mere

---

23. Williams was quoted in the *Joplin Globe* on April 5, 1904—well before he had accepted the deanship. *Columbia Tribune,* September 5, 1908.

record. What journalism records is mere trade. A copyist can do this. When it merely buys and sells news it is a business. When it goes beyond and comments upon, and interprets what it sells and buys, it is a profession. A journalist who comments upon life is a *professional.*[24]

History and Principles of Journalism was part inspiration, part exaggeration, part evangelism—and Walter Williams meant every word.

The catalogue listed seven other courses to be offered by the School of Journalism that first year:

—*Newspaper Making.* This is a laboratory course setting forth, in practice upon the daily newspaper, journalistic work in all departments.
—*Newspaper Administration.* This course is a study of the conduct of newspapers from the viewpoint of editorial direction and control.
—*Magazine and Class Journalism.* This is the study of the making of magazines, of technical, trade and class journalism.
—*Comparative Journalism.* A study of journalistic conditions in all countries with comparison with conditions existing in the United States.
—*Newspaper Publishing.* The business side of journalism, including discussion of advertising and circulation.
—*Newspaper Jurisprudence.* A study of laws that relate to newspaper publication, particularly the laws relating to libel.
—*News-Gathering.* This course considers the methods of getting the news, by individual effort, by press associations, etc., and discusses the relative value of news and its treatment.
—*Correspondence.* This is a study of the special feature in newspaper work, war and other special correspondence and the handling of the telegraph.
—*Office equipment.* This course considers the mechanical equipment of newspaper office, type, presses, etc.[25]

Besides his History and Principles class, Williams also would teach Comparative Journalism, a forum for incorporating much of what he had seen (and hoped to see more of in the future) of the world's press, and Newspaper Administration. Judge John D. Lawson, dean of the law school, agreed to teach the course in Newspaper Jurisprudence, the first college course ever devoted to that subject. Ross and Bent divided the other classes, several of which were to be offered only on alternate semesters. All three full-time teachers worked together in the Newspaper Making and News-Gathering classes, which, as with History and Principles, would be taught every semester.

---

24. Transcript of notes recorded by Battle Williams, an early student in the History and Principles of Journalism class taught by Walter Williams. Gibbany Papers, Western Historical Manuscript Collection.
25. University of Missouri School of Journalism, *Announcement of Courses in Journalism, 1908–09,* 4–5.

Williams's schedule called for the lecture classes to begin at 8 A.M. and end by 10 A.M. At ten o'clock the pragmatic work would start, and before the day was over the students and the faculty would have produced a newspaper.

Newspapers around the country had reported the creation of the world's first school of journalism at the University of Missouri, and as a result the enrollment, from the outset, came from far and wide. More than seventy students cast their lot with the new school during the first two days of fall semester registration, greatly exceeding Walter Williams's most optimistic estimates. The *Columbia Daily Tribune,* monitoring the new school closely, speculated after early registration figures were in that the journalism total would exceed a hundred.[26] It did not, but the beginning enrollment base for a viable program was clearly there. The school would generate enough credit hours—a key index to tuition dollars and state funding—to pay its way. Even more impressive was the diversity of the entering student body: whereas most University of Missouri students came from inside the state, the School of Journalism from the outset attracted students from across the nation: seventeen states, ranging from California to New York, were represented in that entering group, and there was one student from Canada. A few days after classes began and the demands professors would make became clearer, the enrollment dropped to sixty-four, of whom six were women. Fifty-three of these were entering freshmen who would become candidates for the degree of Bachelor of Science in Journalism; eight were special students, pursuing specific courses but not specifically seeking a degree, and three were students in other departments who wanted background work in journalism.[27] This was enough. Walter Williams's bold prediction, that there was sufficient student demand to justify a journalism school, had proven accurate.

But this high student turnout only served to increase the tension for Charles G. Ross, who, at the age of twenty-three, was about to become a teacher in the same academic community where he had been a student only three years earlier. And so, on the morning of September 14, 1908, when he met his Correspondence class for the first time, Ross was a nervous young man. Just before eight o'clock the students began to file in and promptly on the hour they had settled into their seats in a makeshift classroom in the basement of Academic Hall, a classroom with several enormous water pipes stretching across the ceiling. As Ross was about to start his lecture, a drop of warm water

26. *Columbia Tribune,* September 13, 1908.
27. Rucker, *Walter Williams,* 145.

fell from one of the pipes directly overhead and struck the young professor on the head, in full view of his students.

"This might be an omen," Ross told his students, grinning. "I hope it is the last time I am in hot water with this class."

"Even so," he said, "we must begin."[28]

By five o'clock the next afternoon, September 15, 1908, the Newspaper Making class had made its first newspaper. It was Volume 1, Number 1, of the *University Missourian,* centerpiece of the new School of Journalism and, indeed, the heart and soul of the curriculum. "The lecture system is helpful, but it is not sufficient," Walter Williams was quoted in the *Tribune* as saying. "In our department we intend to make use of the laboratory system; that is the routine part of every newspaper."[29]

The *Missourian* was printed at the E. W. Stephens plant initially, though Williams had quietly begun plans to set up a modern newspaper press on the campus. Students were dispatched by their faculty editors on assignments throughout the community, their reports to be written under close faculty supervision. Walter Williams was listed in the masthead as editor, Silas Bent as managing editor and city editor, and Charlie Ross as news and telegraph editor. "A large circulation among University students is anticipated," reported the *Tribune.*[30]

But the *Missourian* was deliberately intended to be a community newspaper, as opposed to one that merely covered the campus. With four pages per issue, six columns per page, the *Missourian* was published each afternoon, Monday through Friday. The paper was filled with news from the city of Columbia, the campus, and the state and world. (The Associated Press, in a goodwill gesture to the new school, had made its wire service available free of charge.) The *Missourian* was also a commercial operation in that it solicited subscriptions and advertising as well as news from the community in direct competition with private enterprise.

The head-to-head competition, not just for news but also for business, ensured that the *Missourian* would become a demanding, realistic training ground and give its eager young student staffers invaluable professional experience. This Walter Williams had envisioned. What he had not envisioned was the vehement reaction the *Missourian* would provoke among some of his powerful friends.

---

28. Farrar, *Reluctant Servant,* 46.
29. September 13, 1908.
30. *Columbia Tribune,* September 3, 1908.

9

For Worse—and for Betterment

 All of the practical activities of the school center around the
University Missourian, a four-page daily evening newspaper
published by students of the school under the supervision
of the faculty. It is the laboratory product of the school—a
daily measure of the practical work done in the classrooms.
It is a commercial enterprise only to the extent that it solicits
business—subscriptions and advertising—in order to pay
expenses.

—Promotional announcement, School of Journalism, 1910

Soon after he took over the *Columbia Daily Tribune* in 1905, Edwin Moss Watson joined his fellow Missouri Press Association members in the campaign to promote the creation of a School of Journalism at the state university. Though Watson's support was less exuberant than some, it was nevertheless genuine. In one editorial on the subject, he wrote:

> There is a tendency among old-fashioned newspaper men to sneer at colleges of journalism. Many people still adhere to the ancient theory that journalists, like poets, are born and not made, and to a certain extent that is true, but even a newspaper man who has been "born" can learn something if he is properly taught.[1]

And when the school did open that September of 1908, Watson heralded the event in approving terms, praising especially the real-world journalistic training for the students to be afforded by the laboratory newspaper, the *Daily Missourian:*

> Experience in gathering facts and writing them out in readable style will be of value to every student who takes the work offered by the department, whether the student who takes the work later becomes proprietor of a metropolitan newspaper or not. The student's powers of observation will necessarily increase with such practice.[2]

---

1. Pike, *Ed Watson,* 124. This excellent work was written by a longtime *Tribune* staffer who knew Watson and Walter Williams well.
2. Ibid.

But two weeks later, as the full implications of the new paper's impact on the community were beginning to sink in, Ed Watson underwent an angry and total reversal. Now he saw the *Daily Missourian* in an entirely different light—as a business competitor that threatened to take away some of his income—and he was incensed. In the first of what would become a steady barrage of heated editorials on the subject, Watson fumed:

> The *Missourian* has a liberal advertising patronage, and is in the field for such business as generally comes to a newspaper. It is submitted that this is competition. The state pays for the paper, the printing, and employs the publishers. If students were merely trained in journalism, there could be no possible objection to the *Missourian,* but in all fairness should the state go into the newspaper business against private individuals?[3]

Watson's indignation resonated with other publishers in the state. The respected *Ledger,* in the nearby community of Mexico, joined in:

> The *Ledger* has always believed that a chair of journalism at Missouri University would not only add strength to the institution and prove of great benefit to the newspaper men of the state, but the management of the *University Missourian* should strenuously avoid competition with the local papers of Columbia. We feel confident that this will be the policy of Dean Williams and his associates.[4]

That same week, the *Hannibal Journal* and the *Moberly Democrat* said much the same thing:

> The *Journal* agrees with the Moberly *Democrat* that the state University Daily, supported at state expense, should not be brought in competition with other Columbia newspapers. The School of Journalism is all right, but it ought to be conducted so as not to come in competition with private enterprise.[5]

The powerful *St. Louis Star,* though favoring the concept of a journalism school, sided with those who thought the *Missourian* enjoyed an unfair commercial advantage:

> What right has the state to set up a business proposition in connection with a state educational institution, and in competition with citizens? The *Missourian* is a bright publication, but it has never been a newspaper in the real sense of the word, and a mistake was made when it endeavored to force its consideration on the people as such. Strictly on its merits as a newspaper it would not command much advertising patronage. As a paper put out by the State University in the Athens of Missouri, however, it commands consideration. There can be no doubt that there are not a few people in Columbia who contracted for advertising space because they thought it unwise to antagonize university interests in a university city.[6]

---

3. Ibid.
4. Rucker, *Walter Williams,* 164.
5. Ibid.
6. Quoted in ibid., 154.

Against this rising tide of protests, Williams scrambled to control the damage. Hurriedly he dashed off letter after letter to newspaper publishers, most of whom he had known for years, and he took pains to reassure his friend Ross Hill that the loyalty of the university president's office had not been misplaced. Requesting permission to speak to the press association, to report on the beginning year of the journalism school, Williams told the state convention at Fulton:

> Our school seeks to do for journalism what schools of law, medicine and agriculture have done for those vocations. Previous to the existence of those schools, training in those fields was obtainable only in the lawyer's office, the doctor's office and on the farm. But now professional schools have taken the place of such individual training. They have attained their high development by the application of the laboratory or clinic to their instruction programs. The School of Journalism is to be conducted on the same plan. . . . The School was to meet doubt and mistrust from some, misapprehension from others, and destructive criticism from a few. The needs of the first year compel the adoption of a plan which was unfortunately seized upon as the "State competing with private enterprise." It was not regarded as proper for the State in training for journalism to pay for the support of such public enterprise. The competition was not large if it really was competition.[7]

Ed Watson, however, was adamant, certain by now that his fellow publishers had been deceived and he personally had been blindsided by the lofty rhetoric of Walter Williams. In the weeks that followed, he published a dozen or more biting editorials demanding that the state cease funding the School of Journalism's laboratory newspaper. Then he took his case to the Board of Curators, sensing that some resentment of Walter Williams, and of Williams's ill-conceived, abortive scheme to be both a dean and a curator, might still linger in the minds of several members of the board. Joined by the publishers of the town's two weeklies, the *Columbia Statesman* and the *Herald,* Watson and the *Daily Tribune* put in writing to the curators their demand that the *Missourian* be ordered to pull out of the local advertising field. But the curators, on cue from President Hill—whose support of Walter Williams never wavered—took no immediate action, promising tactfully to defer the matter to a later meeting.[8] Furious, Watson vowed to deal directly with the Missouri legislature, a venue in which he knew he would get a sympathetic hearing.

Williams and the *Missourian* were particularly vulnerable during these first few months of the school's existence. Lacking time to build up an advertising and subscriber base, the *Missourian,* as might any start-up newspaper, lost money, and there was no capital surplus to absorb it. Keeping the paper

---

7. Viles, *A Centennial History,* 416.
8. Rucker, *Walter Williams,* 150.

afloat required more extensive use of state funds, and 1908 was a tight-money year when the university's budget requests were repeatedly being cut, not increased.[9] One alternative for the *Missourian* would be to redouble its selling efforts, seeking more and more advertising and subscription revenue to compete in a market Ed Watson regarded as properly belonging to private enterprise and his *Tribune.* This, Williams knew, would not play well with the General Assembly at Jefferson City. But the only other immediate possibilities would be to cease publication of the *Missourian* altogether or, perhaps even worse, reduce it to a college-newspaper-only status.

In the meantime, Charles G. Ross and Silas Bent, as news editors, were expected to keep the paper as noncontroversial as humanly possible. This self-imposed blandness lasted for months, and Ross chafed at it. He wrote to a friend: "There is no real news in Columbia that would interest you; indeed, there is no real news of any kind. If there were a bit of real live news, I suppose the *Missourian* would be throttled."[10]

The *Missourian*'s troubles did not provoke, but almost certainly they in-tensified, the sharp personality clash that had developed almost immediately between Williams and his brilliant young assistant professor, Silas Bent. The two men could not have been more different. Bent's urbane wit and irreverent manner, added to a love for fast living and lively parties, did not at all suit Williams, whose approach to life and to his pioneering, evangelistic mission was deadly serious. Only weeks after the first term opened, the two men were arguing openly. Ross repeatedly attempted to intercede, but these were strong-willed men and neither was willing to give ground. Midway through the fall term, Williams called Bent into his office to inform him that he wasn't "fitting in." Bent thereupon tendered his resignation, to become effective at the end of the semester.[11]

And so Silas Bent, who was soon destined to become nationally famous, and nationally controversial, as a leading journalist as well as a biting critic of the contemporary press, left the academic world after less than six months. Ross, who admired Williams and genuinely liked Bent,[12] was deeply disappointed

---

9. Charles G. Ross to Mary Paxton, June 3, 1909, Mary Paxton Keeley Papers, Harry S. Truman Library.

10. Ross to Mary Paxton, October 8, 1908, Keeley Papers.

11. Mary Paxton Keeley, interview with the author, January 5, 1964, and quoted in the author's *Reluctant Servant,* 48. See also Sara Lockwood Williams, *Twenty Years of Education for Journalism,* which, though helpful in so many respects, is devoid of any suggestion of the intramural conflict that marked the early months of the school.

12. The Charles G. Ross Papers in the Harry S. Truman Library contain a number of friendly letters between Ross and Bent.

that some way had not been found to harness Bent's considerable intellect to the task of building the School of Journalism. For the restless Bent, however, an illustrious professional career lay ahead. He joined the staff of Chicago's *American,* then moved to New York, where he would eventually work on the *Times* and three other Manhattan dailies, and edit *Nation's Business* magazine. In 1927, he wrote *Ballyhoo,* a scathing indictment of the tabloid journalism that characterized the Roaring Twenties. In this early and important work of press criticism, Bent angrily charged that the press would "ballyhoo, for the aggrandizement of its own treasury, prize-fighters, channel swimmers, football players, chorus girls, and aviators," and he warned that "freedom of the press has no advocate, no intercessor, no vindicator. It has only defenders and apologists." He urged the press to "shovel less smut and print more news . . . even in public questions which promise no immediate return to its pocketbook." Bent mailed a copy of *Ballyhoo* to Walter Williams along with a note saying "you will not agree with much that I have to say."[13] Probably Bent was right. Some time before, in a comparable context, Williams had written this revealing passage:

> Country printers are more faithful, more intelligent, more efficient than city printers and much more economical. Some of the best printers were never in a city. The training of a city printer is wholly different from that of the country printer and when he comes to the country he usually begins to sneer at country ways and becomes a disturbing element in the office.[14]

To replace Bent, Williams went to the *Kansas City Star* for an old friend, a lanky, easygoing Nebraskan named Frank Lee Martin. They had met some years earlier while Martin was reporting on the terrible typhoid fever epidemic of 1905 that raged through central Missouri. Martin had interviewed Williams, among others who had been stricken, in the Columbia hospital, and the two men had remained on good terms since. Martin had moved up briskly in the *Star* organization and was an associate editor and editorial writer when Williams approached him in 1908. Never really comfortable in the city, Martin jumped at the chance to live and teach in a small town. He was an agreeable individual, certainly a competent one, and both Ross and Williams found him a superb colleague.

---

13. Silas Bent, *Ballyhoo* (Boni and Livright, 1927). In his preface to the book, Bent credited his experience as a journalism professor with forcing him, for the first time, to examine the press field as a whole. Bent to Williams, November 9, 1929. Williams Papers, Western Historical Manuscript Collection.

14. Walter Williams, *The Missouri Editor,* undated, reprinted in Sara Lockwood Williams, "A Study of the Columbia, Missouri, Herald, from 1889 to 1908," master's thesis, University of Missouri, 1931. It should be added that when Bent sent a copy of *Ballyhoo* to Williams he received a cordial, if cool ("Dear Mr. Bent") thank-you note in return.

But as the faculty situation improved, problems with the *Missourian* grew worse. Ed Watson, hard-driving, hard-living, doggedly determined, kept up his editorial offensive. Many politicians were interested in what Watson had to say, instinctively suspicious of the University of Missouri, and sympathetic to his claim that a tax-supported state institution had begun competing unfairly with tax-paying private enterprise. In the spring of 1909, Watson and his publisher-allies made their case at Jefferson City with the General Assembly, and they got what they wanted. When the 1909 funding act was passed, the legislators pointedly inserted a stipulation that "no part of any money appropriated [to the University of Missouri] be used directly or indirectly for the support, maintenance or publication of any newspaper which solicits, receives or accepts paid subscriptions or which prints or publishes advertising."[15] Anxious to protect the university's primary funding source, the Board of Curators then issued a directive that any and all financial support from the university would "be withdrawn from any publication in Missouri or elsewhere that solicited, received or accepted paid subscriptions or which printed or published advertisements." While the *Missourian* was its primary target, the ban also affected the alumni magazine and the *Missouri Farmer,* published by the College of Agriculture. The effective date of the new policy would be the end of the academic year, on June 9, 1909, at which point it was widely assumed that the School of Journalism's *Daily Missourian* would have published its last issue.

Williams, however, did not quit. The *Missourian* was the key to his curriculum and to much else he had in mind for the school. He had no intention of abandoning it.

Moving swiftly over the summer of 1909, Williams formed what he called the University Missourian Publishing Association to take over production of the paper. A board of directors, composed of journalism students to be elected by their classmates, would be nominally in charge, though clearly the defining ideas and decisions were those of Walter Williams. Leasing office space well off the campus, at 1105 Broadway, downtown, Williams set up a small but sufficient printing plant, including a new Mergenthaler Linotype typesetting machine, a Campbell sheet-fed printing press, casting equipment, and an adequate assortment of type. Full details of how this equipment was acquired were not disclosed, and the records are unclear. Minutes of the association report that in 1908 and 1909 only $261.30 was spent on equipment; yet later records recall that "the first press for the School of Journalism was purchased

---

15. Sara Lockwood Williams, *Twenty Years of Education for Journalism,* 98.

and paid for from a State appropriation." Most likely the new printing plant resulted from some combination of state money, industry contributions—Mergenthaler, like the Associated Press and United Press, which had donated their wire services, was also interested in acquainting youthful journalists with their products—and promissory notes. Articles of incorporation for the University Missourian Publishing Association were hastily drafted and filed and, on August 2, 1909, approved by the Boone County Circuit Court. The incorporation was reported tersely and without comment in the *Columbia Daily Tribune*. Installation of the printing equipment was completed in late August, only days before the summer recess ended. When fall semester classes began that September, the *Missourian* triumphantly resumed publication as usual, carrying news and advertising to its regular list of paying customers, this time from its own printing plant. Although there would be glitches—at one point in September the new equipment failed and the *Missourian* would be published briefly on the E. W. Stephens company presses—the transition in general was extraordinarily smooth.[16] The paper had not missed an issue.

The creation of the University Missourian Publishing Association and the move off campus might well have violated the spirit of the legislature's mandate, but the letter of it remained more or less intact. Ed Watson was beaten. And while he would continue to complain, in print and to his friends around the state, about the *Missourian* and its threat to local free enterprise, he came to accept competition from the School of Journalism newspaper as a fact of life. The *Missourian*'s somewhat ambiguous off-campus organizational structure may or may not have survived a challenge in the courts, but neither Watson nor anyone else cared to push the matter any further.

Watson was, in truth, neither a mean-spirited man nor Walter Williams's personal or professional enemy. Proud holder himself of two degrees from the University of Missouri, Watson was a vigorous booster of the institution and most of its activities. One of his cherished possessions was an imposing hat rack, an elk head with massive antlers mounted on a formidable oak cabinet. The hat rack was prominently displayed in the *Daily Tribune*'s newsroom, and if a visitor remarked that the piece was nothing if not hideous, he or she was quickly informed that it had once adorned the president's office of the University of Missouri and was a personal gift to Ed Watson from Dr. Richard Henry Jesse. Watson and Walter Williams were both ardent Democrats, both leaders in the affairs of a small town, thrown together dozens of times each year

---

16. Ibid. "Statement Concerning the University Missourian Association, 1927." This report, signed by the executive committee, was in the Walter Williams Papers. *Columbia Daily Tribune,* August 4, September 21, 1909.

at civic and social occasions. And while Watson would periodically remind his readers that "the *Tribune* is forced to continue to enjoy alone the distinction of being the only newspaper in America which competes with a sovereign state in the elevating business of journalism," he accepted his situation without rancor and remained unfailingly cordial to the dean of the School of Journalism. What discomfort Ed Watson may have suffered would be eased substantially by the *Tribune*'s dramatic growth, both in influence and profits, under his deft and aggressive management. Years later Floyd C. Shoemaker, executive secretary of the State Historical Society of Missouri, would write Walter Williams: "I believe that Ed admires, respects, and loves you, but of course that does not include as yet one of your creations."[17]

Even as Williams had predicted, the *Missourian* was proving to be a superb teaching laboratory. Journalists from far and wide paid visits to Columbia to observe the operation and to seek out promising *Missourian* staff members for future employment. "Every news story must stand the test of publication," reported the *Christian Science Monitor,* in a lengthy and highly complimentary piece, one of many to appear in the national press about Missouri's School of Journalism. "There is no writing for the wastebasket. Student copyreaders edit and headline the copy turned in by the reporters, as well as United Press copy and syndicated material. Students write the editorials, the features, and many of the advertisements. Practically all the work of publishing the paper, except the work of the printers, is done by students."[18]

Williams himself took little hand in the day-to-day operation of the *Missourian,* leaving those chores to Frank Martin and Charlie Ross. Both were disciplined craftsmen and exacting teachers, yet patient with their young charges. The students respected both men and worked hard for them. "The gaunt Martin slouched, his chest seemed to cave in. His legs were a problem when he sat down," one admiring student would write later of the six-foot, four-inch professor. "He would listen patiently to a student, then say something like, 'Why don't you just go ahead and develop the story the way you told it to me?' "[19]

Of Charlie Ross, he recalled:
    Ross, youngest of the faculty trio, was a broad-shouldered man with deep-set eyes that made his cheekbones seem prominent. He was tolerant with students but

    17. Pike, *Ed Watson,* 125, 127, 128.
    18. *Christian Science Monitor,* December 1, 1925.
    19. Dale Wilson, a 1912 graduate of the School of Journalism, to Dr. William H. Taft, April 20, 1977.

sometimes irritated by fellow faculty members from other departments: "They're always complaining about being misquoted."

On one of my first reporting assignments Ross sent me to interview Dr. Charles Elwood, head of the sociology department, who had just returned from England—he had been teaching at Oxford. Elwood talked slowly and I took full notes . . . The story made page 1 in the *Missourian.*

Next day Ross stopped me in the hall. "Elwood phoned that he was accurately quoted," he said. "That's the first time any blankety-blank professor has done anything but gripe over a story."[20]

Early in the fall of 1909 the *Missourian* increased its publication frequency from five issues per week to six, every day but Sunday. But intensified interest in football prompted a season-long Sunday edition as well. The Sunday paper, Columbia's first, was filled with wire service reports of Saturday's college gridiron action across the country. There was the odd extra edition, too, such as on High School Day and whenever unusually big stories were breaking. The paper ranged from four to eight pages per issue, six columns per page, and sold for four dollars a year by carrier or three dollars by mail. Circulation hovered at about one thousand.[21]

The *Missourian*'s news-editorial content, reflecting more and more of a professional polish, symbolized a growing air of confidence in the School of Journalism and all it was trying to accomplish. As one student-written editorial in 1909, the second year of the paper's existence, put it:

The School of Journalism has passed the experimental stage and the *University Missourian* will give this year practical demonstration of the School's success. As a newspaper it will give the news truthfully, graphically, and fearlessly. It will seek to aid the entire University by adequate, helpful exploitation. It will welcome cooperation with student journals, student organizations, and every agency that seeks the best interests of the University of Missouri. It will hold up the hands of those in authority who plan for a greater *University Missourian* to bring their plans to realization. In a word, the *University Missourian* will serve the University of Missouri as the University of Missouri serves the state.[22]

The *Missourian* that year even felt secure enough to publish a self-parody, a "Yellow Extra," in the lurid yellow journalism traditions of William Randolph Hearst and Joseph Pulitzer. More of an inside joke than anything else, the spoof edition was done with the faculty's blessing and served as a welcome release for the staff at year's end. It, and an April Fool's stunt edition, became something of an annual tradition. No longer "throttled," as Charlie Ross had described it, and with its very existence no longer threatened, the *Missourian* had arrived.

---

20. Ibid.
21. Sara Lockwood Williams, *Twenty Years of Education for Journalism,* 98.
22. Ibid., 99.

So, too, it seemed, had the School of Journalism. A retiring president of the University of Missouri, in a speech some years later, remembered those first, tentative months in the life of the journalism program. Entitling his address "Obstacles Overcome," he referred to "mountains removed," the impression he retained from watching the childhood and adolescence of the world's first school of journalism under the leadership of Walter Williams. "The Dean," he recalled, "one by one, removed these mountains by his faith. By his faith . . . he removed them so completely that none remain today."[23]

But if the *Missourian*'s political worries were over, its financial problems were not. Even though many of the paper's operating costs were provided for—the student reporting and editing staff worked without cost, the faculty supervisors were supplied as part of the school's teaching function, the state absorbed the cost of newsroom (as classroom) office space and utilities—there were still production and distribution costs. For all his grousing about competition, Ed Watson still secured for his *Daily Tribune* the lion's share of advertising and subscriber income and dominated the tight Columbia market. At times, the *Missourian* had trouble covering its printing costs. During one lean year, advertising sales had dropped precipitously and the *Missourian*'s ledgers were covered by deep pools of red ink. Walter Williams mortgaged his home as collateral for his personal note of seventeen hundred dollars to tide the paper over. When economic conditions improved, the money was repaid.[24] Williams's willingness to assume so much to ensure the School of Journalism's student laboratory paper's survival would be long remembered, both on and off the campus.

Less well known is the fact that the *Missourian*'s economic times were not always bad. Williams's oft-expressed claim that the laboratory newspaper "is a commercial enterprise only to the extent that it solicits business—subscriptions and advertising—in order to pay expenses" was somewhat disingenuous. Indeed, if Ed Watson had mounted even a cursory investigation for the *Daily Tribune* into the *Missourian*'s books, he would have discovered that the laboratory newspaper in more than a few years turned a tidy profit. And, in its own way, the *Missourian* quietly became a cash cow for the School of Journalism.

The Missourian Publishing Association would eventually be reorganized, and capital stock, a hundred shares at one hundred dollars each, was sold

---

23. President Emeritus J. Carleton Jones, quoted in Viles, *A Centennial History,* 415.
24. Rucker, *Walter Williams,* 153.

to graduates and former students of the School of Journalism, raising ten thousand dollars.[25] Times grew better, and advertising sales flourished. A substantial portion of the profits would be discretely transferred to the School of Journalism. By the mid-1920s, the association's executive committee's minutes noted that fifteen thousand dollars were now safely on deposit in a reserve fund "to be used by the University Missourian Association for any purpose that may arise." At that same meeting, the executive committee formalized its procedure for transferring money from the paper to the school by establishing what it called the Betterment Fund. The initial allocation was for one thousand dollars, the money, according to the minutes, "to be used for any purposes that might make for the improvement and advancement of the School of Journalism in general, warrants upon this fund not to be drawn except upon written request from Dean Williams."[26]

The Betterment Fund would be regularly enriched in future meetings, sometimes by a few hundred dollars, but by four thousand dollars at one meeting in 1928 and three thousand and five thousand dollars at separate meetings in 1929. These were not trifling sums, considering that a dean's salary during that time was less than five thousand dollars and a professor might be earning less than three thousand. In addition, the Missourian Board of Directors authorized payments to cover specific expenditures of the school. In one such action, the minutes noted approval of an order "that travel expenses, railroad and steamship fares, of members of the Journalism Faculty who represent the School of Journalism as exchange professors be regarded as proper charge against the Association."[27] This directive, it turned out, would be implemented later that year to approve allowance of travel expenses amounting to $2,850 for Williams and $2,500 for Frank Lee Martin as visiting professors to Yenching University in China. Indeed, the entire exchange program with Yenching University—scholarships, lectureships, publications, visiting professorships—seems to have been underwritten by association money, including, as the minutes explained, "under the Dean's direction, the Scholarship Fund, the Betterment Fund, and the Reserve or Emergency Fund."[28]

Williams's own international travel bills were substantial. Among other travels, he visited the British Isles in 1909, took a nine-month world tour in

25. J. Harrison Brown, *Business Management History, University Missourian Association, 1908–1952,* School of Journalism, University of Missouri, 1952. This useful booklet, perhaps understandably, makes no mention of the Betterment Fund.

26. Minutes of the Executive Committee of the University Missourian Association, June 5, 1926.

27. Ibid., April 30, 1930.

28. Ibid., November 30, 1930.

1913, visited the Orient in 1918, attended a World Press Congress in Guatemala in 1919, delivered guest lectures in Mexico City in 1926, revisited the Orient in 1927, revisited Guatemala in 1925 and 1930, and took an extensive tour of Europe in 1932.[29] And while he received outside funding at times—the Kahn Foundation subsidized his world tour in 1913, for example—much of his travel expense, both foreign and domestic, was borne by the *Missourian,* channeled through convenient accounting vehicles such as the Betterment Fund.

Williams's small faculty did some traveling as well: before his visiting professorship in China, Frank Martin was sent on a sabbatical to be a sub-editor on the English-language *Japan Advertiser* in Tokyo during 1914–1915. And Charlie Ross was dispatched on a sabbatical to Australia, where he served as a sub-editor of the *Melbourne Herald* in 1916–1917. Arrangements for both these assignments were completed by Williams during his 1913 world tour.[30]

Funds generated by the *Missourian* also provided scholarships for some students in the School of Journalism and were used to purchase other things the school needed, but could not manage on its state-appropriated budget. Various publications, such as an early history of the school, *Twenty Years of Education for Journalism,* were paid for through the Betterment Fund.[31]

In short, the Betterment Fund, and other funds in different times with different names but the same purpose, provided Walter Williams with leverage and visibility he could never have managed otherwise. Through these *Missourian* monies he was able, as if by magic, to take the name and the mission of the School of Journalism across the globe, exerting a unique brand of professional leadership out of all proportion to what might have been expected of a tiny, still-experimental academic department at a financially strapped university in a small town in a remote part of the American Midwest.

Wherever he went on his well-planned, well-publicized travels abroad, Williams would be greeted by the local newspapers with something approaching reverence as the man who had led the fight for professional training and enhanced stature for journalists. "Leading Figure in the Press World," headlined the *Brisbane Telegraph,* as Williams arrived in Australia.[32] Describing him as "the gentle genius," the *New York Sun* reported on a Williams trip to China that "appears to have borne new and exotic fruit":

> A Chinese school of journalism has just been established at Shanghai. Although news reports announcing this fact mention no definite connection between it and

---

29. This compilation comes chiefly from Williams's scrapbooks, Williams Papers.
30. Farrar, *Reluctant Servant,* 48–50.
31. Minutes of the Executive Committee of the University Missourian Association, January 20, 1928.
32. *Brisbane Herald,* June 28, 1928.

the oldest of the American journalism schools, more than fifty graduates of the Missouri institution are at present engaged in newspaper work in that part of the world. Dean Williams has long been interested in the propagation of American newspaper ideals throughout the Far East . . . [33]

In the Far East, yes. And in Europe and Central and South America and the rest of the world as well. Just as he had crisscrossed Missouri years before to bond with editors as president of the state press association, Williams now felt obliged to roam the earth, not only to show the flag of the world's first school of journalism, but also to make his case for journalistic professionalism and unity. Unlikely funding—profits quietly siphoned off from what appeared to be a struggling laboratory newspaper—helped get Walter Williams to visit newspaper leaders of many nations. But his own dedication and diplomatic skills would turn those visits into spectacular and lasting successes.

Williams's discrete transfers involving the Betterment Fund and other profits generated by the *Missourian* may or may not have survived a rigorous examination by the press and, especially, by state auditors. So far as is known, however, no such examination ever took place. Perhaps it was assumed that the *Missourian* was perpetually in dire financial straits, as it sometimes was, and any speculation about profits would seem outrageously irrelevant. For whatever the reason, few questions about the *Missourian*'s finances were raised and little information about them was volunteered.

For his part, Walter Williams was succeeding beyond his fondest dreams. His School of Journalism was now known and admired—and emulated—in many lands. His message, a plea for a heightened sense of responsibility and for professional unity, was getting across. No longer an obscure small-town editor, Walter Williams had become a journalist to the world. And a homely, once-controversial little laboratory newspaper had done much to make it all possible.

---

33. *New York Sun,* April 12, 1929.

10

Losses—and a Gain

 Noblesse oblige *might well have been carved over the doorway of the school which Walter Williams founded at Columbia, Missouri. There, near the geographical center of the country, he established a nerve center—the importance of which cannot be overestimated.*

—Arthur Hays Sulzberger, publisher, *New York Times*

There were no signs or rules posted in the School of Journalism's quarters in Switzler Hall. None were needed. "Dean Williams set the example by his personality, demeanor, conduct, and appearance," a former student explained. "His deep concern permeated everyone and everything in his environment." "When I first saw Dean Williams," another student wrote later, "I thought he must be 70 years old. " 'No,' someone told me. He's about 50." Actually, he was in his mid-forties at the time.[1]

Williams's grave manner epitomized the dignity he insisted the school must present to the world, but it made him a somewhat less-than-exciting lecturer. In the classroom, he tended to sermonize, often at mind-numbing length. " 'Accuracy, terseness and fairness are the chief requisites of a good news story,' Dean Williams said in his History and Principles class, but in his teaching he forgot the terseness," a member of the class of 1916 remembered. "H & P was boring. The dean talked very slowly, a habit he had acquired when he had a speech impediment. Someone said he had overcome stuttering by practicing with marbles in his mouth. His lectures were platitudinous but his personality was inspiring and he commanded respect." "He often paused in mid-sentence until one wondered when he was going to continue," another H & P student recalled. "This was his manner when he served as toastmaster, too. But it seemed to bring emphasis to the point he was making." Others were

---

1. Joe Cowan, an early student in the School of Journalism, to James Atwater, dean of the school during the 1980s, January 10, 1989. Dorothy Baker Suddarth to William Howard Taft, April 19, 1977.

less charitable. "He was an autocrat," another student remembered. "He would get carried away and preach instead of teach."[2]

Often students must have wondered whether they were in a journalism course or at Williams's famed Sunday school class at First Presbyterian Church. He sometimes used the same material for both. "Williams believed the Bible was the best textbook for a journalist," wrote William H. Taft, who would in later years take over the History and Principles of Journalism class. "He considered Christ to have been the first great democrat. He viewed Moses as the first great editor, a man who 'gave more criminal news and told it more graphically than today's newspapers would dare to report.' Luke was the best reporter. Mark had 'too little coloring in his news story' and John had too much. But Luke's story had 'clearness, human interest, a touch of the writer's personality.' Williams also observed 'how the Bible contained portraits, feature stories, personal gossip,' not unlike contemporary newspapers."[3]

Fully aware that students often regarded his lectures as ponderous and dull, Williams sought to liven up his classes with what he called "Gems of Journalism," examples of poorly written news pieces—"sentences," he said, "that appear to have been in an automobile accident"—taken mostly from Missouri weekly newspapers. More than half a century later, a student could recall verbatim one such classroom example. It described a tornado that had struck a country schoolhouse. The storm, Williams read to his class, "that had frightened the students and the brave little teacher tore the roof off the school and threw it a mile away."[4]

Williams saw History and Principles less as a class than as professional indoctrination, the critically important first step in shaping the visions of those who could have an impact on their, and his, profession. Convinced that men and women, as opposed to events, make history, Williams held steadfast in his faith that the young men and women in his class would someday make journalistic history themselves. Thus he insisted that they endure a thorough grounding in the lives and achievements of those who had gone before. If these ancient stories kindled enthusiasm in his students—as they never failed to do so with him—then so much the better. But in any case the names and achievements of those who had shaped journalism must be drilled home. Williams defined his role, as had Tacitus nearly two thousand years earlier,

2. Dale Wilson to William Howard Taft, March 20, 1977. Suddarth to Taft, April 19, 1977. Maurice Votaw, Class of 1919, undated memorandum to William Howard Taft. Votaw, who would work for many years as a journalist and educator in the Far East, later taught at the School of Journalism.

3. William H. Taft, "Walter Williams, The Man," undated, unpublished manuscript, c. 1980.

4. Frank Willmarth, writing in the *Downieville* (Calif.) *Mountain Messenger,* March 3, 1994.

as being "to rescue virtuous actions from the oblivion to which a want of records would consign them."[5] Thus he insisted that names of important journalists and their publications, time frames, and achievements must be mastered. In other words, preparing for a Walter Williams examination required a fair amount of memorization. Typical is this test, from the spring semester of 1915:

FINAL EXAMINATION

Be specific. If you can't give facts, don't give anything. Keep questions in order. Be brief. Don't be afraid to give names and dates. If the question is about a newspaper, name the editor; if about an editor, name the newspaper. Give important facts from *journalistic* viewpoint.

Part A.

1. Just what was it that Gutenberg invented?
2. Explain the point system of type measurement.
3. Name the most striking two improvements in printing in the last fifty years.

Part B.

Describe specifically the various restrictions placed upon the early English press and outline the struggle for freedom.

Part C.

Write 150-word paragraphs on:
1. John Peter Zenger
2. Prosecution of Harry Croswell
3. John Wilkes
4. *Missouri Gazette*

Part D.

Tell in a sentence or two each the important facts about the following:
1. Horace Greeley
2. Sarah J. Hale
3. Junius letters
4. First daily newspaper in the United States
5. First two newspapers in the American colonies
6. First real English newspaper

---

5. Quoted in *The New Dictionary of Thoughts* (Standard Book Co., 1954), 255.

7. First real daily in the world
8. Early Washington newspapers
9. James Rivington
10. Robert L'Estrange
11. Blanket sheets
12. Elizabeth Mallett
13. New Orleans *Picayune*
14. Robert Hoe
15. *Acta Diurna*
16. Ottmar Mergenthaler
17. Benjamin Franklin
18. Henry J. Raymond
19. James Gordon Bennett
20. George Jones

(*Author's note: The answers—or, at least, the author's open-book attempt at the answers—may be found in the appendix.*)

The literature of journalism at that point was thin at best. For his lectures, Williams could draw upon only two book-length histories. One of these was Isaiah Thomas's *The History of Printing in America, with a Biography of Printers, and an Account of Newspapers.* While an excellent source for colonial and early U.S. journalism, this two-volume compilation, published in 1810, was by now outdated by a full century. The other book on press history, only thirty-five years or so out of date when Williams began his classes, was Frederic Hudson's *Journalism in the United States, from 1690 to 1872.* A former managing editor of James Gordon Bennett's *New York Herald,* Hudson wrote a lively and entertaining history, which, though unfortunately flawed by many inaccuracies, became a standard reference work for many years. A few other books available at the time dealt with the history of journalism, but only in passing. Charles A. Dana, brilliant editor of the *New York Sun,* compiled some of his addresses into *The Art of Newspaper Making.* A bitter and cynical treatment by Lambert A. Wilmer, *Our Press Gang: or, A Complete Exposition of the Corruptions and Crimes of the American Newspapers,* published in 1859, was interesting reading, but it presented a somewhat different portrait of the field than the one Walter Williams had in mind for his idealistic journalism students. Other works available in this period included *Hints to Young Editors,* written by staff members of the Yale *Courant,* then the campus newspaper there; Edwin Shuman's *Steps Into Journalism,* and Jesse Haney's *Haney's Guide to Authorship,* considered by some to be the first news reporting textbook, though it was clearly not intended to be a college text. There were a few more, but not many that could be adapted for use in the School of Journalism.[6] Much of the instruction came from contemporary newspapers and magazines. If Williams and his small faculty wanted textbooks, they knew they would have to produce their own.

Shortly after Frank Lee Martin replaced Silas Bent in early 1909, Williams enlisted Martin as coauthor of a text he wanted to write, a book that would inspire students and, in the process, elevate the tone of newpaper work in the public mind. Entitling it *The Practice of Journalism,* Williams and Martin devoted much of the manuscript to polishing the sometimes-tarnished image of the working press. The opening chapter, called "Journalism as a Profession," may well have come from Williams's first-day lecture to his History and Principles of Journalism class. "A journalist," he wrote, is "a recorder, advocate, buyer and seller of news, judge, tribune, and teacher," and journalism was less a vocation than "a call to joyful, fascinating service."

"The Reporter" chapter, probably written by Martin, listed sixteen abilities a good journalist must demonstrate: to ask good questions, to find exclusive information, to accept suggestions for articles, to persevere, be observant, accurate, reliable, friendly, fair, enthusiastic, loyal, honest, promising, thorough, alert, and conscious of detail.[7]

Williams and Martin emphasized the importance of the journalist's personality in helping shape how the news got reported. Their interpretation flew in the face of the view of many other newspaper people and critical observers—a group that included the third and youngest member of the Missouri faculty, Charles G. Ross. Ross argued instead that a detached, objective treatment of news is best; he agreed with James Gordon Bennett's espoused (but not always followed) philosophy: "We shall endeavor to record facts on every public and proper subject," Bennett had written in 1835, describing the mission of his

---

6. Thomas published his book at his printing plant in Worcester, Massachusetts, in 1810. The American Antiquarian Society, which Thomas founded, brought out a reprinted version in 1874. Harper and Bros., 1873. Other journalism texts included Benjamin Drew's *Hints and Helps for Those Who Write, Print, or Read* (1871), *How to Write for the Press,* by George Gaskell (1884), *Writing for the Press,* by Robert Luce (1886), *The Ladder of Journalism,* by Thomas Campbell-Copeland (1881), and *The Blue Pencil and How to Avoid It,* by Alexander Nevins (1890). A very helpful source in this regard has been Joe Mirando, "Journalism's First Textbook: Creating a News Reporting Body of Knowledge," paper presented at the Association for Education in Journalism and Mass Communications national convention, Kansas City, 1993.

7. Walter Williams and Frank Lee Martin, *The Practice of Journalism* (E. W. Stephens Co., 1911), 168–296. Also Mirando, "Journalism's First Textbook."

New York Herald, "stripped of verbiage and coloring."[8] Trained under that most disciplined of city editors, Oliver K. Bovard of the *Post-Dispatch,* Ross had been convinced that the journalist should be an observer, not a judge. But Williams and Martin insisted that the reverse is true:

> Personal journalism has not been succeeded by impersonal journalism. The journalist was never more powerful nor did personality ever count for so much in the profession of journalism as now.[9]

The philosophical differences Williams and Martin had with Ross were never allowed to escalate to the level of the ferocious infighting that so often polarizes otherwise rational members of the academy. The three men remained close friends and amiably accommodated each other's views on journalistic objectivity. Indeed, when Ross wrote his news reporting textbook, Frank Lee Martin, who was teaching reporting that term, enthusiastically adopted the Ross book as his text.[10]

Ross's *The Writing of News,* arguably the first newspaper reporting text ever published, began with a defense of its own reason for being. At a time when noisy elements of the intellectual community were deploring "journalese" and "newspaper English," Ross felt obliged to put newspaper writing into better context:

> "Newspaper English" has often been used as a term of reproach, as if the newspapers, by concerted action, had been guilty of creating an inferior, trademarked brand of English for their own purposes. The term has been hurled indiscriminately at all newspapers, the good as well as the bad, and young writers have been warned in a vague, general way to beware of the reporter's style. As applied to loosely edited newspapers, the criticism is just. It is not true, however, that "newspaper English" constitutes a special variety of language, to be shunned by all who would attain purity in writing. There are good books and bad books, just as there are good newspapers and bad newspapers, and it would be as unreasonable to condemn all books because they are written in a "bookish" style as it is to include all newswriting in a sweeping condemnation.
>
> No defense is needed of the style of writing in a well-edited modern newspaper. Free from pedantry and obsolete expressions, the English of the best newspapers fulfills its purpose of telling the news of the day in language that all can understand. Newspaper English . . . is the language of the people, clarified and simplified in the writing . . . Newspaper English is nothing more nor less than good English employed in the setting forth of news.
>
> The reporter writes his stories for readers of all degrees of intelligence . . . Simplicity is the keynote. This does not mean crudity or slovenliness, for while

---

8. *New York Herald,* May 6, 1835.
9. Williams and Martin, *The Practice of Journalism,* 113.
10. Farrar, *Reluctant Servant,* 76.

the good news story is written with the limitations of the least intelligent reader in mind, it should not offend the educated reader.[11]

Then, in a plea for freshness, Ross concluded his chapter of "Don'ts for the News Writer" with a list of what he called "newspaper bromides," terms which in 1911 he found trite and overworked. Many are still around:

agent of death	Grand Old Party
angry mob	grim reaper
battle-scarred veteran	jury of his peers
better half	last but not least
breakneck speed	calm before the storm
break the news gently	news leaked out
caught red-handed	nick of time
cool as a cucumber	nipped in the bud
day of reckoning	one fell swoop
dull, sickening thud	one fine day
facile pen	pale as death
fair sex	ripe old age
few and far between	sad tidings
goes without saying	silver-tongued orator[12]

A slender volume of just over two hundred pages, *The Writing of News* sold well, and Ross would be continually surprised over the years at the number of people who wrote to tell him how useful the book had been to them. The publication also enhanced Ross's growing reputation as a teacher, and no doubt helped his cause when he was approved for promotion to associate professor the following year.

In 1913 Ross wrote another guidebook, this one a thirty-four-page monograph for rural reporters called *The News in the County Paper.* It was in most respects a rather routine, if useful and welcome, how-to-do-it tract for inexperienced newspaper correspondents. But in one paragraph, dealing with crime news, Ross demonstrated a striking sense of social awareness:

> How crime news should be treated is a constant problem of a newspaper, but certainly if crime news is printed, the underlying causes should be given. The editor of a great Western newspaper in a recent address expressed the opinion that the newspaper of the future would treat news, especially crime news, from what he termed a more socialized point of view. That is, according to his theory, we shall concern ourselves not so much with the details of the crime itself as with an exposition of the social forces that produced the man capable of such a crime. Newspapers more and more should incline toward this attitude. The well-edited paper, the paper that aims to be something more than a mere "common carrier" of

---

11. Charles G. Ross, *The Writing of News* (Henry Holt and Co., 1911), 8 ff.

news, does not want lurid and revolting details, but it does perform a real service to society by exposing conditions that lead men to become enemies of society. All of which means, to sum it up in the terse order of a city editor to his reporter: Find out the motive—dig down under the surface facts to get the story.[13]

Ross, meanwhile, had fallen in love. The girl was Mary Paxton, a member of the first class in the School of Journalism. She, too, had grown up in Independence, but she had been four grades behind Ross in school.[14] Mary's well-to-do parents sent her to Hollins College in Virginia for two years, but the idea of Missouri's new journalism school appealed to her, and she transferred to it. She arrived in Columbia to learn that one of her professors would be Charles Ross, a young man with whom she had gone out on a buggy ride a summer before when they were both in Independence on vacation. It had been a hurried outing, however; the fathers and mothers of Independence insisted that their daughters terminate buggy rides by 6 P.M. or else risk being branded "fast."

She and Ross began dating steadily in the spring of 1909, despite the embarrassments that inevitably accrue to a professor who has one of his students for a sweetheart. It galled him, a man of academic rank, to call for her at the Kappa Kappa Gamma sorority house, where a sorority member would meet him at the door and yell, "MARY! HERE'S CHARLIE!" It was awkward, too, for him to escort her to dances and parties where he would sometimes be the only nonstudent present. He tolerated these and other annoyances, however, because he delighted in Mary's company; if he was uncomfortable at a fraternity dance, the last waltz—almost always "Home Sweet Home," with the lights dimmed romantically—made it all worthwhile. Mary was pretty, bright, and lively. That summer of 1909 he visited her in Independence, and they came to an understanding that they would eventually be married.

Mary, however, was not in a hurry. "There's so much to see, so much to do," she said. Ross, meanwhile, had been unable to save much money for marriage—increasingly, he'd been sending part of his fifteen-hundred-dollars-a-year salary to support his mother and sisters. Mary, meanwhile, had been introduced to Winifred Bonfils Black, the renowned "sob sister" for Hearst newspapers who was one of the most celebrated, and envied, women of her day. Black saw in Mary Paxton a kindred spirit and urged her to apply for a

---

13. Quoted in Farrar, *Reluctant Servant,* 56.
14. However, Ross had skipped two grades and Mary Paxton had missed school for two years because of illness, so there was a difference of only seven months in their ages.

reporting job on the Hearst-like *Kansas City Post.* Here, as the first female journalist in Kansas City, Mary scored success after success with her articles. One of her most famous was a first-person account of a ride in a kite, an exciting variation on the sport of ballooning; another article resulted from a trip through Kansas City's notorious red-light district. Before long, Mary blossomed into something of a celebrity herself, and marriage was not much on her mind.[15] And so the two drifted apart. But though they each would marry someone else, Charlie Ross and Mary Paxton would remain in each other's thoughts for the rest of their lives. Their meetings would be infrequent and then only through professional happenstance. But they wrote each other hundreds of letters, some of them intimate, over the years, and their star-crossed but enduring romance became a part of the folklore of the School of Journalism.

Not unlike many professors before and since, Walter Williams was far more effective with his students outside the classroom than in it. He systematically arranged for each student in the school to meet with him privately in his office. "In these private conversations he was charming," wrote one student who had regarded Williams's classroom lectures as tedious. "He loved to hear and tell good stories. He seemed to know everyone in Missouri and to carry on correspondence with hundreds of them."[16] A female student wrote later about her conference with the dean. "I think he wanted to give encouragement and perhaps some guidance . . . He was so kindly in his manner that he made a person feel good. The only definite thing I remember about the talk was that I told him I was not the least bit clever. He smiled his slow, twinkly smile and replied, 'Well, you remember the fable of the tortoise and the hare.' "[17]

Williams was determined to show off his students, to gain exposure for them, and for the School of Journalism, at every opportunity. To Ovid Bell, publisher of the *Fulton Gazette,* he wrote:

> Would it be worthwhile, as an advertisement to the *Gazette,* for you to pay the traveling expenses of one of our senior students in Journalism, who would write two columns or more for the University Missourian about you . . . and the *Gazette?* I am planning to send some of the senior class in Journalism out to neighboring towns for serious interviews upon subjects that make for Missouri's larger prosperity. It seems to me a story of the *Gazette,* its building and its owner, his views on country journalism, &c, would be a fine contribution to Missouri history of the best type. Unfortunately, we have no appropriation to meet such

---

15. Interview with the author, quoted in the author's *Reluctant Servant,* 51.
16. Wilson to Taft, March 20, 1977.
17. Suddarth to Taft, April 19, 1977.

expenses and I am selecting a half dozen public enterprises like the *Gazette,* thinking the advertising features would be worth their meeting the cost of the student's journey.[18]

Hundreds of such individual arrangements were worked out between Williams and his publisher-friends. Each agreement usually resulted in a nice trip and a byline or two for an ambitious journalism student, a promising contact for the student with a publisher (Bell, at the moment Williams wrote this particular letter to him, was about to become president of the Missouri Press Association), a bit of unexpected publicity for the publisher's newspaper, and, not so incidentally, still another public relations success for Williams and the School of Journalism. With the publisher himself paying for it.

Drawing upon his carefully kept notes from travels abroad, Williams invited foreign publishers to hire Missouri journalism students as summer interns or, better yet, as full-time reporters and editors after graduation. Two graduates per year, personally selected by Williams, would be automatically employed by the *Japan Advertiser* in Tokyo. More than fifty alumni were hired in Asia alone during the first two decades of the school's existence. Three early graduates of the school would become directors of journalism programs in China: Don D. Patterson launched a journalism department at St. John's University in Peking; he would be succeeded by Maurice E. Votaw, class of 1919. Vernon Nash, class of 1914, would begin the journalism program at Yenching University.[19]

Walter Williams often told his History and Principles students, "He who has not set eyes on the outside world is not a journalist."[20] Another of his classroom platitudes, perhaps, but students realized their solemn dean fervently believed what he was telling them and, more to the point, that he understood how to secure the opportunities he wanted for them and which they knew they needed. Henry J. Haskell, editor of the *Kansas City Star,* was among many journalists across the nation who praised Williams for

> his great contribution in sending out into the world young men and women trained in his ideals, inspired by his spirit of disinterested public service. No one could come in contact with Dean Williams without being permanently enriched from that abounding personality.[21]

The far-flung alumni of the young school were mostly men—sixteen of them were working as reporters and editors in Tokyo alone before 1918—but,

18. Williams to Ovid Hill, January 21, 1911, Williams Papers, Western Historical Manuscript Collection.

19. Votaw manuscript. Taft manuscript.

20. Quoted in Taft manuscript.

21. *Kansas City Star,* July 30, 1935.

increasingly, female graduates of the school were landing newspaper jobs also. Wrote one grateful columnist in the *Washington Post:*

> Women journalists particularly owe him a great debt. Before the coming of schools of journalism, newspaper offices were largely closed to them on the basis of any dignified, professional status. Most editors accepted them only as sob sisters, muckrakers, or stunt reporters. Their writing was expected to be flashy and maudlin. But through their training in schools of journalism and through Dean Williams's personal sponsorship of them and belief in them, they were graduated into professional respectability and new fields of opportunity are opened to them.[22]

At the spring commencement of 1909, Charles A. Arnold, who had transferred into the School of Journalism from the College of Arts and Science, became the first person ever awarded the Bachelor of Journalism degree. Previously a student in the English department, Arnold had joined the original class in the School of Journalism the previous year and Williams, never hesitant to use his deanly powers, granted young Arnold credit for some newspaper work he had done earlier. These waivers permitted Arnold to move quickly through the remaining coursework in the School of Journalism and win his diploma. Though he had obvious talent for journalism, Arnold opted instead for an academic career and in time became a professor of English at the University of Pittsburgh.[23] Those who followed, for the most part, sought newspaper jobs, and promptly landed them.

Six students earned BJ degrees the following year, including the first woman to graduate, Mary Paxton. Her engaged-to-be-engaged relationship with Charlie Ross now irrevocably broken off, she plunged into a whirlwind newspaper career that would one day lead to her being identified, perhaps with more local pride than accuracy, as "The First Lady of Journalism."[24] Ten students were graduated by the school in 1911 and ten more in 1912. By 1913 the number of graduates had risen to twenty-three, including at least two whose names would loom large in the school's history. One was Frank W. Rucker, destined to become a distinguished newspaper publisher and prolific author whose works would include an important textbook on newspaper management as well as an affectionate biography of his friend and tutor, Walter Williams. The other was Ward A. Neff, son of a wealthy publisher and former mayor of Kansas City. Ward Neff would soon be looking for a way to honor his late father, and Walter Williams would figure prominently in his plans.

---

22. Malvina Lindsay column in the *Washington Post,* July 29, 1935.
23. Sara Lockwood Williams, *Twenty Years of Education for Journalism,* 413.
24. Barbara Zang, "The First Lady of Journalism," *University of Missouri School of Journalism Alumni Magazine,* 1987, 11.

In the autumn of 1912 Lee Shippey, one of the school's first graduates who had just begun as a cub reporter in Kansas City, sold his first article to *Collier's*. It was quite a coup for the youthful journalist, made even more satisfying when the magazine commissioned him to write another piece. But when he sent in the second manuscript, the editor at *Collier's* demanded better photographs to accompany the text. Shippey knew his old mentor at Missouri, Dean Williams, possessed some photos that would be perfect to illustrate the piece, and he wrote Williams asking to borrow them. To Shippey's great surprise, an entire week went past without an answer. The *Collier's* assignment was his first from a New York publication, and Shippey was close to panic at the thought of muffing it. Furious at Williams for failing to answer his letter, Shippey borrowed enough money to put in a long-distance telephone call. Hours went by before he got through. "You're awfully hard to catch," Shippey complained. "I wrote you days ago and got no answer. And now I've had to take most of today to get you by telephone."

"I'm sorry," Williams said. "I am telephoning from the hospital. My son is very ill."

"Then I was conscience-stricken and begged him to forget the matter," Shippey would write years later in his *Los Angeles Times* column. "But he knew it must be something very important to me, and looked up the letter, which had been unopened in his office for days. The next day I received the pictures I wanted, by special delivery, and hurried them on to New York. And when the evening paper came out that day I saw that Dean Williams's son had died. In the midst of his worry and grief he had realized what those pictures might mean to an eager boy."[25]

Walter Williams, Jr., died on November 8, 1912, still another victim of typhoid fever. His brief life had held enormous promise. Like his father, he had learned to read at a very early age, and he disciplined himself for a life of hard work and achievement. But while he strived manfully to emulate his father, it was the approval of his mother that he seemed to need most of all. While still in elementary school he wrote his own personal code of conduct:

(1) to pretend nothing that is not so; (2) to spend as little time as possible in idleness or useless occupation; (3) to learn to see farther into the future; (4) to do without some pleasures in order that I may obtain self-control; (5) to keep myself free from taint and wickedness; (6) to study harder that I may obtain my ambitions; (7) to be cheerful and considerate toward others; (8) to take nothing that I do not deserve; (9) to think only of things pure and noble; and (10) to do nothing that I would not be willing for her [his mother] to know.[26]

25. Lee Shippey column in the *Los Angeles Times,* July 29, 1935.
26. Quoted Rucker, *Walter Williams,* 208.

At the age of eleven Walter, Jr., had served as a page at the Democratic National Convention at St. Louis. In his senior year he was editor of his high school newspaper. He entered the University of Missouri at sixteen, and impressed his parents and his professors by writing freelance articles and selling them to metropolitan newspapers, magazines, and agricultural journals. When stricken with typhus he was a junior in the School of Journalism, talented, popular, well known throughout the campus and the community, headed for what appeared to be certain success in journalism. The death of his son would be one of the great sorrows in Walter Williams's life.[27] His grief was almost unbearable.

Helen, the daughter, was growing up to be much like her mother—attractive, vivacious, well liked by the older generation as well as by her contemporaries. She was especially devoted to her shy, reserved, younger brother, Edwin, and an unwavering source of comfort to him, and to her parents, after the death of Walter, Jr.

During the world war year of 1917, she married her longtime sweetheart, John Franklin Rhodes, in the sanctuary of the Presbyterian church. The groom, a captain in the army, and his best man wore full military dress uniforms, and the church was decorated with red, white, and blue trim. It was, as the *Columbia Tribune* described it, "one of the prettiest weddings ever solemnized in Columbia."[28]

A year later, and pregnant with Walter's and Hulda's first grandchild, Helen vowed to name the baby, if a girl, Hulda, after her mother. It was an affecting, bittersweet tribute; she knew her mother was in the throes of a lingering, fatal illness and would not live to see her namesake, Hulda Gordon Rhodes, who was born on September 25, 1918.

When she died on April 9, 1918, Hulda Harned Williams had been married to Walter Williams for twenty-six years. At the time of her wedding he had been an obscure, though promising, editor of a small-town weekly newspaper. Now he was internationally recognized as the unchallenged leader in the field of journalism education and, beyond that, as a spokesman to and for the press of the world. But his dramatic success did not come without some cost to their marriage. Neighbors and a few intimate friends noted, a trifle sadly, that since the death of their first-born son Walter Williams had spent more and

---

27. Rucker, *Walter Williams,* 208. Sara Lockwood Williams, unpublished Walter Williams biography.

28. Quoted in Rucker, *Walter Williams,* 70.

more of his time at work, less and less at home. At least one neighbor bitterly accused Williams of taking his wife for granted.[29] But if Walter Williams had appeared to be career-driven and autocratic, occasionally brusque with neighbors, Hulda Harned Williams seemingly had time for everyone. She ran an exemplary household and was regarded with affection throughout the town. "She identified herself with every worthy project in the community, lending every encouragement, aid and assistance," proclaimed Ed Watson's *Columbia Daily Tribune*. "It would be impossible to ever approximate the womanly virtue, the Christian character, the generosity, kindness and graciousness of Mrs. Williams."[30] The cause of her death was never made public. All the press accounts noted guardedly, in the fashion of the time, that she had been ill for about a year. She was fifty-one. Her funeral, held at ten o'clock the morning of April 10, 1918, before a packed congregation at First Presbyterian Church, was conducted by a team of ministers, one of them the Reverend H. B. Banks of Mexico, husband of Walter's sister Elizabeth; he had also officiated at her wedding more than a quarter-century earlier. A black-bordered box on page one of the *Missourian* announced the funeral arrangements, noting that the list of pallbearers included longtime family friends E. W. Stephens, Charlie Ross, Frank Lee Martin, and A. Ross Hill, the president of the university. She was buried in a family lot at Columbia Cemetery.

Afterward Williams went home, accompanied only by his remaining son, Edwin Moss. Their house, suddenly empty and cheerless, was nevertheless a thing of beauty. It had been completed just a few months earlier on two large lots at 102 South Glenwood Avenue. The well-landscaped grounds, maintained by an elderly gardener, were full of memories: the ivy on the house had been transplanted from a sprig Walter, Jr., had insisted upon planting at the old house on Hitt Street some years before. One hardy rosebush, sprouted from a favorite bush of Walter's mother, had come from the old family homeplace in Boonville. An iron step at the garage, with the name "Walter" embossed on it, had once adorned the old Boonville carpentry workshop of Dr. John Walter in Boonville, in whose honor Walter Williams had been named. Shrubs and trees had been brought back by Williams from his travels in Europe and Hawaii and the Orient. Every growing thing there seemed to have its own story: the Japanese maples were a personal gift to Williams from a Japanese ambassador, and the Japanese cherry was personally planted by another ambassador from

---

29. Margaret Dorsey Fuqua, interview with the author, August 4, 1993. A great admirer of Hulda Harned Williams, Fuqua had visited often in the Williams household as a child.

30. *Columbia Daily Tribune,* April 10, 1910.

Japan who had wended his way to Columbia, Missouri, for a reunion with his friend, the dean of journalism.

The interior of the two-story home was roomy and tasteful, decorated with curios and museum pieces from Williams's travels, and dominated by his expansive, book-lined study. In every way, this house was unlike any Williams had lived in before. Their earlier homes—the cottage on Waugh Street where the marriage had begun and the somewhat larger bungalow on Hitt Street where the children had grown up—appeared to be extensions of the effervescent personality of Hulda Williams. The new home was more like Walter: sedate, worldly, even elegant.[31] It was the home Walter Williams had dreamed of all his life. But now it had become a terribly lonely place, a stylish sepulchre.

The relationship between Walter Williams and Edwin at that moment was affectionate, but at times painfully awkward. As a relative would write later, Edwin was "so much younger, so different, so difficult for his father to understand."[32] Walter Williams, stiff and somewhat formal at the office, found it hard when he got home to converse naturally and easily with a teenaged son. At times, the boy seemed almost a stranger. Throughout his married life, Williams, like Edwin, had thrived on the boundless love and devotion Hulda had bestowed on them. Williams was a loving and sentimental husband and father, but he was more reserved than Hulda, and manifestly less skilled than she had been in communicating with their children. He grew increasingly preoccupied and remote. So did Edwin. Eventually things would improve; Edwin left home a few years afterward, embarking upon a journalistic career that ultimately propelled him to a vice presidency of the wire service, United Press. But that was to be much later. The immediate future for both of them appeared bleak, and was certain to bring more than a few moments of melancholy.

World War I cut the School of Journalism's enrollment almost in half. At the beginning of the 1916–1917 academic year 305 students were enrolled in the school; the following September there were only 173. The number of female students remained essentially the same, but the male enrollment had dropped from 246 to 113. Draft summonses and enlistments exacted a heavy toll, and Charlie Ross, in particular, was fuming. Unlike Walter Williams, Ross had always detested teaching women. He was convinced that their journalism studies were merely something to occupy their time until their

---

31. Sara Lockwood Williams, unpublished Walter Williams biography.
32. Ibid.

wedding day, when they would forget about their academic and professional training entirely.[33]

Ross's discontent was gently nurtured by O. K. Bovard, who had been in touch with Ross several times with job offers since Ross had returned early in 1916 from a sabbatical in Australia. Bovard's latest proposition was the most tempting of all; he wanted Ross to go to Washington and become a special correspondent from there. Before long, Bovard pointed out, there would be a Washington bureau of the *Post-Dispatch* and Ross would be chief of it. The offer was hard to refuse.

As the months wore on, Ross's frustrations increased. He fumed silently day after day as apathetic students handed in work he regarded as sloppy and indifferent. More and more Ross felt trapped by academic committee assignments and routine work while so much of real import was happening in the world outside.

One hot day in August, near the end of the summer session, Ross had produced a lecture of which he was especially proud. His best effort had gone into the writing of it, and he was putting all he had into the delivery. But as he neared what he considered to be the key part of his text, he looked up from the manuscript. Just in front of him sat one of his brightest students, Pauline Pfeiffer, gazing absently out the window and munching from a sack of sticky candy.

This, for Ross, was the last straw. In one blinding moment something inside him said the hell with it and his frustrations, pent up for months and even years, suddenly surfaced. Pauline Pfeiffer and her candy represented the stark futility of it all. Then and there he knew he was through forever as a teacher. Mechanically, he finished the lecture. He walked out of the classroom toward the Western Union office. Minutes later he was writing out the text of a telegram to Bovard of the *Post-Dispatch*. "If you still want me," Ross wrote, "I am now available."[34]

And so Charlie Ross went to Washington, where he would in time win a Pulitzer prize for interpretative reporting and earn the respect of the Washington press corps for his distinguished service as bureau chief, editor, and political columnist for the *Post-Dispatch*. Years later he would become even more famous as press secretary, adviser, and confidant to his boyhood friend from Independence, President Harry S. Truman. For her part, Pauline Pfeiffer would

---

33. Farrar, *Reluctant Servant,* 68.

34. Ibid., 68–70. Ross said nothing publicly about why he left teaching until 1950, when he met with Pfeiffer in Florida and obtained her permission to use this story, which he did in a speech just before he died.

prove to be something more than the empty-headed student whose classroom indifference had so devastated Charlie Ross. She went on to graduate from the School of Journalism and swiftly landed a job in New York as a writer for high-fashion magazines. While on one of her fashion-writing trips to Paris she met and was married to a promising young novelist named Ernest Hemingway.

Walter Williams and Charlie Ross would remain close friends. But for the moment, the departure of Ross was a difficult blow for the dean to absorb. World War I had already cost him half his student body. Now it had cost him the best and brightest faculty member he would ever hire.

Jay Holcomb Neff had a knack for making money. Born poor in Hartford, Indiana, in July of 1854, the eldest of seven children, he supported himself by working at odd jobs, mostly as a hod carrier, while he studied for his high school diploma. Then he peddled enough books to pay his way through Asbury College (later DePauw University) at Greencastle. Two years later, while keeping himself afloat largely through some part-time teaching, he had read enough law to pass the state bar exam. After practicing law for two years at Peru, Indiana, he pulled up stakes and headed west, arriving at Kansas City in 1881. Discouraged at his attempts to build a thriving law practice there, he abruptly changed course, abandoning the legal profession for a news reporter's job with a publication serving the livestock industry. It seemed an unlikely career move, but Neff knew what he was doing. With his eye on the main chance, he began buying stock in the publishing company, and before long had become sole owner of it. His ascendancy coincided beautifully with the dramatic surge in the livestock industry that brought new prosperity to Kansas City and points west. Shrewdly changing the name of the paper from the *Kansas City Daily Price Current* to the *Daily Drovers Telegram,* he saw his circulation shoot upward and his profits accumulate. He purchased substantial interests in other livestock publications, headquartered at Omaha and St. Louis, and soon after the turn of the century he was recognized as one of the leading trade journal publishers in the country. From 1904 to 1906 he served as mayor of Kansas City.[35] When he died, in 1915 at his summer place in the mountains of Wyoming, he was a very rich man.

His publishing empire was inherited by his only son, Ward Andrew Neff, who had been graduated from the School of Journalism in 1913. Ward Neff was proud of his journalism education, and he personally admired Walter Williams.

Like most of his classmates, Ward Neff had chafed at the school's cramped, inconvenient quarters at Switzler Hall, a building that had once housed the

---

35. Sara Lockwood Williams, *Twenty Years of Education for Journalism,* 36–37.

College of Agriculture.[36] Unlike his classmates, however, Ward Neff suddenly found himself with the wherewithal to make things better.

He invited his former dean to breakfast with him at a Kansas City hotel one morning during the spring of 1918. As Walter Williams was beginning to pour maple syrup on his pancakes, young Neff blurted out what he had come to say: he had been thinking for some time of a suitable way to honor the memory of his father. And that he had decided to donate funds for an entire new building, to be designed for and presented to the School of Journalism. Stunned, and for once speechless, Williams could only nod—forgetting his thumb was still pressing down the pourer on the maple syrup. Only after the syrup overflowed onto the tablecloth did the news sink in.[37]

Neff's gift, announced by President A. Ross Hill at commencement that June, would mark the first time, until then, that an entire campus building had been donated to a single academic program. And it would also be the largest gift ever made, at that time, to the University of Missouri. Almost as an afterthought, Ward Neff asked if the new building might be named after his late father. Williams said he felt sure it could be.

36. The building had been named for the late Colonel William F. Switzler, at one time editor of the *Columbia Statesman* and an early and prominent political supporter of the University of Missouri.

37. This story, more of the folklore of the School of Journalism, is quoted in Rucker, *Walter Williams,* 159.

11

Sara

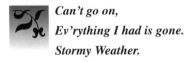 *Can't go on,*
Ev'rything I had is gone.
Stormy Weather.

—Ted Koehler and Harold Arlen

Groundbreaking ceremonies for the new building were held on May 8, 1919, with young Ward A. Neff shoveling up the first sod, and on September 1, 1920, Jay H. Neff Hall was dedicated. It was a handsome redbrick structure, well situated on a shaded, gentle slope at the northeast corner of the campus quadrangle, and designed with care to integrate the classroom teaching and professional laboratory facilities into a functional, comfortable theater of operations. On the main floor were the dean's office, a large newsroom for the *Missourian,* an office for the paper's business manager, two faculty offices, and, covering one entire end of the building, the journalism library. Upstairs were the 276-seat auditorium, two large faculty offices, three classrooms, and a small room with a stairway leading to the attic, space that would later be devoted to a laboratory for students interested in the emerging medium of radio. In the basement were darkrooms and photo labs, photoengraving facilities, an advertising layout room, and a complete printing plant, including three Linotypes and a Duplex web-perfecting press capable of producing five thousand eight-page newspapers in an hour.[1] From now on, the *Missourian* would be published in School of Journalism quarters, not in a rented building far off the campus. The paper's legal standing, once controversial and murky, was no longer in question. Only hours after the new building was dedicated, a confident Walter Williams personally threw the switch in the basement of Neff Hall cranking up the press for that day's run of the newly redesigned *Missourian.* If he had ever needed tangible proof that his dream for a School of Journalism was being fully realized, that moment—bringing to life a roaring newspaper press inside a splendid new building—must have provided it.

From the outset, Williams had envisioned the School of Journalism as more than a training ground for students; he believed the school should also provide a

---

1. Sara Lockwood Williams, *Twenty Years of Education for Journalism,* 36–40.

forum for the entire industry. Williams wanted journalism's big names to know, and be known by, his students, and he thought it essential for the industry's important ideas and trends to be discussed there. But getting journalism's big names to the campus wouldn't be easy. Little money was available for honoraria, or even travel expenses, for the visiting dignitaries. But Williams boldly invited the industry's leaders anyway, and, to a remarkable degree, journalism's best and brightest welcomed the invitations and accepted them. Thus Williams's effortless, almost mystical rapport with newspaper editors, first demonstrated many years previously when he was the youngest-ever president of the state press association, now brilliantly connected him to a national constituency. From across the land, and usually without compensation for doing so, editor after editor trooped into Columbia, Missouri—no easy trip, in most cases—to meet journalism students and to talk shop with Walter Williams and his small faculty. In the process, students developed important contacts in the industry and editors, in return, enjoyed the recognition as well as the opportunity to get an early line on promising young talent. And Walter Williams had a grand time of it as host.

After surviving his first year of operating the new school, Williams felt secure enough in 1909 to begin orchestrating a week-long program to climax the spring semester. Calling it Editors Week, Williams laid on an all-star lineup of journalists, headed by the famed editor of *Collier's,* Will Irwin. Eleven separate speeches were packed into the five-day celebration, and several dozen Missouri editors and high-powered university administrators joined attentive undergraduates in the audience. Each visiting editor was assigned at least one greeter-and-guide, a bright-eyed journalism student who assured the visitor of a warm welcome and an enthusiastic escort. Two or three lecture sessions or panel discussions were presented each day to a crowd that overflowed the College of Agriculture auditorium in Switzler Hall, and Williams presided at every one. From beginning to end, Editors Week proved a solid success, and a tradition was born.

The following year Williams arranged a repeat performance, but one even more ambitious—not just an Editors Week, but a Journalism Week. This time the speakers included Oswald Garrison Villard of the *New York Post,* acknowledged for two generations as one of the leading newspapermen in the country, and top-of-the-line news professionals from Chicago, Baltimore, Detroit, and St. Louis. The year after that Williams arranged with no fewer than ten different professional journalism organizations to hold their annual conventions on the Missouri campus during Journalism Week.[2] Each spring

---

2. Ibid., 158–245.

Journalism Week seemed to grow in prestige, as Williams landed one nationally famous star after another as headline speakers.

The climax to Journalism Week was the annual banquet, featuring Williams at the top of his game as a toastmaster. Resplendent in his white tuxedo, the diminutive dean formally opened each occasion with a toast—not with champagne, but with "sparkling clear water from the deep springs of Missouri"—to the president of the United States.[3] Famous speakers addressed the huge crowds at these dinners: William Jennings Bryan and Champ Clark, each of whom made a serious bid for the presidency; Antonin Barthelemy, the ambassador from France, and Karl A. Bickel, president of United Press, along with other distinguished publishers, editors, and foreign correspondents. Missouri governors, the university's president and curators, and other celebrities dutifully put in an annual appearance at the banquet, but they tended to remain in the background. This was Walter Williams's show. He was not only the author, producer, and director, but also the star.

Eventually, Williams would add another important dimension to Journalism Week, the awarding of about half a dozen distinguished service medals each year to those who had, in the view of Williams and his faculty, brought honor to the field of journalism. At least one of the awards might go to a Missourian, but the others recognized achievement on the national and even international scale. Journalism's top talents would travel happily to the School of Journalism to receive their medals. "This to me is a more meaningful award than the Pulitzer prize," no less a personage than Walter Cronkite of CBS News would say many years later, accepting his Distinguished Service Medal from the School of Journalism. "A Pulitzer is awarded for a single report or series, but this medal acknowledges the cumulative work of an entire career."[4]

Journalism Week turned out to be a perfect vehicle for Williams to enhance the credibility of the school, contacts for his students, and visibility of journalists to the world outside. In a deeper sense, Journalism Week helped articulate to the general public a feeling about his profession that he never lost. As a *New York Times* editorial would describe it later, "Dean Williams himself has said of journalism that it is 'the great, unfinished, fascinating new adventure.' "[5] The dean was enjoying himself immensely.

Journalism Week also became the venue for recognizing the academic achievement of the brightest scholars in the School of Journalism, many

---

3. Rucker, *Walter Williams,* 86.
4. Walter Cronkite, remarks at Journalism Week, April 1964.
5. *New York Times* editorial, July 30, 1935.

of whom would be declared ineligible for the oldest and most prestigious scholastic society, Phi Beta Kappa. Steeped in the liberal arts tradition, Phi Beta Kappa members often dismissed coursework done in journalism as being too professionally oriented, and as a result some otherwise deserving journalism students were passed over each year when Phi Beta Kappa keys were being awarded. Frustrated at what he regarded as an affront to his students, Williams decided to create his own honorary society, which he named Kappa Tau Alpha. (The Greek letters, in this case, were to symbolize Knowledge, Truth, and Accuracy.) Kappa Tau Alpha members, according to the by-laws and ritual Williams wrote, must rank in the upper 10 percent of their graduate or undergraduate class, based on grade averages. The annual Kappa Tau Alpha selections and initiation ceremony became an important part of Journalism Week.

A few years later, Lawrence Murphy, then head of journalism at the University of Illinois, asked Williams about establishing a local chapter of Kappa Tau Alpha on that campus. Williams readily agreed. Murphy, most likely with prodding from Walter Williams, then campaigned to make KTA a truly national organization, later to be recognized as one of the oldest societies dedicated to the encouragement and recognition of scholarship. In time there would be more than ninety Kappa Tau Alpha chapters scattered across the country, and nearly fifty thousand men and women from the nation's journalism schools would be initiated into the society. The initiation ceremony, gracefully written and idealistic in tone, would remain virtually unchanged from Williams's original text.[6]

Kappa Tau Alpha would never eclipse Phi Beta Kappa, nor was it intended to. But Kappa Tau Alpha keys would be coveted, also, in their own way, and to the extent that they reflected academic attainment, they fulfilled the aspirations Williams had for them. Few people venerated collegiate scholarship honors more than he, perhaps because he had never gotten the chance to compete for them himself.

Still another offshoot of Journalism Week turned out to be its role, informal but significant, in beginning the national organization of journalism educators. A handful of journalism professors had met one time before, in 1910 at the University of California. In 1911, Williams invited representatives of all known journalism programs to convene during Journalism Week that April. Through

---

6. Interview with Keith Sanders, professor of journalism and national executive director of Kappa Tau Alpha, June 29, 1997. The society's national headquarters remain at the University of Missouri School of Journalism.

a questionnaire he had mailed to two hundred institutions of higher learning in the United States, Williams had been able to identify thirty-two colleges and universities then offering some form of journalism instruction. It was time to organize for the common good, and the American Association of Teachers of Journalism, as the new organization became known, was created. In giving direction to the emerging organization, Walter Williams was joined by a man also destined to become a towering figure in the field, Willard Grosvenor Bleyer of the University of Wisconsin. "Daddy" Bleyer, who had been teaching various classes in journalism at Wisconsin since 1904 and whose intellectual leadership would help give journalism a liberal arts context and lead to wider acceptance within the academic community, was chosen as the AATJ's first president.[7]

The following year's convention, held in the lecture room of the historical library at the University of Wisconsin, attracted twenty-four teachers from seventeen institutions, and reflected Bleyer's intellectual standards and his sure-handed guidance. Where only one research paper had been presented the previous year, this time there were a dozen or more dealing with scholarly and professional concerns—the relationship of journalism to the English department, improving classroom teaching, what should be taught in newspaper management courses, the use of the city newspaper and laboratory newspaper as teaching tools, the emerging field of agricultural journalism and how it might best be taught, and, significantly, a paper dealing with "the journalist's responsibility."[8]

Bleyer's contributions to journalism education have been published elsewhere and will not be detailed here. But the point should be made that his role in the founding of the AATJ was decisive, and his leadership in that organization and in his discipline was exemplary. A brisk, hardworking, professional man with stout convictions and the courage to back them up, Bleyer would be widely credited with establishing meaningful standards of scholarly and professional performance, with introducing research into the field, and with much else of enduring support to the academic discipline. His most significant book, *Main Currents in the History of American Journalism,* illuminated generations of journalism students about the development of their industry; it remains a classic work of scholarship. Frank Luther Mott, the historian and Pulitzer prize winner

---

7. This discussion is drawn heavily from the author's essay, "The Push for Standards and Recognition: A Brief History of the American Association of Schools and Departments of Journalism," in *Seventy-Five Years of Journalism and Mass Communications Leadership* (Association for Education in Journalism and Mass Communications, 1993), 54–71.

8. Edwin Emery and Joseph P. McKerns, "AEJMC: 75 Years in the Making," *Journalism Monographs* 104 (Association for Education in Journalism, 1987), 5.

who would one day be dean of journalism at Missouri, credited Bleyer with "raising the banner for high standards in the field."[9] What Walter Williams did to promote journalism education to the newspaper profession—that is, to gain an early, gratifying measure of acceptance for journalism education—"Daddy" Bleyer did for his discipline within the academic community.

While Williams was elated with the initial success of the AATJ, he soon realized that his own sternly held notions of what a journalism school should be were not universally shared by his colleagues around the country. Journalism programs were spreading from campus to campus with astonishing speed. And as other colleges and universities by the dozens were beginning to teach journalism, they often adopted a very different approach—that of journalism-as-social-institution, something to be analyzed and critiqued within the accepted liberal arts environment, not unlike courses in Music Appreciation or Understanding Art. This view contrasted sharply with that of Williams, who regarded journalism as a professional school designed to prepare young men and women for a career in the field. Williams described his concern in a speech to the American Society of Newspaper Editors:

> Some courses in journalism are used mainly, if not entirely, to enliven instruction in English and make it more palatable. Other courses are employed as publicity promoters for the institution, the students as unpaid press agents. Others afford opportunity for consideration of current events and yet others, more serious in character, discuss the history of journalism and its place in society. The teachers in these various courses have had, as might be expected, different degrees of preparation for teaching journalism. Some have had helpful journalistic experience and are men of genuine ability as teachers. Within the limitations of their institutions they are doing excellent work. The personality of the teacher overcomes inadequacy of equipment and insufficiency of courses.[10]

By 1916, the year before wartime conditions disrupted enrollment figures, the larger and stronger professional programs had begun to stand out sharply from the others—those institutions where journalism was offered only in the form of scattered courses, perhaps within the English department—and Williams felt the time had come to distinguish what he regarded as the more professional programs from all the rest. That year he contacted administrators

---

9. See especially Harold L. Nelson's tribute in Emery and McKerns, "AEJMC," 5–6. A partial list of subsequent leaders in academic journalism who studied under Bleyer, most of them as graduate students, would include Chilton R. Bush of Stanford, Ralph D. Casey of Minnesota, Blair Converse of Iowa State, Robert W. Desmond of California–Berkeley, Roy L. French of Southern California, H. H. Herbert of Oklahoma, Hillier Krieghbaum of New York University, Frederick Merwin of Rutgers, Curtis D. MacDougall of Northwestern, Niel Plummer of Kentucky, O. W. Riegel of Washington and Lee, Frederick S. Siebert of Illinois and Michigan State, and Henry Ladd Smith of Washington.

10. Sara Lockwood Williams, *Twenty Years of Education for Journalism,* 419.

in the American Association of Teachers of Journalism, inviting them to join with him in a separate organization—not apart from the AATJ, but within it. He would call the new organization the Association of American Schools and Departments of Journalism. In Williams's opinion, there were but a few—"perhaps ten or fifteen, of which I speak"—journalism programs designed

> to give professional purpose, that the student may know how to use his knowledge, may be trained in accuracy and clarity of expression, terseness of statement, force, persuasiveness in writing; that he may be taught, as far as it is possible to teach, to observe for himself, to write rapidly and accurately and comprehensively, to view and interview and review, with open eyes and unshuttered, understanding mind; to interpret; to evaluate; that he may have ingrained in him the ideals of the profession, that he may know its history; that, as far as wisdom that comes from observation may teach, he will learn to avoid its pitfalls, and seek its summits, know of libel and public opinion, and high purpose and achievements . . . [11]

Williams decided to contact his fellow administrators and, a few months later, had secured pledges from five universities—their names were not recorded—to join the American Association of Schools and Departments of Journalism. This was enough to convince Williams, Bleyer, and their colleagues that a second organization was viable, and that it was time to call a meeting. It began at 2:30 P.M. on April 5, 1917, at the La Salle hotel in Chicago, just prior to the AATJ convention. By that time, ten institutions were on board, and they became charter members of the AASDJ: Columbia University, Indiana University, Ohio State University, and the Universities of Kansas, Missouri, Montana, Oregon, Texas, Washington, and Wisconsin. Bleyer called the meeting to order, Williams was elected president, and the AASDJ was officially in business.

By the end of World War I more than two hundred colleges and universities were offering journalism instruction in some form. Walter Williams, especially, pushed hard to further distinguish the more fully and professionally developed programs from the rest. A first step in this regard came in 1922 with the appointment of a Committee on Classification, charged to designate each journalism program as either an A, B, or C. The proposal was highly controversial among faculty, as might be expected, but a number of prominent editors expressed their approval, among them H. L. Mencken:

> Soon or late the Class A schools, demanding more sound educational qualifications for entrance and offering well-planned and thorough courses of study, will be sharply differentiated from the one-room schools that now flourish, just as Class A medical and law schools are differentiated from the other kind. When that time

---

11. Ibid.

comes the graduate of a Class A school will be practically assured of a good job on a newspaper the day he is graduated.[12]

While the journalism professors as a group balked at classifications, efforts at some sort of recognition, other than acceptance into membership in the American Association of Schools and Departments of Journalism, continued. Eventually, the AATJ and AASDJ voted to establish a form of accreditation. The accrediting process for each program would begin with gathering reams of preliminary material, such as the records of graduates, budgets, curricula, faculty backgrounds and experience, library holdings, laboratory facilities, and teaching standards. Next would come an on-site visit by an outside accrediting team, consisting of mass media professionals as well as academic members. The visiting team's recommendation, always delivered in person to the college or university president involved, would ultimately be acted upon by the national accreditation council. Eventually, national accreditation of journalism programs quietly became accepted as a matter of course. Thus membership in the American Association of Schools and Departments of Journalism—essentially, the accredited schools—became less and less important. By 1983, the AASDJ was clearly redundant, and at the brief business meeting that year a motion was made to, in effect, dissolve the organization altogether.

Few voted against the motion. There was little reason to, for AASDJ's time had passed. Walter Williams had led the founding of the American Association of Schools and Departments of Journalism more than sixty years earlier in an attempt to give journalism education two things it urgently needed but did not possess: standards and recognition. Those objectives had been won, and the organization that had done so much to win them had, by doing so, succeeded itself into oblivion. All in all, it was a nice way to go.

As he entered his fifties, Walter Williams had begun to age a bit, but, as those who worked around him hastened to point out, he did so gracefully. His deep blue eyes were as penetrating as ever, enhanced, perhaps, by the wrinkles that were starting to line his fair complexion. He wore spectacles now, but only for reading. Though he would never become bald, his once-blond hair had long ago turned white and his hairline was receded at one side of his forehead. His lower lip had always protruded somewhat, a condition that became more

12. Edmund G. Blinn and Robert L. Jones, "A History of the American Association of Schools and Departments of Journalism," 1960, 6. This mimeographed compilation, which the authors themselves describe as a "first draft," for distribution chiefly to AASDJ members, is detailed and authoritative for the period it covers and has proved invaluable to the present author.

noticeable as he grew older. His slender frame, which had suggested frailty in his youth, seemed less delicate in middle age as he gained a good fifteen pounds or more. He announced his height as five feet, eight inches, but many who met him would place him as shorter than that. Diminutive stature notwithstanding, he cut a distinguished, dignified figure, but his features were distinctive and lent themselves readily to caricature. One noted cartoonist, writing Williams a thank-you note following a Journalism Week appearance, simply drew a cartoon of Williams on the envelope, adding only "Columbia, Mo." The letter reached him promptly.[13]

Williams walked and sat erectly, and was rarely seen in a slouching position. In conversation, he punctuated his words with gestures, often spreading his short, almost dainty fingers on the arm of a chair or thrusting his hands quickly downward in a chopping motion. "He rumpled a dinner napkin or a handkerchief in his hands when he made speeches," a relative recalled, "often rocking back and forth on his feet while he talked, seldom standing still."[14] A restless pacer in his office, Williams would crisscross the room as he interviewed visitors or dictated letters to his secretary. A stubby, thick-leaded copy pencil rarely left his right hand; during lengthy dictation sessions, he might accidentally make black marks on his scalp or a sleeve while gesturing vigorously as he talked.

He was something of a fashion plate, well turned out in a Prince Albert—a long, double-breasted frock coat—for church and for his dressier daytime speeches. His top hat and tails, often his costume for evenings out, had been custom-made for him in London, as were many of the white shirts, with detachable collars, he always wore. His wide selection of linen suits, appropriate for hot Missouri summers, had been tailored for him on his visits to the Far East. He affected a walking stick while abroad, but never at home lest the locals think him arrogant or, worse yet, decrepit. He often wore bow ties, but never quite mastered the art of knotting them himself, relying instead on store-tied models when no one was handy to assist him. His four-in-hand neckties occasionally ran to bizarre colors, a subject of intense, whispered student discussion during his History and Principles lectures. "For someone so meticulous in his grooming," his wife once noted, "he wore terrible hats. He hated to buy a new hat, so the older a hat the better he liked it. He never kept the original crease in it properly, he just pulled it on or off in the most comfortable way."[15]

---

13. Sara Lockwood Williams, unpublished Walter Williams biography.
14. Ibid.
15. Ibid.

Once, in Washington, Williams strode out of the Willard Hotel just a few steps, as it happened, behind the Chief Justice of the United States, Charles Evans Hughes. Once on the sidewalk, the Chief Justice suddenly stopped and adjusted one sock and garter. Williams caught up with him and the two walked together up Capitol Hill. Williams never forgot that incident, and thus when his own socks, garters, or shoestrings needed adjusting he invariably stopped whatever he was doing and tended to them. "If Chief Justice Hughes can do it in public, so can I," he announced.[16]

What little physical exercise he got came from walking, and even that he limited to brief, quiet strolls in the evening. He was fond of wandering in his well-manicured backyard, enjoying the beauty and symbolism of the place, absently inspecting the gardening done by a servant known only as Will, his handyman for eighteen years. Even in his backyard in the evenings, neighbors noticed, Williams would be dressed in a business suit. No one could recall seeing him when he was not wearing a coat and tie.

His hobbies, such as they were, were confined chiefly to collecting souvenirs of all kinds, mostly from his travels, and clipping articles from newspapers and magazines. He carried a pair of smallish, blunt scissors in his vest, and when he went home after work his pants pockets would be bulging with the day's harvest of clips. Articles in which he was featured—and there were increasing numbers of these—would be pasted into personal scrapbooks. Other articles gleaned from his voluminous reading would find their way into files he maintained for his lectures and speeches, or perhaps suggested as story ideas to the editors of the *Missourian.* Still other pieces would be clipped because he thought someone he knew would especially appreciate them. Through the years friends from all over the world received clippings from the dean. He maintained a remarkably extensive network of friends and professional associates. Cordial relationships he enjoyed in great abundance, but there were precious few intimates. Only a handful of individuals ever got really close to him, even for a brief period. For all his notoriety, Williams was very much alone. His guard was never let down.

Well, practically never.

In the closing years of the nineteenth century, John and Mary Jane Lockwood decided to move from Rock Port, in Missouri's far northwestern corner, to Columbia. The Lockwoods were of modest means—he ran, but did not own, a general store—and they decided that living in Columbia might make it easier to educate their large family. The relocation worked out as they had hoped. All

16. Ibid.

seven of the Lockwood children went on to attend the University of Missouri, and six of them—five sons and a daughter—would earn their degrees. The daughter, Sara, studied in the School of Journalism.

A member of the class of 1913, Sara Lockwood was personally recommended by Walter Williams to the publisher of the *St. Joseph Gazette,* and within weeks of her graduation she was being publicized in St. Joseph as "the *Gazette*'s first girl reporter." The owner of the paper frankly regarded any female reporter as a dubious experiment, but he valued Dean Williams's judgment, which Sara Lockwood promptly vindicated with her crisp, professional performance. Red-haired, short, and energetic, Sara was worked hard and was soon producing far more than her publisher, who was paying her only seven hundred dollars a year, expected. She proved adept at handling all types of assignments, but was especially effective with her tear-jerking human-interest stories. Sara detested the term "sob sister," but nevertheless found it gratifying that some of her feature stories helped raise money for the city's poor.[17]

Her enterprise and resourcefulness permitted her to obtain the only interview Mary Garden, the popular opera star, gave while in that portion of western Missouri. Sara also interviewed Ignace Jan Paderewski, the Polish statesman who was then regarded as perhaps the greatest pianist in the world, during his extensive concert tour of the United States. She helped organize the St. Joseph Press Club, which then claimed to be the only press club in the country to admit women as members. By the time she resigned from the *Gazette* in August 1915, her byline was known throughout the area and her yearly pay had been increased to $1,040.[18]

Sara left St. Joe to return to Columbia and assist at the bedside of her mother, who was gravely ill and needed Sara at home. When he heard of Sara Lockwood's planned move back to Columbia, Walter Williams offered her a part-time job in the School of Journalism. She would become a laboratory assistant, charged with setting up a reading room for the School of Journalism and also establishing the *Missourian*'s "morgue"—so called because it would contain "dead" material, clippings from past issues, file photos, and other reference information reporters would need for background purposes in developing current, or "live," articles. In her spare time, Dean Williams said, she might help faculty members grade papers. If she had any more spare time after that,

---

17. Very helpful in this passage has been a profile sketch of Sara Lockwood Williams in Mary K. Dains, ed., *Show Me Missouri Women* (Thomas Jefferson University Press, 1989), vol. 1, 154–56.

18. Sara Lockwood Williams's curriculum vitae, containing a remarkably detailed work record and salary history, is among her papers in the Western Historical Manuscript Collection at the University of Missouri.

she could do some freelance magazine writing on her own—not a bad idea, in view of her salary, which would be only $180 for the academic year.[19]

Still, it was better than nothing and she looked forward to being around the School of Journalism again. And, especially, to being close to Dean Williams, whom she idolized. On a warm, overcast Tuesday in mid-August of 1915, she telephoned him to let him know she was back in Columbia. He invited her over to the journalism offices at Switzler Hall later that afternoon to chat.

The visit did not go as Sara had expected.

In a long, emotional, remarkable letter written three days after that fateful meeting, she described what had happened:

Marguerite dear—

I have wanted you this week more than I ever wanted anyone in my life. Before I left St. Joe you said "write your troubles" and my first impulse was to do that. But this is so big—so different—and so hard I can't understand or believe it myself. At first I didn't dare put it on paper for fear I would be doing a man the greatest injustice. And then I loathed myself for thinking such thoughts. I feared that I was to blame, that there was something about me that I myself did not understand. Oh, I *wish* you were here, for there isn't another soul on earth who would understand the least little bit of what I feel. I have waited three days, weighing the matter in every possible way, trying so hard to get *his* point of view and to make myself feel that he is just deeply interested in me as my father might have been. I have stayed here in the country and studied over it until I feel as though I must have *dreamed* it. I can't make myself believe it of the man I have almost worshipped for years.

Please forgive me for this prologue, when I know you are frantic to know all about it. But this letter is as much to clear my own mind as to ask you advice and love. I want to put it down as it happened as nearly as I can remember, as honestly and frankly as possible. Perhaps it will make things clearer to me.

Oh, Marguerite! It was hard enough to leave St. Joe, when I was coming to work beside the man who has had so much influence in my life already, whom I have regarded as my ideal of a Christian gentleman, whom I have quoted as above reproach. I have poured my troubles into his kind, sympathetic ears for years and gained courage and inspiration. I have regarded him from afar as an ideal—a model from whom all men and women could pattern and grow better.

You know now, surely, whom I mean—Dean W (even now I daren't write his name for fear someone else would see it and I can't tell anyone else of a fallen idol!)

That is what hurts! If it had been anyone else but *him,* the man I have believed in as surely as though he were my own father—no more than that. I believe I have thought of him as almost superhuman. Perhaps that is why it all happened. At least that is why the hurt is so great. My faith has been shattered. Marguerite, if *he* isn't good—is any man good? Or is it I? Am I to blame?

He kissed me, and I let him.

---

19. Ibid.

That may mean everything or nothing. I have tried to know how, why, and a thousand other questions and the only answer I can find to all is: He had no *right* to do it—no matter *why* he did it. Whether fatherly or not, it was not right. There are better ways of proving one's friendship and devotion.

Do you think I am silly and prudish? Is it all right for an old man, a man with a lovely wife and grown children, to kiss a girl? If so, why should I have that awful feeling of hurt, of disappointment in him, of loathing for myself for permitting it? Surely it isn't all caused by the fact that our beautiful friendship, in which he served as an ideal far above me, has been in one moment changed to a basis of familiarity, of commonness. That sounds foolish, but it is true. It has spoiled everything! My confidence in him is gone. I can't look up to him any more.

Even though he regarded me sincerely, sweetly and truly as though I were his daughter, that moment of familiarity has changed our friendship. I can never again feel the same trust in him or feel that I can speak so freely to him. *I shall have to be on my guard with Dean W*—the man whom I had thought to trust always.

But let me tell it as it happened. I called him up Tues. morning to tell him I had arrived and was ready to begin work. He asked me to come talk things over that afternoon. When I entered the big main office, it was empty, and I remembered Miss Quinn [Cannie Quinn, Williams's secretary] was on her vacation. Everything in the big empty building was quiet and I was afraid Dean W had gone. But when I rapped at his private office door, he opened it. He smiled his glad, winsome smile and his right hand grasped mine. I remember now (though I thought little of it at the time, merely regarding it as a little extra demonstration of his gracious gladness in seeing me) that his left hand clasped my arm and seemed to draw me closer to him. As I say, I didn't think of it at the time, for I was *glad* to be welcomed heartily for I was a bit sorry I had left the jolly bunch in St. Joe. He found me a chair and before he would talk news business had to hear all about the parties given for me in St. Joe—about my good times there and the work and play I liked best. He showed me a stack of clippings he had saved from St. Joe papers, things I had written and things written about me. He told me I was getting prettier every day and I laughed at him. His interest and his compliments pleased me as such evidence from my friends always do, when honestly given. Then he asked me, teasingly and yet in earnest, to tell him about "The Man." And I laughingly and frankly admitted there was "no such animal," that I was still heart free. "You didn't find anyone up there you liked better than your Dean?" "Not a soul." "Then it's all right and I'm happy."

Before I knew it there had been nearly an hour of friendly visiting with scarcely a word about my new work.

I was in no hurry and Dean seemed happy to forget any work he may have had, so we talked on. It was all chatty and pleasant and he did tell me something of my work. But all the time I felt strangely restless, slightly embarrassed and there was a scarcely realized wish that Miss Quinn were in the next room, that the big building were not so quiet.

It had begun to rain in torrents, and I had neither umbrella nor coat, so I stayed on. He took me to my new office in the back room of the building. We met Mr. [Charles] Ross, one of the profs, there and the three of us planned my new work. Mr. Ross went back to D's office with us and we talked business for half an hour. I was ready to leave, but waited for the rain to slack. Mr. Ross left and I rose, but

D waved me into my seat again. I supposed he had thought of something else concerning my work, but when we were alone he began chatting again.

"No," he said, "your work won't begin till Sept. 1, but I'll need you to help boss the furnishing of your office. You must come in every day. There won't be anything to do but you must come to see me anyway."

I rose to go and he said, "Oh, don't leave me. Surely you don't need to go." I insisted and he followed me into the main office. It was still raining and he took his umbrella from the rack to hand me. I didn't want it. I thought I could get to Mildred's before it rained hard. If I were talking with you, I couldn't explain the queer feeling I had that I *must* get away, and yet I never for an instant crystalized that feeling into the thought that I was afraid of him. He had not said or done one thing that was out of place. He was just my kindly interested and good friend. There was no earthly reason why I should have feared him. He put the umbrella in my hand. "You must take it. I won't have you getting wet." "Yes sir, if you command it," I said, meaning to be playful, but my voice sounded rather trembly. As I took the umbrella his left arm went around me and with his other hand he raised my face and kissed me on the lips. "I can't tell you how much it means to have you back here, Sara," he said.

And then I found myself in the hall with the door closed between us. I have no recollection of how I got out the door—whether he or I opened it. There was just chaos inside of me, but the greatest feeling was horror—a sort of terror and astonishment, an actual feeling that I had just done the wickedest thing I ever did in my life. And yet, Marguerite, I can't see that I was to blame.

Do you think it was wicked? Do you think I am prudish?

That was Tuesday and I had promised him I would come back Thursday to help plan the furnishings of my office and outline catalogues, books, etc., with him. I haven't been back and won't go until next week when Miss Q will be back from her vacation.

I would have wept (and I did for a few minutes) but I have been constantly with people and I didn't *dare* let anyone know what had happened. I was so miserable one day they all thought me homesick for St. Joe, and truly I was! I believe that was the first tangible feeling I had after I left his office—loathing for myself. It was as though, by some thoughtless missteps of my own, I had lost my balance and swung in mid air, hopelessly, frantically and helplessly trying to gain a firm hold upon something that would at least steady me, even though I couldn't climb up on it to the same height I had been before.

Perhaps you are sighing with relief, or calling me an idiot, or saying I'm making a mountain out of a mole hill. Please wait judgment, both of him and me, until *you* read it all. Perhaps in another man I should not have called it wrong. I have sought excuses for him in my own mind—it was a rainy, lonesome afternoon. We were alone in that great old building and had been for more than an hour.

Is it just prudishness—because I haven't . . . no it couldn't be that, I started to say because I hadn't been with men—but I have worked with men and among men for 2 years without their being familiar or in the least disrespectful.

Could it be because I have heard so many wild stories, so many wicked things that do happen in the world, that my mind is poisoned and I suspect even sincere and good men?

Do I feel this way because I am cold hearted and caresses do not appeal to me anyway? I have been told by both girls and men that I do not seem to feel deep emotion—that I am undemonstrative . . .

Coming as it did at a time when Hulda was still living, the incident flew in the face of the strong religious and moral code that Williams embraced so publicly. There is no indication that his feelings toward Hulda had cooled; so far as can be determined, he remained devoted to her as long as she lived, and certainly he was grief-stricken when she died. The indiscretion with Sara Lockwood would appear an aberration, a fleeting moment of weakness in a disciplined man whose feelings normally remained under tight control.

Sara's letter to Marguerite was never finished. But obviously it was never thrown away, either.[20] It was as if Sara wanted never to forget that extraordinary, thunderstormy Tuesday afternoon, and her utter despair at discovering her hero was all too human.

By the beginning of the fall term in September, Sara had come to terms with her emotions and resolutely settled into her duties with the School of Journalism. So far as is known, Dean Williams's indiscretion was not repeated.

Sara resigned at the end of the academic year. There was nothing more she could do for her mother, her assignments at the journalism school had been well begun, and she felt a longing to reenter the newspaper field. She secured a job in Oklahoma as a general assignment reporter on a new paper, the *Tulsa Times and Democrat,* at a tenfold increase in pay, $1,820 a year. Two years later, she headed east to Philadelphia, joining the staff of the *Philadelphia Evening Public Ledger* in May 1918 in time to cover war-related stories: new ship launchings from the massive Philadelphia navy yard, features about women's war work, the first troopships returning doughboys from the battlefields of France, other ships bringing war brides to America, the ambitious war relief efforts headed by Herbert Hoover to provide food for European refugees. She traveled up and down the Eastern seaboard on assignments for the paper, and she also did publicity work for various nonprofit organizations in Philadelphia.

Back in Missouri, meanwhile, Walter Williams's life had also undergone a change. He had long since become a widower. Three years after Hulda's death in 1918, and five years after he had made an amorous pass at Sara Lockwood, the dean got in touch with Sara again. Perhaps she had never been long out of his thoughts. Now he wanted her to come back to the School of Journalism,

---

20. The letter was included in the extensive papers she donated to the Western Historical Manuscript Collection at the University of Missouri. "Marguerite," no last name given, presumably was a friend of Sara's in St. Joseph.

not as a laboratory assistant but as a member of the faculty. He offered her an assistant professorship at twenty-six hundred dollars a year. And Sara, once again, accepted. Perhaps he had been in her thoughts as well. Her circumstances had changed also. For all its excitement, Philadelphia had proven to be a tough town. A broken love affair and a broken leg, which left her with a lifelong limp, figured prominently in her decision to return. "Everyone is kind and sympathetic," she wrote bitterly in a letter from Philadelphia, "making me realize now more than ever that I'm a cripple. But I guess I needed some sort of affliction or it [her decision to return to Missouri] wouldn't have happened."[21]

Sara herself later maintained that she had become the first woman to hold a professorship at a journalism school in the United States.[22] While this may or may not have been the case, she did in fact handle a full schedule of classes that included reporting, editing, trade journalism, feature writing, and literary and dramatic reviewing. Outside the classroom, she worked closely with the *Missourian* and set up the paper's first weekly magazine section.

She also entered discretely into what turned out to be a prolonged romance with Walter Williams. Theirs was a comfortable, private arrangement, and over the next six years little was said—or, perhaps, even noticed—of the special relationship Sara Lockwood enjoyed with a man twenty-five years her senior. Indeed, their low-key romance might have gone on indefinitely had not Sara taken a leave of absence in June 1926 to spend the summer as a feature writer on the *Honolulu Star-Bulletin*. Missing her desperately, Williams bombarded her with romantic telegrams throughout her sojourn in Hawaii.[23] In one of these, he proposed. She returned from Hawaii and accepted.

"He was fun," Sara wrote in a diary entry before the wedding, which they scheduled for that fall. "We teased one another, laughed much. So many amusing things in wedding plans. Sheer nonsense, talking in rhyme . . . making up words. Our shared jokes."[24]

Whatever others—faculty, students, townspeople, newspaper friends— thought about their forthcoming wedding, she added, they mostly kept to themselves. But one friend had to know: "How could you do it?" she demanded of Sara. "It would be like marrying Jesus!"[25]

———————

21. Dains, ed., *Show Me Missouri Women,* 156. Notes for a letter, c. April 1921, found in her papers. The recipient of the letter was not identified.

22. Technically, she may have been correct, though it is likely that other women held professional rank in journalism teaching by 1921, though perhaps not in schools of journalism.

23. Dains, ed., *Show Me Missouri Women,* 156.

24. Undated notes found in the Sara Lockwood Williams Papers, Western Historical Manuscript Collection, University of Missouri–Columbia.

25. Ibid.

12

"I Believe in the Profession . . ."

 To forbear, to fight bravely and to forgive; to protect and comfort friends; to hold the Vision unobscured and in patience; to work, to hope, and to make glad; to keep the Dear Ones happier by our nearness; to bear in silence Disappointment and Dismay; to live agreeably with other people for other people's good . . . and, above all, neither to reproach, nor to trifle, nor to turn away; but, with Faith unswerving, to press onward—Shall not these bring Joy?

—Walter Williams, "The Joy of Life"

Williams's marriage proposal to Sara Lockwood that summer of 1927 appeared on the surface to be an act of spontaneous ardor—Sara herself thought so—but in fact the dean had been pondering the decision for some time.[1] And, characteristically, he had sought the counsel of others. "Now as to the advisability of a new Mrs. Dean," wrote F. M. Flynn, a School of Journalism alumnus then working in Tokyo, in response to a query from Williams, "I do not believe your judgment will go wrong on so important a decision as this. If it means happiness and comfort and help to you, I would say 'bravo' . . . Nothing can break the hold you have on the hearts of your students and your position in the journalistic world is secure."[2] Others whose opinions he trusted said much the same thing. Still, Williams moved the wedding plans along with discretion and a certain amount of caution.

The ceremony itself, he and Sara decided, would not take place in Columbia, but in faraway Utah. The venue they chose was the home of Sara's cousin, Dr. Sherman Brown Neff, in Salt Lake City. If friends and relatives were to raise their eyebrows at this May-December marriage, they would have to do so from afar. Salt Lake City was, in fact, on Williams's route home from a trip to the Far East, where he had been visiting Missouri alumni in China, Japan, and Hawaii. Sara had quietly taken the train from Missouri to Utah. The private

---

1. Dains, ed., *Show Me Missouri Women,* 154–56.
2. F. M. Flynn to Walter Williams, September 6, 1927, Williams Papers, Western Historical Manuscript Collection.

wedding, performed on October 22, 1927, by a local Presbyterian minister, was a joyous one, but subdued and uneventful—except for the moment when the groom was asked to produce the wedding ring. Williams fumbled absently in his vest pocket and came up with snub-nosed scissors instead.[3] So far as is known, however, the dean clipped no newspapers that day.

From the Rockies, the newlyweds headed back east. Their train was met in Kansas City by Williams's daughter Helen and her husband, John F. Rhodes, his son Edwin, and a nephew, Judge Roy Williams. News of the wedding had appeared by now in papers across the country. An informal reception, hastily arranged in Kansas City, brought greetings from a crowd of western Missouri journalists, many of them alumni. Once back in Columbia, Walter and Sara were toasted at several receptions and dinners in their honor.[4] Congratulatory letters and telegrams poured in by the dozens. Any fears Williams may have had about public acceptance of his remarriage seemed, in retrospect, silly.

Sara's happiness was complete. "Evenings at home are more exciting than a schoolgirl date," she confided to her personal journal. "He reads aloud (my sneaking feeling that he was educating me—and he was!) . . . Exchange of ideas about things read. His stories of experiences—how I love them!"[5]

The memory of his first wife, Sara wrote, was dealt with directly. "Long before we were married we talked together of Hulda. . . . I wanted him to feel free to mention her whenever the impulse came—never to feel he must suppress any intimation of his first wife, his children's mother. I knew he had loved her devotedly and I honored him for it. I never felt the slightest jealousy. I accepted Hulda as a part of his life, an influence. I knew that he loved me sincerely and deeply—that I filled a need in his life. There is an eagerness in his love."[6]

Sara was convinced, and much relieved, that she now enjoyed the full support of Williams's daughter, Helen, who came to Columbia to help her father and his bride set up housekeeping. The two women got along well, and soon Helen's nine-year-old daughter, Hulda, was referring to Sara as "my grandmother." ("What would you have expected?" the child asked. "My

3. Sara Lockwood Williams, unpublished Walter Williams biography.

4. Rucker, *Walter Williams,* 71.

5. Sara Lockwood Williams, undated journal found in her papers. The term "journal" is used here for convenience; actually, these entries are her own notes dashed off from time to time on whatever writing material she found handy. This particular entry, for example, was written on stationery from the Hotel Muehlbach in Kansas City. Possibly she intended to write her own memoirs, though she never did so.

6. Ibid.

grandfather's wife?") "Helen is understanding," Sara wrote in her journal. " 'You are more of a companion for father than my mother could be [Helen said]. You have so many interests in common and you understand and love his profession. You not only appreciate intimate relations, you can travel with him and share foreign experiences. That was difficult for Mother, who had to think of her children.' "[7]

Some adjustments were required. His friends were usually much older, and when they came calling Sara often found herself by twenty-five years the youngest person in the room. There was a momentary awkwardness, Sara admitted in her journal, as she first began calling her husband by his given name. Too, he sang in the bath, she added, without further comment.[8]

Just after the wedding Sara resigned her faculty position, occupying her time by writing a history of the school, *Twenty Years of Education for Journalism*, which would be published in 1929. Eventually she would start on her master's degree in journalism. She already knew what her thesis topic would be: a history of the *Columbia Herald*, from 1889 to 1908, and she would have a great many nice things to say about the man who had edited the paper during most of that time.[9]

Sara also took her new role as the dean's wife seriously. Too seriously, in the eyes of some. "Many of Walter's friends were weaned away by Sara," snapped the outspoken Mary Paxton Keeley. "She was jealous of his friends, both men and women."[10]

But if Sara was fiercely possessive, or merely protective, of her husband, Williams himself didn't seem to mind. Friends commented that he looked better, certainly more relaxed, than he had in years. An alumna, attending a reception for the former president of the university, A. Ross Hill, remarked to Charles Ross—back from Washington for the occasion—about how fit Dean Williams appeared. "Well," Ross replied, "perhaps having a young wife has made him feel younger."[11]

Sara was, in fact, something of a celebrity in her own right, admired within the mass communications field as the first woman to hold a professorship in a school of journalism. She had freelanced articles to various magazines and maintained many of her Eastern contacts from her days as a reporter in

7. Ibid. Later the child referred to Sara as "Grandma Sally."

8. Ibid.

9. *Twenty Years of Education for Journalism* is especially valuable as a compilation of source materials. Sara Lockwood Williams, "A Study of the Columbia, Missouri, Herald."

10. Quoted in Pike, *Ed Watson,* 137.

11. Dorothy Baker Suddarth to William H. Taft, April 19, 1977.

Philadelphia. At the time of her wedding, she was in her second term as national president of Theta Sigma Phi, a society for professional women in the field of mass communications. She had come to terms, finally, with the knowledge that she would limp for as long as she lived. "Sometimes I feel terribly rebellious," she had written in her journal while still living in downtown Philadelphia. "It is so awful to have people staring at my swollen leg and making comments. Some days I feel as tho I just *couldn't* get courage to walk down Broad Street."[12] Her condition was less noticeable now—shoe lifts helped—and her old energies returned. She proved to be, among much else, a superb traveling companion for her new husband.

This was as it should be, for Walter Williams was gone from Columbia a great deal of the time, restlessly roaming the country and the world. The contacts he had developed during his 1902–1903 round-the-world tour to promote the St. Louis World's Fair were cultivated, and recultivated, time and again in the years that followed.

His first substantial trip as a journalism school dean, however, was a purely American one: it was an automobile journey retracing the legendary trade route he had heard about all his life, the Santa Fe Trail. No one, it was said at the time, had completed this expedition by car before. He set out, in July 1911, from Old Franklin—just across the Missouri River from his birthplace—along with Hulda and Edwin Moss, and a chauffeur. Walter Jr., then seventeen, was along for part of the journey. So was the dean's secretary, Miss Cannie Quinn, then vacationing in Colorado, who joined them en route. Her main task was to transcribe the thousands of words Williams dictated along the way. Williams admitted undertaking this adventure partly for the history and romance the Santa Fe Trail represented; but also, he said, he wanted to call attention to the need for better highways. "The transportation problem . . . is vital to the progress of civilization," he wrote. "No economic question more deeply concerns the welfare of all the people than the road question."[13] While bumping along over cow paths and the mostly unpaved roads, Williams dictated dozens of pieces. Most were for the *Missourian,* but many were reprinted by newspapers in Denver, St. Louis, and Kansas City. The 2,850-mile journey was not without incident. Portions of the route were impossible to cover via automobile, so Williams improvised with a rented horse and buggy, reuniting with the others and his Buick, which followed alternate routes, when road conditions permitted. The entourage frequently took a wrong fork on an unmarked dirt

12. Sara Lockwood Williams, undated journal entry.
13. *University Missourian,* July 12, 1911.

road, at times remaining lost for hours. Walter Jr., riding in the second car that was sometimes needed, once strayed off the trail and was not located for half a day; the lad knew the next emergency rendezvous point was the railway station in Kansas City. He waited there for more than twelve hours. Williams arrived, finally, explaining he, too, had encountered difficulty: "I have been explaining to the police that we lost our license tag on the trail, a story they seemed to doubt, I regret to say. Now we'll go to supper if you've seen enough of the depot."[14] Williams's writing style, folksy and yet authoritative, might remind latter-day readers of an Ernie Pyle or Garrison Keillor or Charles Kuralt. A typical dispatch, after his viewing of an elaborate mural in a dusty hotel lobby in Kansas:

> They make much of the past in Kansas, perhaps because they have so little out there that is not present and future. They mark historic places, have anniversary celebrations and recount the glory of yesterday for the inspiration of today. The Santa Fe Trail is really a Missouri product, but it is first marked in Kansas, where it only crossed the state and never tarried. True, the wrong places have been sometimes marked and the wagons shown in bas-relief are impossible wagons, but the marking is done, a proper tribute to the historic age of the American plainsman . . . [15]

Williams himself was greeted along the way with press coverage that bordered on adulation. The *Santa Fe New Mexican* proclaimed his arrival in a lengthy front-page article that began:

> The first man in the world to go over the entire Santa Fe Trail in an automobile is here.
>
> His name is Dr. Walter Williams, dean of the School of Journalism of the University of Missouri at Columbia, Mo., and a noted newspaper man and magazine writer, and who will be the noted historian of this famous trail which begins in Old Franklin, Mo., and ends in Santa Fe . . . [16]

His safe return to Missouri prompted these headlines from the *Denver News:*

COMPLETES ROUND
TRIP OVER TRAIL

• • •

First Time by Motor

• • •

Establishment of Trans-con
tinental Highway Over
Route is Urged

Columbia, Mo.—The first automobile trip over the Santa Fe Trail, from trail's end to trail's end and return was completed yesterday when Dean Walter Williams of

---

14. Ibid., August 26, 1911.

15. Ibid., September 7, 1911.

16. *Santa Fe New Mexican,* August 18, 1911. Like many other publications, this newspaper referred to Williams as "Doctor," a mistake the dean never corrected.

the School of Journalism of the University of Missouri arrived at Columbia from Lexington, Mo. Mr. Williams completed the journey from Franklin, where the trail began, to Santa Fe, New Mexico, where it ended and returned a week ago as far as Lexington. Here heavy rains delayed the automobile and only yesterday was it possible to finish the entire trip.[17]

Publicity from the trip was credited with assisting the "good roads movement," as it was called, in Missouri. Williams soon found himself serving as president of the State Highway Improvement Association and, later, of the Missouri Old Trails Association. His newspaper articles about the Santa Fe Trail were never compiled into the book he hoped to produce. But much good came of the journey, which he felt was as important as any he ever took.

He began another world tour—it would be his second—in 1913. Much of the cost was underwritten by the Kahn Foundation for Foreign Travel of American Teachers. Williams claimed to have visited some two thousand newspaper offices on this nine-month journey across Europe, the Orient, and Australia. He planned to use this trip to conduct research for a book, which he tentatively entitled *The World's Journalism.* The book turned out to be far slighter than he had envisioned; it ran to only forty-four pages, and was printed in 1915 by the School of Journalism as one of its periodic Bulletins.[18] Much of the text was a comparison and contrast of various newspaper styles:

> The types of journalism most conspicuous and most easily differentiated as national products are the British, French, German, and American. The British type has long been and is today in many parts of the world the most potent in making and molding newspapers—they are literary productions. The German newspapers are weak in news and newsgathering facilities, but strong in political articles, in art, music and literary criticism, in informational discussions. The American newspaper is more audacious than any of its foreign contemporaries, more smartly written, more attractively printed. In news facilities, in persuasive appeal to all classes, as a general medium for exchange of thought, it is unsurpassed.[19]

The Press Congress of the World, which grew out of the World Press Parliament Williams had organized during the St. Louis World's Fair, met for the first time in 1915 as part of the Pan-Pacific International Exposition at San Francisco. Some eighteen nations were represented, enough to convince the journalists who attended that a permanent global organization was needed.

---

17. *Denver* (later *Rocky Mountain*) *News,* September 12, 1911.

18. Sara Lockwood Williams, *Twenty Years of Education for Journalism,* 31. The School of Journalism Bulletin series, begun in 1912, dealt with various phases of journalism. Mostly written by members of the faculty, the bulletins were distributed to a limited mailing list composed chiefly of journalism professionals and educators.

19. Walter Williams, "The World's Journalism" (School of Journalism Bulletin, 1915), 11.

Williams, who had kept in touch with many of the delegates over the years, was elected president.

Six years later, at Honolulu, Williams convened the World Press Congress again, this time against the backdrop of the international Naval Disarmament Conference, then in session at Washington. While President Harding and other world leaders were viewing with alarm the ominous military buildup in Japan and other countries, Williams issued to the Press Congress an eloquent plea for better communication rather than better weaponry:

> A league of journalists—keeping open and free the avenues of world communication—and speaking just and fair may do even more to preserve sacred institutions of society, to promote and maintain world peace, to give large life to all, than even the most skillfully balanced league or association of nations. In the last analysis, public opinion rules. Recorded, crystalized, interpreted, expressed by journalism, it is supreme. Ideas, not navies, rule the sea. Ideas, not armies, dominate the land. Let us disarm the typewriters of the jingo press in every land and limitation of—nay, abandonment of—armaments, even without the Washington conference, is an accomplished fact.[20]

Williams served for ten years as president of the Press Congress of the World, presiding again at the next convention, in Geneva and Lausanne, during 1926. He stepped aside after that, only to be chosen honorary president for life. He had no illusions that the Press Congress could change the world. It did not, any more than would kindred organizations more than a generation later: the Federation Internationale des Editeurs de Journaux, the International Press Institute, the Inter-American Press Association, and others. But, as Williams would explain, the potential of such a global organization was breathtaking, and far too important to ignore:

> If the Press Congress of the World shall make fearless the timid editor who trembles at telling the truth about party, friend or foe; if it shall strengthen the arm of him who strikes at iniquity entrenched; if it teaches better business methods to the shiftless or unlearned; if it elevates the standard of the doubtful and gives new hope to the despairing; if it replaces filth with purity, and sensationalism with sober truth; if it inculcates true ideas of the dignity of journalism and its responsibility; or if it adds, in smallest measure, to the equipment of the editor, making him a better citizen and a better man, the existence of the organization has been amply justified.[21]

Between meetings of the Press Congress of the World, Williams scheduled a number of other trips abroad, averaging perhaps one lengthy voyage about every other year. Indeed, there was grousing about his prolonged absences

---

20. Quoted by William H. Taft in "Walter Williams: International Journalist," *Journalism Quarterly* 36:2 (1959): 221.
21. Ibid.

from the campus; some students and faculty, and even friends in the Missouri Press Association, complained that the dean was nurturing personal contacts abroad rather than tending to business at home.[22] And if the general public had known that these trips were largely funded by (unpublicized) profits from the School of Journalism's commercial newspaper, the complaints likely would have been far more intense than they were.

But when he returned, all was forgiven. Seldom arriving empty-handed, Williams would bring with him, or report the forthcoming arrival of, exotic gifts to the School of Journalism: intricate scrolls from China; rare books from Germany; a seven-foot-tall stone lantern from Japan; a stone that had been quarried in 1724 and was a part of St. Paul's Cathedral in London; two massive stone lions from Nanking, China; early printing presses; Babylonian-inscribed tablets.[23] Even more impressive were the intangibles: arrangements with foreign publishers to hire Missouri graduates, sabbatical leave opportunities for faculty, news of exuberant reunions overseas with alumni, and, above all, still more publicity for the School of Journalism.

"Dr. Williams," editorialized the *Shanghai Evening Post,* "stands out as the greatest journalist-educator of the modern age." Homer Croy, a Missouri graduate who gained fame as an author and humorist, put it less reverently: Williams, to him, was "a small man with a homely face and a down-hanging underlip," who also happened to be "one great Midwestern journalist."[24] Croy saw Williams frequently in Washington and New York. Other alumni encountered him in Chicago and Tokyo and London. The dean was everywhere.

For all his travels—or perhaps because of them—Williams never wrote the truly important books he had dreamed he would. His official biography, prepared by the publicity department at the University of Missouri, lists him as author of seventeen books. But four of these were law books that he edited for law professors; several others were compilations of proceedings that he edited and for which he wrote a preface, and still others were little more than pamphlets or in-house publications, such as School of Journalism Bulletins. His textbook, *The Practice of Journalism,* which he had written with Frank Lee Martin, did enjoy a brisk sale and later appeared in a revised edition. But his really important writing, he told Sara, would have to wait until he retired.[25]

22. Rucker, *Walter Williams,* 112.

23. Ibid., 113; see also Sara Lockwood Williams, *Twenty Years of Education for Journalism,* 223 ff.

24. *Shanghai Evening Post,* July 30, 1935. Taft, "Walter Williams: The Man."

25. The books listed in the university biography include: *How the Cap'n Saved the Day* (1901); *Some Saints and Some Sinners in the Holy Land* (1902); *The State of Missouri* (1904);

He continued to deliver speeches, many of them memorable, to diverse audiences throughout the country and abroad. He dwelt on three favorite themes—professionalism in journalism, faith in God, and peace on earth. In what was probably his most famous address, he swung from the heels and hit them all. Entitled "The Bible: A Text-Book for Journalists," it was first delivered to the Iowa State Press Association in February 1918. In response to repeated requests, Williams delivered essentially the same text again and again over the years. The speech concluded with these ringing paragraphs:

> We have been thrust as a nation from a secluded place into a central position among the peoples of the world. We have become a world's spokesman. Have we as journalists risen to the vantage ground of opportunity? Knowledge of the world, not of the village only, is needed for the journalists of the village to count aright in the world today. Journalists who would lead must know . . . We need to know ourselves and other peoples. This means study; it means an open mind and a sympathetic heart, and above all, unflinching faith.
>
> World leadership is not a matter of a full treasury nor of a heaped granary, nor of a mailed fist. World leadership is spiritual. It is not a matter of faith in food, or in fuel, but faith in man and in God . . .
>
> To lack faith is the highest treason; to have faith and to exemplify it in written and spoken speech is the truest, most genuine, most helpful patriotism.
>
> We are experimenting, we are playing at democracy. Will we, can we, make democracy real in this republic and in the world? We can, and will, only as we keep the faith in war time and in peace in journalism. Are we not, you and I, interpreters, carriers, crystallizers, creators of public opinion? The supreme court of the world, the arbiter under God of the destinies of men and of nations; are we not come unto the kingdom for such a tremendous time as this?
>
> Let us then fight the good fight, but let us also, God helping us, keep the faith.[26]

Speeches such as that would reach thousands of people, and the articles Williams wrote for newspapers and magazines reached, in the aggregate, hundreds of thousands, perhaps even millions. But the most enduring and influential thing he ever wrote was a brief philosophical statement that he called *The Journalist's Creed*. This one-page testimonial would inspire generations

---

Personal Injuries in Mines (1905); *History of Missouri* (1908); *Personal Injuries on Railroads* (1909); *Missouri Since the Civil War* (1909); *Eloquent Sons of the South* (1909); *From Missouri to the Isle of Mull* (1911); *Law in Shakespeare* (1910); *Legal Antiquities* (1911); *The Practice of Journalism* (1911); *History of Northeast Missouri* (1914); *The World's Journalism* (1915); *History of Northwest Missouri* (1915); *Journalism—The Newest Weapon for Democracy* (1919); *The Press Congress of the World in Hawaii,* with a Foreword by President Warren G. Harding (1922). Sara Lockwood Williams, unpublished biographical outline materials about Walter Williams.

26. From *The Bible: A Text-book for Journalists,* privately printed at Columbia, Missouri, by Sara Lockwood Williams, c. 1936. This speech was sometimes entitled "Keeping the Faith in Journalism."

of journalists everywhere. It would also do much to revise the opinion an entire industry had of itself.

It is ironic that one of American journalism's great cynics, Charles A. Dana of the *New York Sun,* also composed what is arguably journalism's first code of professional ethics. Much of his own writing was brazen and biased, as he cheerfully admitted: "If we choose to glow or cry out in indignation, we do so, and we are not a bit frightened at the sound of our own voice." When a rival publisher, Adolph S. Ochs, created a slogan for his *New York Times,* "All the News that's Fit to Print," he could compare that lofty philosophy with Dana's, which was somewhat less restrictive: "I have always felt," Dana declared, "that whatever the Divine Providence permitted to occur I was not too proud to report." It was Charles A. Dana, not William Randolph Hearst or Joseph Pulitzer, who was accused at the time of creating the sensationalistic, inflammatory reporting that would later be branded "yellow journalism." But it was also Dana's *Sun* that was idolized throughout journalism for its intellectual qualities, literary standards, and thoughtful presentation of the news. Despite his bluster and his hard-bitten sarcasm, Dana cared deeply about his newspaper, which even critics admitted was not merely manufactured, but created with affection and precision. Near the end of his career Dana was told by a friend that the *Sun*'s legacy was not its influence for good or evil, but that it made a contribution to journalism. And this, his ablest biographer wrote, was the tribute he coveted most and the one he most deserved.[27]

In 1888 Dana was invited to address the Wisconsin Editorial Association, and he used that forum to deliver a valedictory, of sorts, on the subject of journalistic behavior. He knew of no set of professional rules in existence for newspaper people, he said, but just as there were ethical codes for physicians and attorneys, there should be one for journalists. He offered these maxims:

Get the news, get all the news, get nothing but the news.
Copy nothing from another publication without perfect credit.
Never print an interview without the knowledge and consent of the party interviewed.
Never print a paid advertisement as news-matter. Let every advertisement appear as an advertisement; no sailing under false colors.
Never attack the weak or defenseless, either by argument, by invective or by ridicule, unless there is some absolute public necessity for so doing.
Fight for your opinions but do not believe that they contain the whole truth or the only truth.

27. Frank M. O'Brien, *The Story of the Sun* (Harper, 1918), 302–3, 241. Candace Stone, *Dana and the Sun* (Dodd, Mead and Company, 1938), 404.

Support your party, if you have one; but do not think all the good men are in it and all the bad ones outside it.

Above all, know and believe that humanity is advancing; that there is progress in human life and human affairs; and that, as sure as God lives, the future will be greater and better than the present or the past.[28]

From his first day as a college professor, Walter Williams had decided that newspaper ethics must become an integral component of his History and Principles class. "It proves to be more difficult," he wrote, "to avoid than to include discussion of the ethical principles involved."

"There is no appearance of preaching," he added, perhaps knowing that some of his students might not agree. "The principles taught are not only matters of ethics, but of good newspaper work."[29] Williams sensed, or perhaps he *knew,* that many of his young charges would soon move into positions of journalistic leadership. So, in a more advanced class, called The Editorial, Williams required each student to develop his or her own code of professional behavior. The terms of each code were to reflect individual choices: "The instructor making it his chief business not to voice definite principles," Williams explained, "but to see that all angles of each problem are taken into consideration and to guide the arguments—for there are arguments in plenty—along worthwhile lines." But each student code had to address a number of specific journalistic concerns, among them:

What should be the attitude toward political partisanship?
    Should an editor hold office?
    What news, if any, should not be published?
    Should a newspaper make corrections? And, if so, how?
    Should a newspaper make news?
    Should a newspaper play the detective to uncover wrongs?
    Should newspaper men accept "courtesies" to the press?
    Should news ever be colored? Suppressed?[30]

By 1914, Williams had decided to write his own ethical statement. It was more than a set of guidelines, though one distinguished observer later ventured that Williams brought to this task a vision of the Ten Commandments, as applied to the field of newspaper work. An admiring editorial in a medical journal compared Williams's code with the Hippocratic Oath.[31] But Williams

---

28. Stone, *Dana and the Sun,* 52.

29. Undated notes by Williams, presumably the text for a talk to newspaper professionals on the subject of his History and Principles of Journalism class.

30. Ibid.

31. Taft, "Walter Williams: The Man." *Missouri Medical Journal,* c. July 1935. As quoted by Rucker, *Walter Williams,* the editorial added: "The crowded life of this noted journalist and educator has not prevented him from giving thought to the profession of medicine, nor did the

did not intend what he had written to be a code or an oath; it was, instead, an affirmation:

THE JOURNALIST'S CREED

I believe in the profession of journalism.

I believe that the public journal is a public trust; that all connected with it are, to the full measure of their responsibility, trustees for the public; that acceptance of lesser service than the public service is a betrayal of this trust.

I believe that clear thinking and clear statement, accuracy and fairness are fundamental to good journalism.

I believe that a journalist should write only what he holds in his heart to be true.

I believe that suppression of the news, for any consideration other than the welfare of society, is indefensible.

I believe that no one should write as a journalist what he would not say as a gentleman; that bribery by one's own pocketbook is as much to be avoided as bribery by the pocketbook of another; that individual responsibility may not be escaped by pleading another's instructions or another's dividends.

I believe that advertising, news and editorial columns should alike serve the best interests of the readers; that a single standard of helpful truth and cleanness should prevail for all; that the supreme test of good journalism is the measure of its public service.

I believe that the journalism which succeeds best—and best deserves success—fears God and honors man; is stoutly independent, unmoved by pride or opinion or greed of power, constructive, tolerant but never careless, self-controlled, patient; always respectful of its readers but always unafraid; is quickly indignant at injustice; is unswayed by the appeal of privilege or the clamor of the mob; seeks to give every man a chance and, as far as law and honest wage and recognition of human brotherhood can make it so, an equal chance; is profoundly patriotic while sincerely promoting international good will and cementing world comradeship; is a journalism of humanity, of and for today's world.

The Journalist's Creed was incorporated into the 1914 edition of the *Deskbook of the School of Journalism,* a basic style manual developed by the faculty for the *Missourian* and for the classroom work produced by the students. All students were required to commit the *Creed* to memory, for they would be tested on it early in their undergraduate careers.

But the *Creed* would soon reach audiences far beyond the campus. Copies were circulated to newspaper offices throughout the nation. Translations, frequently undertaken by enthusiastic graduates of the school as well as by overseas friends from the Press Congress, began appearing throughout the world. "Will you please inform the Dear Dean," wrote Roy C. Bennett of the *Philadelphia Bulletin,* in one of many letters from alumni on this subject, "that I had *The Creed* translated into twelve dialects of the Philippines while I was

---

long hours spent in the editor's chair and in the self-made man's study interfere with his helping to elevate medicine to the high plane it enjoys today."

there?"[32] In time, *The Journalist's Creed* would be published in more than a hundred languages and would adorn newspaper offices all over the world.

"Walter Williams . . . promotes the highest type of newspaper ethics," editorialized the *Indianapolis Star. "The Journalist's Creed* touches a lofty plane for the guidance of veteran and neophyte." *Editor and Publisher,* the international trade journal for the newspaper field, went even further, describing the *Creed* as "exactly what Walter Williams believed and advocated for the American democracy, for the Japanese Empire, for the struggling Chinese Republic, for lands where kings rule or dictators beat their breast, and all the rest. When the people of the world accept that formula of enlightened self-government, life will have a sweeter, safer and happier meaning for all mankind." *"The Journalist's Creed* . . . formulated the standards for the profession to aim at," declared the *New York Times*. "It had a wide influence on editors, publishers, and reporters, young and old, and was one of the potent factors in eliminating the subjective element in the objective reporting of news."[33]

Within a few years there appeared other codes, their terms more specific and their rhetoric less evangelical than *The Journalist's Creed.* One of the most thoughtful of these would be the *Canons of Journalism,* adopted in 1923 at the first annual meeting of the American Society of Newspaper Editors. This ASNE statement would be followed by a detailed, high-minded *Code of Ethics* of the Society of Professional Journalists, then called Sigma Delta Chi. These and the other codes of journalism ethics developed since the *Creed* would deal with professional concerns—there being little further discussion in them, at this point, about the status of journalism as a profession rather than as a trade or business or craft. Whether journalism is indeed a true profession, in the sense that medicine, law, and the clergy are defined as professions, remains to many an open question. But while others may challenge journalism's right to call itself a profession, Walter Williams emphatically did not. If there is a key sentence in his *Journalist's Creed,* it is the opening one, proclaiming his belief in the *profession* of journalism. This assertion, said Arthur Hays Sulzberger, publisher of the *New York Times,* "was Dean Williams's opportunity to contribute greatly towards stirring the consciousness of his fellow workers in their great trust . . . Walter Williams found journalism a trade and helped to make it a profession."[34]

The spring of 1929 was, for Williams, a grand time. His School of Journalism, begun as a controversial experiment, had survived for more than two

---

32. Roy C. Bennett to Sara Lockwood, October 1, 1924.

33. *Indianapolis Star,* July 31, 1935. Marlen Pew, editor, in *Editor and Publisher,* August 8, 1935. *New York Times,* July 30, 1935.

34. Arthur Hays Sulzberger, remarks at Journalism Week, University of Missouri, 1932.

decades and could now be considered, by most accounts, the strongest program at the University of Missouri; indeed, it was the one unit on the campus with a reputation for excellence of international proportions. Through his leadership of the World Press Congress, as well as his extensive travels, speeches, and writings, Williams had become, in the words of Governor Guy B. Park, "the greatest Missourian of his generation and certainly the best-known of his time." The worldwide acceptance of his *Journalist's Creed* served as testament to his stature in his chosen profession. "He could have been governor of the state," editorialized the *St. Charles Banner.* "The nomination was offered to him on a silver platter by the editors of Missouri at the conclusion of Governor [Arthur M.] Hyde's term of office in 1925. A man of less wisdom and more flaring ambition might have accepted the offer." Frank Luther Mott, director of the School of Journalism at the University of Iowa and author of *History of American Magazines,* for which he would win the Pulitzer prize, visited Williams that spring of 1929. Following the annual Journalism Week banquet, Mott noted in his journal, "Never in my life have I seen such adoration from students as I have seen tonight for Walter Williams." William Jennings Bryan, who knew something about running for national office, asked permission to list the name of Walter Williams among those he thought well qualified to be president. Williams declined, gracefully, just as he would when President Franklin Roosevelt's White House sounded him out about being U.S. ambassador to China.[35]

Williams was well into his sixties by now and a trifle less energetic than he had been. He cut back sharply on what had been a rigorous schedule of club meetings. He accepted fewer speaking engagements, attended fewer conventions of journalism educators and newspaper publishers. To Sara he admitted that, for the first time, he was looking forward to retirement at sixty-five, to living out his days in travel and, at long last, writing the big books that had eluded him throughout his career. He accepted only one commitment for the year ahead, 1930, and that was to do a lecture tour of South America.[36]

But his plans—perhaps his nonplans—would be rudely shattered by two dramatic events, one national, the other local. The national event was, of course, the stock market crash that October, an economic catastrophe that would plunge the country into a dreary and prolonged depression. The local

---

35. Quoted in the *Columbia Missourian,* July 30, 1935. *St. Charles Banner,* July 31, 1935. Frank Luther Mott, journal entry for April 25, 1929. Mott's journals are in the Western Historical Manuscript Collection at the University of Missouri. Cosgrove, *An Old House Speaks,* 125.

36. Williams was a Mason and holder of the thirty-third degree of the Scottish Rite; a member of two press clubs in England and the National Press Club in Washington and an author's club in Paris. Locally, he held a membership in the Round Table Club, which was a quite active group of business and professional men, and the Columbia Country Club. Sara Lockwood Williams, unpublished Walter Williams biography.

event was the increasing lack of confidence in the central administration of the University of Missouri, and the toppling of the university's president by, of all things, a sociological research project involving what came to be known as "the sex questionnaire." After one day-long session of the Board of Curators, President Stratton D. Brooks was summarily dismissed. To replace him, the curators turned to the one man they thought could restore the university's political and social credibility and guide it through the economic crisis ahead: Walter Williams. The minutes of the board meeting indicate that the choice was made without consideration of any other candidates. Williams had refused the presidency before, back in 1921, when times were good.[37] Times were not good now, and he could not refuse again.

---

37. Stephens, *A History of the University of Missouri,* 530. Sara Lockwood Williams's Walter Williams manuscript and various other sources affirm that Williams was informally asked to take the presidency in 1921 when the curators' candidate, Frank McVey, then of the University of Kentucky, declined. When Williams asked not to be considered, no formal offer was made.

13

Depression

The University of Missouri is not a cheap institution, despite the cheapness of its appropriations, sometimes; it is a distinguished institution—distinguished because of the men we have been able to keep during these last few years.

—Walter Williams

By just about any standard of measurement, Stratton D. Brooks's seven-year presidency of the University of Missouri was a disappointment. In his previous job, as president of the University of Oklahoma, he had earned widespread respect for his deft leadership style and aggressive, determined resistance to politicians who were out to inflict the spoils system on that state's major institutions of higher learning. His grit traveled well to Missouri, but his management skill, alas, seemingly had not. He was also unlucky. Through no fault of his own, he was hammered by the press early in his administration about the high costs of the remodeled president's home. "Nearly $68,000 has been spent," grumbled the *St. Louis Post-Dispatch,* among many others, "to remodel a $10,000 house." The renovation had been planned long before Brooks assumed the presidency, but he endured the criticism anyway, and it put him on the defensive from the outset. Though he was a native Missourian—he had been born on a farm near the tiny community of Everett in 1869—Brooks never quite connected with the Missouri legislature. As a result, state appropriations actually declined during the 1920s, though student enrollment was increasing and Missouri, like the rest of the nation, was prospering. Brooks also found himself at odds with his own faculty over admissions requirements and a number of other governance issues. Thus did the university flounder and stagnate during the Roaring Twenties, a period of what should have been dynamic growth and development.[1] With only a handful of solid supporters among the curators, the legislature, the faculty, and in the news media, Brooks felt increasingly isolated and powerless. And vulnerable. One more public controversy could do him in. During the spring of 1929, there was one, and it did.

---

1. *St. Louis Post-Dispatch,* January 23, 1926. Stephens, *A History of the University of Missouri,* 500 ff. Olson and Olson, *The University of Missouri,* 65.

It was neither faculty governance nor the dreary condition of the university's finances that brought Brooks's troubles to a head, however. Instead, it was a small-bore research project done by a sociology class that got sensationalized in the press and distorted by those who learned of it. Thus a relatively innocuous affair escalated to the point where, as one historian put it, there was "raised an insuperable barrier between President Brooks and his faculty on the one hand, and between Brooks and the Board of Curators on the other, and which led eventually to his dismissal."[2] Students in a sociology course, The Family, had been divided into several small committees, each assigned to study some aspect of family life. One of those topics was how the economic status of women might affect sexual relations between men and women. The group appointed to examine this phenomenon was led by an energetic graduate student who hoped to write a paper on the subject for his major professor, Max F. Meyer. The student developed a questionnaire, to be mailed to six hundred men and women, each of whom would be asked to respond anonymously. Professor Meyer helpfully provided the graduate student with University of Missouri envelopes he had on hand bearing the return address "Bureau of Personnel Research." Newspaper reporters got wind of the survey, however, and wrote accounts of it so lurid they triggered an uproar throughout the state. Angry editorials denounced the "sex questionnaire," as it was called, as an irresponsible use of the state university's resources. Irate citizens across Missouri circulated petitions demanding that everyone associated with the questionnaire be summarily fired. Brooks was furious with the sociologists; when he was interviewed by the press, he blasted the survey, as one observer put it, "in picturesque and intemperate language,"[3] expelled the graduate student who had developed the questionnaire, and placed Meyer and another sociology professor on suspension.

Brooks's tirade against members of his own faculty touched off an extensive and prolonged investigation by the national office of the American Association of University Professors. The AAUP's well-researched report on the matter, circulated nationwide, deplored the university president's refusal to defend academic freedom and, worse, his lack of fairness and honesty in explaining the research to the general public. Or, even, to the curators. Through what must have been gritted teeth, the curators nevertheless issued a weak statement of support for Brooks, pointing out that they, too, believed the questionnaire was reprehensible. But the faculty felt betrayed, and their anger at Brooks threatened to erupt into open warfare. Further charges and countercharges

2. Stephens, *A History of the University of Missouri,* 523.
3. Ibid., 524.

would follow, but Brooks had been damaged beyond repair. The curators stalled for a few months, hoping that tempers would cool. When they did not, the curators—a majority of them, at any rate—realized that their only hope for peace was a change in the presidency. On Saturday, April 5, 1930, they fired Stratton Brooks. As the excruciating, day-long session ended, the curators tried valiantly to place a positive spin on the decision by issuing an official statement placing Brooks's firing in a larger, seemlier context. "The sex questionnaire has no place in this controversy," the statement said. That portion of the statement was false. "The charges made in some quarters that the objections to Dr. Brooks are due to political influences are absolutely untrue," the statement continued. "Every member of this board bears witness to the fact that never at any time has any influence of such character shaped the course, purpose or conduct of this board as to any matter."[4] And that portion of the statement was a whopper.

In any case, Brooks, who badly wanted another opportunity to salvage his presidency, was out; Williams, who didn't want the job even under the best of circumstances, was in.

Officially, Williams retained his title as dean of the School of Journalism. He would be referred to as acting president while Stratton Brooks was given a six-month leave of absence with full pay. After that, the curators decreed, Williams would be president in his own right. But Williams was expected to take command immediately and thus was very much in charge from the moment he strode into the president's office on June 5, 1930. The room was a familiar one; he had spent endless hours in it years before as chief curator and counselor to his friend, Richard Henry Jesse. The office was situated in an imposing building that dominated the old campus quadrangle. Once known as Academic Hall, it had since been renamed Jesse Hall. That morning the president's office was bedecked with flowers, sent by proud newspaper colleagues, hopeful alumni, and relieved faculty members, people convinced they now had a friend in power.

Williams's early moves reassured them they did.

In a dramatic gesture that earned him valuable political points, Williams sent a formal request to the curators to cut the president's salary (but only after Brooks's leave ended) from $12,500 back to $10,000 a year. Williams also declined the fifty-dollar-a-month car allowance Brooks had received. But, he

---

4. University Presidential Archives indicate that two members of the board opposed Brooks's dismissal. *The Missouri Alumnus,* an officially sanctioned publication, printed the text of the board's statement in its April 1930 issue.

made clear, this was a personal, Depression-era sacrifice on his part, not part of a larger plan. "I do not wish this reduction to be regarded as a precedent for reductions in other University salaries," Williams wrote the curators, "which, in most instances, are too low rather than too high." The curators accepted Williams's recommendation without delay and publicly thanked him "for his unselfish and fine-spirited act."[5] A positive note had been struck, and the president's office badly needed one.

He shored up relations with the faculty by recommending to the curators that the beleaguered sociology professors, and especially Max F. Meyer, be restored to full faculty status. The faculty generally admired Meyer, regarding him as an emerging intellectual leader in the field of behaviorist psychology. But if his fellow professors considered Meyer a martyr, the curators thought him an obnoxious, troublemaking jerk. Relegated to academic exile on an obscure research project in St. Louis while on suspension from the Columbia campus, Meyer delivered a highly publicized speech comparing the board's behavior with that of the Spanish Inquisition. Still smarting under this attack and the AAUP report, the curators would go only partway with Williams's recommendation; they agreed to take Meyer back for one year, in which he was to do research but no teaching, and ordered his dismissal after that. Williams acquiesced for the moment, then later quietly pushed for, and got, an additional year of faculty status for Meyer. By then Meyer had landed a job at the University of Miami. Still, the faculty was heartened that Williams had fought for one of them and, by extension, for academic freedom. The "condition of mental or mortal terror among the professors of the University," as a curators' statement had disdainfully described it the day they jettisoned Stratton Brooks, no longer traumatized the campus. Or, as the historian Jonas Viles would put it, "In simple fashion but with characteristic tact and adroitness, he [Williams] made the faculty feel it once more had an important, even decisive, part in determining policies, that this was in the fullest sense of the word their university."[6]

Next, Williams set about mending the political fences. Early on he drove to Jefferson City for a chat with his friend, Governor Guy B. Park. The two men talked for some time, then took a long walk together across the Capitol grounds. As they strode toward a pool of goldfish, Governor Park remarked, "I do not know how on earth these goldfish live, for nobody ever feeds them, and, so far as I know, they have no means of sustenance." Williams was quick to reply, "Just like the University of Missouri, Governor."[7]

---

5. Quoted in Rucker, *Walter Williams,* 190.
6. *Missouri Alumnus,* April 1930. Viles, *A Centennial History,* 267.
7. Cosgrove, *An Old House Speaks,* 125.

Park got the message, and so did many members of the legislature. But as the political fortunes for the university improved, the economic crisis for the state and nation worsened. In just a few months desperate Missouri poultry farmers would be selling eggs at ninety cents per case—three pennies a dozen.[8] Shocked at the poverty and despair of so many of his constituents, Governor Park launched a campaign to provide some relief from what he called "the yoke of oppressive taxation," and challenged state agencies to do more with less. "Drastic reduction of expenses—state, county, municipality—is an implied pledge that must be kept," he declared. "Now, at the very beginning, is the time for action."[9] The cuts would be severe; they would profoundly affect Guy Park's alma mater and the plans his friend Walter Williams had for it.

The university's appropriation for 1931 was cut by 25 percent.[10] Among the first casualties was the university cafeteria at Ninth and Conley, a modest facility where hundreds of students took their meals. The cafeteria was shut down because it had run up a deficit in 1930 of twenty-four hundred dollars. Students who had relied on the cafeteria were advised to form food cooperatives instead. Faculty on temporary appointments were terminated. Faculty with full-time appointments were urged to take leaves of absence at half salary or to seek positions elsewhere—as if other jobs might be open. The College of Agriculture, faced with a sixty-five-thousand-dollar cut in budget, laid off twelve extension agents and much of its clerical staff, and took a month's salary from each of the remaining extension agents. The agriculture dean, F. B. Mumford, was not required to slash his own salary, but he did so anyway. Comparable reductions affected every unit on the campus. Within months some 114 members of the academic staff would lose their jobs. Only one new construction project was then underway, but the additional appropriation required to complete it was vetoed; thus the Home Economics building would remain a stark, half-finished skeleton for years. Science labs were compelled to function with only the most meager supplies; many classroom experiments and research projects were simply abandoned. The university's student loan fund, then one of the largest of its kind in the country, was depleted to the point that each upperclassman could borrow only a maximum of one hundred dollars.[11]

A faculty committee undertook an exhaustive study of student finances and found that the average student lived on $417 a year, an amount that included rent, board, fees, books and supplies, laundry, recreations, and contributions.[12]

---

8. McReynolds, *History of the Crossroads State,* 368.
9. Ibid.
10. *Missouri Alumnus,* November 1931.
11. Stephens, *A History of the University of Missouri,* 550 ff.
12. Ibid.

Even this was far more than most young Missourians could afford. Enrollment at the Columbia campus dropped off sharply, from 4,335 in 1930–1931 to 3,487 in 1933–1934.

Williams at first thought the financial crisis was transitory and could be dealt with by short-term, stopgap measures. His highest priority was to protect faculty salaries.[13] He argued that because salaries had been raised slowly during prosperous times it seemed only fair to trim them slowly when times were hard. More than gradual adjustments were required, however. As the weeks and months wore on he realized that his dreams for the university, which included raising faculty salaries and an extensive building program, would have to wait. "We will continue every possible economy and reduction," he wrote Governor Park, "but not to the extent of closing the University or lowering the efficiency of the state's chief educational institution."[14] But his hands were tied. He had to forgo not only any thought of building new classrooms and labs but also efforts to maintain existing ones. Reluctantly, Williams ordered that only urgent repairs be attempted on the physical plant. Perhaps his thoughts wandered back to those other impoverished days, thirty years ago now, when his friend Richard Henry Jesse complained about not having enough money to water the campus lawn. Yet he must have sensed that conditions could grow even worse before they got better. The early 1930s were far more than hard times; they were a challenge to survive.

Journalistic observers and faculty gossips were fond of noting that the man charged with leading the University of Missouri through its darkest fiscal hour, and with nursing back to health a faculty still recovering from anger and frustration, had no college education himself. Ordinary folk, on the other hand, didn't seem to mind at all. "What if the Dean didn't go to college?" a lawyer from St. Louis said to a reporter for the *New York Herald-Tribune*. "Degree or no degree, we know Dean Williams in Missouri. He is one of our learned men and into his care we will gladly commit our children." A thoughtful historian, Frank F. Stephens, described Williams as "a fine and cultured man, far above the average graduate in learning . . . he never ceased to enrich his own mind with knowledge gained from literature, from travel, and from contacts with university-trained men . . . [he is] also blessed with an unusual degree of common sense, of patience, of good humor, and of ability as a public speaker."[15] But if being "the only college president who never went

---

13. Viles, *A Centennial History,* 267.
14. Quoted in Rucker, *Walter Williams,* 190.
15. Ben Robertson, "He Never Went to College," *New York Herald-Tribune,* November 23, 1930. Stephens, *A History of the University of Missouri,* 531.

to college," as some newspapers headlined the feature articles they published about Williams, bothered him, he never said so, at least in public. He did, in fact, hold three honorary doctorates—from Missouri Valley College (1906), Kansas State College of Agriculture (1909), and Washington University in St. Louis (1926). So if admirers wished to refer to him as "Doctor Williams," that was all right with him too.

There was some grumbling about Williams, however, and it came mostly from alumni of the School of Journalism—not because Williams had become president, but because he refused to give up his dean's title in the process. Frank Lee Martin, a popular professor and much the senior person left on the journalism faculty, had been awarded the title of associate dean, but only when Williams went to the president's office. Thus Martin was entrusted with the responsibility of running the School of Journalism, but not with the title and whatever honor the title symbolized. Eventually Martin would be named acting dean, a distinction that still struck many as unfair. Students knew that for years it had been Frank Lee Martin who had kept the School of Journalism functioning smoothly while Williams was, as often as not, on the road. Mary Paxton Keeley, among a number of alumni, felt that Martin's role had never been properly appreciated. "Williams contributed to the world opinion of the journalism school," she said. "Martin contributed to the organization of the school." Martin himself did not complain, though others did in his behalf.[16] Long accustomed to being in the shadow of Walter Williams, Martin accepted his new situation without a whimper.

Williams never explained his decision to keep both titles, and the curators were loath to force the issue. Perhaps Williams regarded his accession to the presidency as a fluke, a momentary solution to an academic crisis; there was no guarantee that he, or anybody else, could succeed as president with the state's, and the university's, finances in such dire straits. His qualifications to be a university president, on paper at least, appeared ludicrous. Thus the deanship may have represented to him his only real security. Not that he needed security; he was already sixty-five and could retire comfortably at any time. No matter. He had dedicated his career to establishing and sustaining the School of Journalism, and was determined to hang onto the dean's title as long as he lived.

Sara delighted in her new role as the university's first lady. An enthusiastic hostess, she enjoyed entertaining guests in the President's House, a gracious, Italianate mansion situated on the old quadrangle midway between the School

---

16. Taft manuscript. Rucker, *Walter Williams,* 186.

of Journalism and her husband's primary office in Jesse Hall. Built in 1867, the President's House was the oldest building on the campus. Its graceful, redbrick exterior was surrounded by an elegant garden. Thomas Jefferson's original grave marker, a plain, elegant stone obelisk, stood on the grounds. The interior still glistened from the expensive renovation completed just a few years earlier for Williams's predecessor, Stratton Brooks. It was a splendid venue for receptions and parties and distinguished visitors—Mark Twain, among many others, had stayed there—and Walter and Sara fell in love with the place. Acutely interested in everything her husband did, Sara soon came to exert considerable power over the scheduling of his appointments, an influence some found preemptory and objectionable.[17] But she knew, far better than anyone, the extent to which the grinding demands of the presidency posed a threat to his health, and she was fiercely protective of his time and energies.

She generated a fair amount of press coverage herself, virtually all of it favorable. Regarded as a role model by working women for her success as a journalist and teacher, she was often called upon for speeches and interviews. During these occasions she pushed for increased opportunities for women in journalism, but she did so in moderation. "MRS. WALTER WILLIAMS ENJOYS SUCCESSFUL CAREER BUT RESISTS THE ULTRA MODERN VIEWPOINT," headlined the *Baton Rouge State-Times* during a visit to Louisiana.[18] And in an interview that might have dismayed feminists of that (or any other) period, she told a reporter for the *Christchurch* (New Zealand) *Press:*

"We are always told that we American women are spoiled; perhaps we are; we like it and go on with it; it is very pleasant to be spoiled," said Mrs. Williams, a charming and interesting visitor from Missouri, United States of America, who is spending a few days in Christchurch with her husband, Dr. Walter Williams, president of the University of Missouri.[19]

In other interviews, however, she was quick to point out that she herself had paid her professional dues. And when she talked about journalism, she was on solid ground, said the *St. Louis Globe-Democrat,* "for she has been at it since 1913, when ladies knew nothing about newspaper offices." "Sara Lockwood Williams," the article continued, "decidedly is among those women of the country who have journalistically arrived."[20]

Mostly, though, Sara—intimates called her Sally—was there for her husband, sensitive to his thoughts, anticipating his needs, happy to be his partner.

17. Pike, *Ed Watson,* 137.
18. December 30, 1929.
19. March 1, 1934.
20. *St. Louis Globe-Democrat,* undated clipping, c. 1938, Sara Lockwood Williams Papers.

Williams's toughest battles as president were fought with the appropriations committees in the legislature, and the toughest of these concerned the 1933–1934 budget. Through painful cost cutting, Williams and the curators submitted a bare-bones budget request of $3,991,146 for the 1933–1934 academic year. The state tax commission, however, proposed only $1,496,980—barely enough to keep half the campus on life support. In speech after speech, Williams took his case to not only the statehouse in Jefferson City, but wherever in Missouri he could find a forum. His chief arguments were that the university had already absorbed Draconian cuts, that it was asking for only its fair share of available revenues, and that the entire state would be crippled for years to come if the university's request were denied.[21] His rhetoric, those who heard it said, was powerful:

> I would rather have a deficit in the state treasury—though I don't seek it—than in the intellectual and spiritual education of the children of this state. You can't issue bonds for their deficit in education.[22]

Departing from his usual oratorical style, which ran heavily toward generalities, Williams pounded home specific implications of the budget cuts and detailed breakdowns of current expenditures. Before the legislative Appropriations Committee, Williams exposed errors in the state tax commission's analysis, prompting the committee chairman to reject the commission's figures and to lean toward those Williams supplied. In the state senate, the *Kansas City Star-Times* reported, Williams scored another direct hit: during the question-and-answer period, state senator Jerome M. Jaffee asked about what he suspected was an exorbitant use of vehicles at the university. "We have a few trucks and small cars for agricultural extension work," Williams replied, "but that is all. They [the curators] voted me a car, and I said 'Thank you, gentlemen,' and bought my own. Like Daniel, I saw the handwriting on the wall." But the senate was a tough sell. When one senator publicly praised Williams for voluntarily cutting his own salary by 25 percent, another senator, O. B. Whitaker, retorted: "That's fine. Let him cut it another 25 percent. As long as those salaries remain as high as they are I'm going to oppose this educational bill."[23]

Williams's dramatic efforts carried the day—after a fashion. The final appropriation, just under $2 million, still fell well short of what had been asked, but it was far more than had been originally offered. There was some consolation: of the fifty state agencies to be funded that year, the harsh recommendations of the state tax commission were adopted in all but one,

---

21. *Columbia Daily Tribune,* February 9, 1933. Quoted in Adams, "Walter Williams," 122.
22. Ibid.
23. *Kansas City Star-Times,* April 11, 1933. Adams, "Walter Williams," 133.

that for the University of Missouri. It was perhaps Williams's most important legislative victory. And though he got little credit for it at the time, the political goodwill Williams generated would soon make things better. Later that same year, Governor Park called a special session of the legislature to introduce bills calling for new forms of taxation. These were enacted, making it possible to increase the university's appropriations. The corner had been turned, and from that moment on the healing process was well begun.[24]

Williams had not been a young man when he moved into the presidency, and though he brought wisdom and patience to the office—where they had often been missing—his energy levels were diminishing to a marked degree. His intensive, prolonged confrontation with the General Assembly in 1932 drained him both physically and emotionally. Still, bowing to the demands of his office, he kept up a demanding schedule of public appearances and speeches. The invitations poured in. When he could, he created a fresh, well-researched new text for each gathering, which could range from high school teachers' meetings to science colloquia to wildly diverse conventions of businessmen. When the Ice Cream Manufacturers of America met on the campus, for example, he welcomed them with "Eating Ice Cream as a Means of Grace," a fact-filled historical review, replete with references to Dolley Madison and Thomas Jefferson; he praised the nutritional wonders of ice cream and noted, appreciatively, that "the hand that prepares the meal is the hand that rocks the world."[25] This talk, among many others, was widely reported in the press. He spoke to several audiences a week, delivering official greetings, civic club talks, remarks at faculty and staff meetings, commencement addresses throughout the region. One of his briefest talks became one of his most famous; it was at a ceremony at the campus's Memorial Tower in which Williams, on behalf of the military, belatedly conferred the Distinguished Service Cross (a medal for valor ranking just below the Congressional Medal of Honor) upon the mother of a former student who had lost his life in World War I. The remarks, which he called "The Joy of Combat," concluded with this quotation:

> For how can man die better
> Than facing fearful odds
> For the ashes of his fathers
> And the temples of his god.[26]

---

24. Stephens, *A History of the University of Missouri,* 576–79.

25. Adams, "Walter Williams," 98. This well-researched dissertation, written by a professor of speech, presents a highly detailed analysis of Williams's rhetorical techniques.

26. "The Joy of Combat," text found in Sara Lockwood Williams Papers. The medal was presented to Mrs. Emma Karls, mother of Roy Karls. The verse was not attributed and presumably was written by Williams.

Other speech texts were recycled again and again, tailored only slightly to fit new audiences. Perhaps his most celebrated address, which he trotted out with considerable frequency, was one he sometimes called "The Seven Marks of an Educated Man," "The Seven Results of a Sound Education," or "The Seven Lamps of Journalism." Delivered initially as a commencement speech in 1926 when an honorary doctorate was conferred upon Williams by Washington University, the text specified the abilities an educated person (or, depending on the audience, a good journalist) should possess: (1) to express oneself clearly in written and spoken language, (2) to see clearly and completely, (3) to think straight, (4) to do worthwhile things right, (5) to imagine, (6) to live comfortably and helpfully with other people, and (7) to develop the belief in the supremacy of the spiritual over the material. While those seven points remained more or less intact, the emphasis could be readily shifted to fit specific situations. For U.S. audiences, Williams placed great stress on the spiritual, while to a foreign audience he dwelt more on "the ability to live cooperatively with others." Another tried-and-true inspirational speech was "The Things Not Caesar's," which he listed as "conscience and character and culture and the freedom of the human spirit." Williams conceded that Caesar had the world's goods in his grasp, but "what a mess Caesar, the practical man, has made of human life!" This venerable warhorse of a text, which Williams kept going for forty years, was actually a reincarnation of a talk he first developed in the 1890s called "The Things Unseen."[27] Old wine in new bottles, perhaps, though audiences never tired of it.

(Some of his former students must have marveled at how effective Williams could be at a luncheon speech, yet how dull as a classroom lecturer. The respective subject matter obviously had something to do with it; a deeply emotional, half-hour luncheon speech on, say, the Meaning of Life was almost certainly more interesting than a fifty-minute history lesson, delivered three times a week to a class that met at eight o'clock in the morning. Too, Williams's rhetorical techniques, so effective with an audience that heard him only rarely, might have worn a bit thin over the duration of a long academic semester. But if his students found his lectures pedestrian and unexceptional, his after-dinner speech guests clearly did not. Wherever he went—outside the classroom—he drew great applause and left the listeners wishing for more.)

It was a grueling pace for a man now approaching seventy years of age, however, and the speeches took their toll on Williams's declining strength. And though he still looked fit—trim, dapper, tiny, yet somehow charismatic— he was in fact overworked if not burned out, and he tired easily. His batteries

---

27. Adams, "Walter Williams," 110.

ran down more quickly and needed recharging, in a way that only travel could provide for him.

Only three months into his presidency in 1930, he used his vacation to attend the World Press Congress in Mexico City and to accept a few speaking invitations from journalism groups in Central America.[28] The following year he delivered lectures in Panama and Buenos Aires, honoring a commitment he had made much earlier.

In 1932, he toured Europe as a guest of the Oberlander Trust, a foundation then interested in a study of newspapers and higher education in Germany. He was made an honorary member of the student society at the Berlin School of Journalism—a training program patterned after Missouri's—and cited as one "who upholds the highest standards of the press."[29] For this extended trip Williams used his month's vacation, then obtained the curators' permission to stay a second month at no pay. Thankful to Williams for the relative serenity that had returned to the campus, the curators happily concurred. Each year of Williams's presidency, the Board of Curators dispatched a report to the governor expressing, as a preacher might put it, an Attitude of Gratitude that peace had been restored. "We are pleased to say that the affairs of the University have been managed with efficiency," one such affirmation read, "the president and faculty are working harmoniously and are endeavoring to promote the interest and efficiency of the school."[30] If Williams wanted a few extra weeks in Europe, the curators weren't going to quibble about it.

Throughout his travels, Sara was at his side, comfortable now in her role as the trusted aide and boon companion Williams wanted, and increasingly relied upon. This was heady stuff for her, and she reveled in it. "Only one incident, in France," Sara recorded in her journal, "A dashing, elderly gent [presumably noting the difference between her age and Walter's] took it for granted I was W's mistress & suggested I might transfer my affections!"[31]

The 1932 trip to Europe evolved into a trip around the world, with well-publicized appearances in every port of call. As the Nieuw Holland liner steamed into Brisbane, Williams found a cluster of journalists and publishers

---

28. Rucker, *Walter Williams,* 116.

29. Ibid.

30. Board of Curators, *Report to the Governor, 1934.* Presidential Archive, University of Missouri.

31. Sara Lockwood Williams Papers. As has been mentioned previously, the term "journal" is used here for convenience; she wrote hundreds of entries, most of them undated, on various kinds of papers. At one time, she planned to write her autobiography, and these notes presumably were written with that manuscript in mind.

waiting for him. This was not unusual. Neither was it unusual that he was well prepared for them. The page-one story in the *Brisbane Telegraph* was headlined:

"BRISBANE PAPERS
ARE A.1"
-0-
Praise by Dean Williams
of Missouri
-0-
Leading Figure in Press
World

In the admiring piece that followed, Williams was quoted as saying, "The Brisbane newspapers that I have perused are really good papers and rank in the A1 class. I have made out a list of the 200 best papers in the world and there are many of the Australian newspapers which come within that group." His list was not produced, then or, so far as is known, ever. But it made good copy. So did his reason for being in Brisbane in the first place: "I desire to be designated a working journalist, as I am making my rounds," he said to the *Telegraph* reporter. "My University officials said to me, 'Now you go round the world and have a holiday.' They said this because my job is to travel and study. It is the job of a newspaper man to travel and study and thus gain information that will be helpful not only to himself but to the readers of the journals he represents. I am a working journalist of the old type."[32]

The following year, 1933, Williams and Sara went to Europe again as guests of the Oberlander Trust. This time, as Sara noted proudly in her journal, they would be "received by Hitler."[33] The interview, in early November 1933, was described, in the official translation of it issued by Hitler's office, as a "Conversation between the Reichskanzler and the President of the University of Missouri, Professor Walter Williams."

The transcript read, in part:
Question [from Williams]: Has the Chancellor any message for the Americans of German descent in the United States?
Answer [from Adolf Hitler, who referred to himself in the third person]: He has only one message for the German-Americans and that is the request not to believe unquestioningly all that they read in the papers about Germany. He would like to see as many German-Americans as possible visit Germany next summer so that they can convince themselves that law and order and contentment rule in Germany.

32. *Brisbane Telegraph,* c. August 3, 1932.
33. Throughout the 1930s her biographical materials, press releases, and speech introductions mentioned that she had been "received by Hitler."

Question: And to the American press, where it is a question of writing about Germany?

Answer: The Chancellor can only give the same advice to the American press as he has given to the German-Americans. The press is in danger of losing its reputation if it continually reports what is not true. There have been many examples of this in recent times . . . The press must not forget that it has a mission to fulfill. He, the Chancellor, would welcome it if the American newspapers would send sober-minded men to Germany who did not have as their sole aim the spreading of sensational news but who would report on what they had seen and give their own well-considered verdict.[34]

Williams consistently misjudged Germany's leaders and their intentions. After his 1932 visit to Berlin, where he had been royally entertained by high-ranking German officials, Williams told the *New York Herald Tribune:*

I found the greatest friendship for the United States in Germany. We are better liked there than we are in any other country in Europe unless it be in England. The German hatred of the French amounts almost to an obsession. That, of course, has resulted from the French attitude. Germany is in a desperate condition but the American can have nothing for them except the profoundest respect. Their bravery, their courage is superb. There is not sufficient sentiment, I am sure, to bring back the Hohenzollerns. All, however, are certain that there must be some form of strong centralized government brought about soon . . .

All those who talk of high tariffs and armaments and all of those who favor isolation should go to Germany now. There they would see what war and armaments, what barriers to trade have done for a nation. Germany is almost a smokeless nation, industrially. Her harbors are filled with idle ships, her factories are empty, her hotels have few guests. The pity of the situation is to be found in their courage, in the manner in which these people are facing their problems. It is profoundly impressive that with it all they still grow flowers and they still keep their music.[35]

A year later, just after his meeting with Hitler, he had grown slightly uneasy about the Nazi leader, though he remained optimistic about world peace. On the trip home Williams granted an interview with the *Melbourne Herald,* which headlined the article

A MESSAGE OF
HOPE
-0-
"War Talk Is
Only Talk"

Williams described Hitler as "an obscure-looking little man with a fierce look, protesting his desire for peace and swaying thousands through platitudes

---

34. Walter Williams Papers.
35. *New York Herald-Tribune,* August 4, 1932.

delivered with the orator's art." But under Europe's troubled surface, he said, a better feeling between Germans and Frenchmen existed. He said Europe, despite its thunder, was not at all in a warlike mood. Of Williams himself, the *Herald* reporter wrote, "he finds the world a pretty good place, not nearly so close to catastrophe as some of its nervy people think."[36]

Like much of the rest of the world, he was naive and misguided in his assessment of Hitler and Nazi Germany. But Williams would not live long enough to know just how wrong he had been.

The last leg of the return trip, by steamer from the South Pacific, was completed early in 1934. Far from being the tonic he had wished for, the lengthy cruise left Williams feeling weaker than ever. When he arrived back in Columbia, he was examined by doctors, who told him he had prostate cancer.

The medical team pushed for immediate surgery, but Williams refused, saying he needed to finish up the academic year; he especially wanted to deliver the speech at the spring commencement. Against doctors' orders he postponed his full medical workup for two months, then checked himself into Barnes Hospital in St. Louis. His only treatment there was for a kidney infection. The doctors told him he would probably live for several years with his cancer.[37] But he would not. His commencement speech, that June of 1934, would be his last public appearance.

He met quietly with the curators, informed them of his condition, and offered to resign on the spot. Not yet, the curators said, as long as he was physically and mentally able. "Walter Williams sick is worth more to us than any new man we could bring in at this time," one of them told him. Behind the warmth, which was genuine, the curators had one eye on the calendar. The Missouri legislature's appropriations were done on a biennial basis; a legislative year was just ahead, and Williams's influence with the legislators, even from a sickbed, could be decisive.[38]

He hung on throughout the summer. He would not enter Jesse Hall again, though he put in full days at his desk in the President's House. But the beginning of the fall term found him too weak to be much more than a figurehead. In early September, he sent the curators his resignation, to take effect at their pleasure. Reluctantly and without specifying a date for the changeover, they accepted the resignation, at the same time issuing an eloquent statement praising his

---

36. *Melbourne Herald,* February 8, 1934.

37. Stephens, *A History of the University of Missouri,* 569. Sara Lockwood Williams, unpublished Walter Williams biography.

38. Sara Lockwood Williams, unpublished Walter Williams biography.

service to the institution. "Dr. Williams," the statement concluded, "brought to the presidency a mature experience, a broad vision, and an inspiring leadership which have enabled him to guide the University safely through one of the most difficult periods of its history."[39]

To handle the day-to-day business of the president's office, the curators promoted the able and energetic dean of the School of Business, Frederick A. Middlebush. But where major decisions were concerned, Williams was still president, and he did what he could. The spreading cancer now ravaged his system, and powerful medications could make him comfortable for only limited periods. But for several hours each day he would dictate to his secretary, hold conferences with deans and other administrators, and meet with curators, all in his President's House study. When the legislature convened, Williams was much too weak to take his case for the university appropriation to the capital in Jefferson City. So, for the first time in its history, the Senate Appropriations Committee, which had once treated him as an adversary, traveled to the President's House in Columbia and listened respectfully to his report and recommendations.[40]

He made several speeches, but delivered them by telephone from his sickbed. Through sheer force of will, he personally signed a diploma for every member of the graduation class of 1935. On June 5, much too ill to appear at the commencement ceremony in person, he addressed the graduates by telephone. Because he had officially resigned, this was billed as his last commencement speech as president. But students and faculty, all who heard it, realized it indeed was his life, not just his presidency, that was near an end. Williams talked only for a few minutes, but his voice held steady:

> Men and women of Missouri and visitors to our Commonwealth: We are come to the 93rd Commencement, and as I must quit the stage in a brief moment, permit me to give my sincere and heart-felt benediction and Godspeed to the members of the Class. The world is yours, but only if you are willing to pay the price for it. Hard work, moral and intellectual integrity, continuing education, love, preservation and cultivation of the imagination, unshakable faith in God and in fellow men, holding fast to the things of the spirit, without which the ownership of the whole world and the things thereof are a bane, not a blessing. Live in no sheltered house-board in a tideless eddy, but cast your lot along your own coast, in the swift-moving, however dangerous current of humanity's progress, to higher things, and then paddle your own canoe. May all your ways be righteous and your paths be peace.[41]

---

39. Board of Curators statement, September 10, 1934, Presidential Archive, University of Missouri.

40. Sara Lockwood Williams, unpublished Walter Williams biography.

41. Quoted in Cosgrove, *An Old House Speaks,* 128.

Many students, and more than a few faculty, wept openly. For once at a commencement, the conferral of diplomas was an anticlimax.

A few days later, on July 2, 1935, his seventy-first birthday, he convened the curators to insist that his resignation be accepted immediately. He planned to vacate the President's House at once, he said, to return to his own home on Glenwood Avenue. The curators were welcome to visit him there, he added, "at their convenience from time to time for social converse." After the meeting, Sara steadied him as he walked slowly through the President's House, giving it what he knew would be his final inspection.[42]

Once back in his own home, Williams was beset with pneumonia, and his condition declined rapidly. Sara screened his visitors as best she could, limiting them to family and close friends. He did talk at length with his minister, the Reverend Joseph A. Garrison, pastor of the First Presbyterian Church. The two men reminisced about a speech Williams had written back in 1917 and which he entitled "The Blessings of Death." In the text, which ministers had since quoted many times, Williams had likened death to a covered bridge: "We shall all go forth from the covered bridge to our tryst with Him into the meadow lands beyond." And to his family he spoke at some length of the long journey he was about to make. For this, as for his every lecture and meeting and speech, he had prepared. At precisely nine o'clock on the evening of July 29, 1935, his family at his bedside, Walter Williams died peacefully in his sleep.[43]

---

42. Rucker, *Walter Williams,* 197. Sara Lockwood Williams, unpublished Walter Williams biography.

43. "In Memoriam: Walter Williams, 1964–1935," University of Missouri Bulletin, February 10, 1936, 13. The death certificate listed the principal cause of death as "cancer of the prostatic gland," with bronchial pneumonia as a contributing factor. His most recent position was listed as "retired President of the University of Missouri," but his life's work, the certificate said, was "journalist."

"As Much As Any Man . . ."

 Printer's ink is black and of no great worth, but Walter Williams of Missouri mixed it with courage and honor and caused it to shine like gold.

—Editorial in the *Dallas Journal*

The funeral was held in the ivy-covered First Presbyterian Church where Williams had served as an elder for forty-one years. Hundreds of friends and acquaintances were assembled well before the ten o'clock service began, their automobiles lining the streets for blocks around. The church sanctuary, which Williams once had filled Sunday after Sunday with his Bible class, was heavily banked with lilies, roses, gladiolas, and asters, and even the window ledges were covered with floral arrangements.[1] The stores of Columbia were closed for much of that warm Wednesday morning, and classes at the university were dismissed. The university bell tolled from 9:30 until 11 A.M. School of Journalism students attended in a body, adding to a crowd that overflowed the sanctuary and jammed the doorways and entrance halls that led to it.

The simple, elegant funeral service began with some of Williams's favorite music, including "A Mighty Fortress is Our God," a stirring hymn written by Martin Luther. It ended with a eulogy by the Reverend Joseph M. Garrison, who read the Twenty-third Psalm, reminisced about his own close friendship with Williams, and then quoted from one of Williams's own speeches:

> The supreme blessing of Death is his who may, when the hour of leaving earth has come, say, with Paul, in trust unwavering, "I have fought a good fight, I have finished my course, I have kept the faith."[2]

It may not have been the biggest funeral ever conducted in Columbia, but it did receive the most attention from the world outside. Messages of sympathy poured in from across the country and abroad. Dozens, perhaps even hundreds, of newspapers published editorial tributes:

> Walter Williams . . . came to know the earth as widely and as intimately as the astronomer [Harlow] Shapley, born in the same state, knows the stars in the night

---

1. *Columbia Missourian*, July 31, 1935.
2. Quoted in ibid.

skies. And probably no one of mortals could make a more comprehensive report to Him to whom a thousand years are as a day than this journalist to whom the world was made new every day.

—*New York Times*[3]

Walter Williams . . . in the estimation of his fellows and in that of the thousands who sat under his instruction, is the personification of their highest concept of a journalist.

—*Christian Science Monitor*

Dr. Williams, as much as any other one man, was responsible for the improved complexion and attitudes of much of the national press today.

—*Washington Post*

He had genius, a charming personality, tremendous energy and principles. He not only knew things, he understood people. Such a man in any age, almost in any social group, was bound to be eminent, bound to be respected, bound to achieve things, bound to inspire others. He inspired thousands . . . Walter Williams's death takes one of the best loved characters of contemporary life. His institution will go on, for he built solidly.

—*Des Moines Register*

Walter Williams was known to the newspaper profession all over the United States. More than that, he was better known by personal contact to the foreign newspaper world than any other representative of American journalism.

—*Brooklyn Eagle*

Great as the recognized debt of the newspaper profession to Dr. Walter Williams is today, one may predict that such recognition will be even greater in time to come. Fine principles make their way slowly. Pioneer that he was in advocating strict ethics in journalism, Dr. Williams must have felt at times that his words of guidance met with no hearty response. He lived to see a new spirit enter the newspaper profession, largely drawn from his inspiration, and to see progress in setting higher standards, such as he urged upon all of his host of students. Others will carry on and bring to a still higher level conceptions of honesty and courage which he so ardently expressed.

—*Chicago Daily News*

In a personal column, Arthur Hays Sulzberger repeated an observation he had made in a Journalism Week speech some years earlier: "Walter Williams . . . found journalism a trade and helped to make it a profession."[4]

And from Missouri newspapers, edited by friends who knew him best of all:

---

3. One of the nation's foremost astronomers, Shapley was a native of Nashville, Missouri. From 1921 to 1952 he was director of the Harvard Observatory.

4. August 3, 1935.

A student of Missouri University in speaking of the late Walter Williams, says: "Walter Williams dead? How mistaken is that statement. He never will be dead as long as a student who knew him lives, or as long as his journalistic creed hangs on the wall of a newspaper office."

—Neosho Mechanic

And so, Walter Williams . . . we who have served beneath your banner, or who have caught the inspiration of your matchless journalistic creed, salute you. To us you will always remain teacher, counselor, friend.

—Columbia Herald-Statesman

For all the accolades, however, Walter Williams had his detractors. At various times in his life he was described as arrogant, pompous, mean-spirited, and self-centered.[5] And while these may have been petulant remarks and minority viewpoints, reflecting only one aspect of a personality that was most often characterized in far more affirmative terms, Walter Williams did project a certain amount of vanity. And ambition.

Much of what he did was calculated—not in the devious sense, to make himself noticed at the expense of someone else, so much as simply to gain recognition of his program or, often, himself as symbol of it, in ways large and small. "He knew how to attract attention," recalled Jack Hackethorn, a prominent photographer and public relations man. "Whenever a group photo was to be taken, Williams would hurry to position himself at the far end on the right. That way, he told me, when the photo appeared in print, the caption would always list his name first: 'Pictured above, left to right, Walter Williams . . .' "[6]

Throughout his deanship Williams presided at well-publicized presentations of gifts to the School of Journalism: scrolls from China, lanterns from Japan, rare books from Europe, treasures enough to fill a small museum. Each gift was announced with considerable fanfare, Williams implying, somewhat disingenuously, that it had been a spontaneous gesture of goodwill and appreciation to the world's first School of Journalism from grateful journalistic leaders in other lands. In fact, some—perhaps most—of the gifts had come about because Williams had asked for them. In one such solicitation, directed to a French newspaper publisher and political leader, Williams wrote:

Dear Senator Dupuy:
    The University of Missouri, which you honored by visiting, is as you know the oldest university in the Louisiana Purchase Territory, acquired from France in the days of the first Napoleon. The School of Journalism of the University of Missouri is the oldest school of journalism in the world. One purpose of the

---

5. Votaw manuscript. Mary Paxton Keeley, interview with the author, January 5, 1964. Mrs. Margaret Dorsey Fuqua, interview with the author, August 4, 1993.
    6. Interview with the author, August 4, 1993.

School of Journalism is to educate for international journalistic services, seeking that knowledge and sympathetic understanding which best promotes the interests of good journalism everywhere. In recognition of the work of the School of Journalism and helping to promote it, there have come to us in the last two years two gifts from other nations, helpful gestures of goodwill.

The first was a stone from St. Paul's Cathedral, at London, presented by the British Empire Press Union, through its president, Viscount Burnham of the London *Daily Telegraph.* The bronze tablet upon the stone shows that it came from "the birthplace of English Literature, the English Newspaper Press, and the English Publishing Business." It was presented in a notable address by Sir Esme Howard, the British Ambassador to the United States, who came to Columbia from Washington for that purpose.

The second of these gifts was presented through the America-Japan Society, of Tokyo, at the instance of the Japan Foreign Office and the Japanese journalists. It is a Japanese stone lantern from the estate near Tokyo where the first American envoy to Japan established his legation. The Japanese Ambassador to the United States, Mr. Tsuneo Matsudaira, made the presentation address.

In both cases the press of the United States and throughout the world gave news stories and helpful comment upon the presentations and the ceremonies incident thereto. The University of Missouri conferred upon each ambassador the highest honor in its gift, the honorary degree of Doctor of Laws.

I am wondering whether an association of the journalists of Paris, or of France, or the newspapers of which you are the distinguished owner, or some organization, official or otherwise, in France might not also present a gift to the School of Journalism of the University of Missouri, helping thereby the spirit of journalistic comradeship and international goodwill. If so, I believe that the presentation thereof with an address from your Ambassador to the United States, M. Claudel, could be made a most significant occasion and one of far-reaching influence.

It is not, of course, the cost of the gift but the spirit of the presentation that counts. Particularly appropriate it seems to me would this presentation be from the country from which we came into the United States and from the people whose language was used in the first newspapers published in this territory. What form this gift should take and how it should be brought about is, of course, for you to decide, if the suggestion meets your approval. Possibly something associated with Benjamin Franklin, great journalist and great ambassador to France, or with the transfer of the Louisiana Territory or of some other historic and journalistic association.

I hope that, should favorable consideration be given to the suggestion and the gift be brought about, you as well as His Excellency, the Ambassador, will honor us with your presence on the occasion.

The University of Missouri published the proceedings of the other presentations. Copies thereof I am sending you today.
With high regard,
Very sincerely,
Walter Williams[7]

7. January 25, 1927. Walter Williams Papers.

This particular appeal was not successful.[8] But others were, bringing to the school many noteworthy expressions of international fellowship—with attendant publicity, both in the United States and abroad.

Williams regarded publicity as not only desirable but essential. He made no apology for seeking it. In a remarkably candid speech he once acknowledged:

> While I will not contend that all really great teachers have adopted methods of direct publicity, I will contend that practically every successful teacher has done so, and the Biblical injunction not to hide one's light behind a bushel is the soundest apologetic for advertising. The ancient who said . . . "Good wine needs no bush" is right, perhaps, after two necessary preliminaries. First, that we know the wine is there at all; secondly, that we know it to be good wine according to our individual tastes. The importance of this qualification can be seen from the variety of choice on any wine list. As a matter of fact, the better the wine the bigger the bush it deserves, for no bush in existence can create a permanent demand for a bad wine.
>
> Those old physicians in ancient Greece who conducted their operations on a platform in view of all beholders in order to get custom were, at least, actually showing the degree of skill they had attained, and were thus putting into practice one of the axioms of the most modern advertisers, that to exhibit the actual goods to the critical inspection of the buyer is the challenge which honest value alone can sustain.[9]

One of Williams's favorite quotes was from the British historian and critic, Lytton Strachey: "The most useful man in the world is the man with the matches—the man who gives you the light, who enables you to know where you are and what you are doing, and who will prevent you from running into other people."[10] Throughout his life, Williams never wavered in his determination to generate as much light as he could for his profession, his program, and, if it would help, for himself. He was the man with the matches, and he wasn't shy about striking them.

But if Walter Williams was ambitious, he was not consumed by ambition. He was a hard-working idealist, determined to overcome his own shortcomings, a man with a passionate faith in journalism. He never pretended to be anything more than that. Had his ambition indeed been for self-aggrandizement, he probably would have accepted one of the numerous gilt-edged invitations from powerful organizations and individuals who sought him as a candidate for political office. "If the Hon. Walter Williams can be induced to go to

---

8. Not immediately, at least. A search of the record of gifts to the University of Missouri reveals nothing from France to the School of Journalism during that time period.

9. Walter Williams, undated, untitled speech, Williams Papers.

10. Quoted in ibid. The image of the matches was important to Williams and he talked of it often. His widow, in fact, had tentatively entitled her unpublished biography of Walter Williams "One Candle Lights Another."

Congress," editorialized the influential *Mexico Ledger,* "he should be sent there by acclamation." But he repeatedly declined opportunities to run for the Missouri legislature, for Congress, and for governor of Missouri, just as he politely declined an overture from Franklin Roosevelt's White House to be nominated as ambassador to China. "He would have made a master politician," Charles Ross, now Washington bureau chief of the *St. Louis Post-Dispatch,* wrote of Williams. "He could have had the governorship for the asking, with its prospect of further consideration. He had the right flair for politics—tact, liking for human contact, the skill to win and keep loyal support—but preferred to use it in other directions."[11] He did his share of politicking, overtly and behind the scenes, in behalf of his central passions, journalism education and world harmony through the free flow of information and ideas.

Williams's unique blend of compassion and command, so often found in effective leaders, would be confined to journalism, a force he believed, with everything he had in him, to be more potent than politics or even government. "In the last analysis, public opinion rules," he once told an audience after the end of World War I. "Recorded, crystalized, interpreted, expressed by journalism, it is supreme . . . Increase the avenues of communication between nations and free news sources from the poison of propaganda and we thereby help to make a sick world well. Permit these avenues to be clogged, congested and corrupted, and the fever of war returns apace."[12]

But to fulfill its true purpose, Williams was convinced, journalism had to raise its standing in the public eye. As a first step, journalism's practitioners must become better educated. The more they knew, the prouder they would become of themselves and of their calling. He made this point again and again, with some success. "As much as any man dead or now alive, he helped to rebuild the craft of journalism and make it the profession of journalism," John C. Martin, publisher of the *Philadelphia Public Ledger,* wrote of Williams. "He believed that journalism—the editorial making of newspapers—could be taught and lived and practiced as a profession by professionally trained men and women."[13]

Williams had never attended college as a student, never burned the midnight oil prepping for an exam, never won a Phi Beta Kappa key or a varsity letter. Perhaps missing these things created in him some deep-seated, almost reverential appreciation of higher education. Or possibly it was his early exposure to dedicated academic leaders such as Richard Henry Jesse that

---

11. Quoted in Sara Lockwood Williams, unpublished Walter Williams biography.
12. Walter Williams, undated, untitled speech text.
13. August 3, 1935.

convinced him a university degree could open any door and make all things possible. Whatever the reason, Williams was certain that sustained public confidence in journalism could not be achieved without respectability within the academy. Among much else, a school of journalism symbolized a form of acceptance where it mattered greatly to him: in the intellectual community.

The School of Journalism he founded, over such massive objections from some professors and many newspaper leaders, opened up an avenue that many young men and women have since traveled. More than a thousand institutions of higher learning in the United States now teach journalism in some form, and more than a hundred schools and departments and colleges of journalism are nationally accredited—by an agency Williams helped found—after satisfying stiff requirements laid down by academic as well as professional leaders. His was an idea whose time truly had come. Other professions draw their young men and women from the campus. So, to an increasing degree, would journalism. The journalism school is not the only route to success in the field, of course. It is a humbling experience for journalism professors to realize that many of the industry's most brilliant successes never saw the inside of a school of journalism. Lincoln Steffens, widely regarded as one of the greatest reporters of all time, never took a course in newswriting, and Horace Greeley's professional credentials do not include completion of Editing I. David Sarnoff, who founded the Radio Corporation of America, never enrolled in a class in Media Management, nor did Ivy Ledbetter Lee ever sit through a college course in public relations. While it is unlikely we shall ever encounter a self-taught brain surgeon or meet a Supreme Court justice who never attended law school, plenty of people in the mass media field, including many of today's top-of-the-line stars, have yet to undergo an hour of formal study in their chosen profession.

It was ever thus. Throughout much of American history, journalism was not regarded seriously as a career field, much less as a subject worth intensive investigation at a college or university. The earliest publishers were, in fact, postmasters who produced newspapers primarily as a service to their constituents. Later newspapers were published by printing-house proprietors as a sideline to their larger and more lucrative printing businesses. During the formative years of the Republic, politicians often operated newspapers by and for themselves. While some editors of the period wrote brilliantly, they did so almost as an afterthought. The main goal was to perpetuate a philosophical point of view and to root for a political party; journalistic techniques, and providing honest and complete information, remained pretty far down on the editor's list of priorities.

Eventually newspapers became less partisan, courting more readers of all political stripes. To boost sales, the publishers offered more extensive news coverage. This required larger staffs, more reporters to be hired and trained. But many publishers were unwilling or ineffectual mentors, and on-the-job training for new reporters was, at best, a hit-or-miss proposition. A product of the practical school, Williams realized its limitations.

As a group, journalists are far better educated today than they have ever been; they bring to their work a better understanding of the humanities and the social sciences than most of their predecessors, and their grasp of mass media processes and effects aids them enormously in gathering and presenting the news. Journalism schools—then and now often misunderstood, sometimes stumbling—are now generally accepted by leaders in educational as well as mass media circles.[14] And to the extent they are successful, the credit belongs largely to Walter Williams and his vision.

From the moment he took on the deanship, Williams conducted himself as if he were an attorney with only one client, the School of Journalism. All he did and said—and didn't do and didn't say—reflected his determination to promote and protect the fragile standing journalism education had attained within the academy. So vocal and opinionated as an editor, Williams became strangely silent on important political issues after he became a dean. As an editor he might have passionately embraced Woodrow Wilson's internationalism, but as a dean he kept his opinions to himself—perhaps because some of the most ferocious opponents to the League of Nations were centered in the Midwest, with Missouri's Senator James Reed prominent among them. As a journalist and humanitarian, Williams was almost certainly shocked at political, social, and economic conditions in China, but as dean, he had carefully cultivated professorial and student exchanges and other alliances with the Chinese press, and he was not about to place these at risk by speaking out against policies of the Chinese government. He was well aware of heavy-handed authoritarian regimes in Central and South America, but rather than publicly condemning military dictators, Williams chose to have the World Press Congress honor courageous local editors in those countries instead. Part of this reluctance to speak out against the evils of the world may have stemmed from his own well-meaning, and sometimes naive, view of the world; he liked to think the best of everyone he met. He even managed to find good things to say, at least initially, of the Nazi leadership in Hitler's Germany. If Williams was cautious and diplomatic, he was driven by the politics of inclusion. His mission, self-imposed, was for the School of Journalism to develop many friends—and few enemies. More than most men, he achieved almost precisely what he set out to do.

---

14. Frank Luther Mott, *The News in America* (Harvard University Press, 1952), 217.

While Williams was concerned with journalistic knowledge and skill, he cared even more about values. "The journalist who undertakes his high mission will be the daysman [arbiter or umpire] who stands between the extremes of society," he promised—or warned—from the speaker's dais. "He will be the keeper of the conscience . . . and woe be unto him if he neglects his primary duty to the weak, the friendless, and those who have no helper!"[15] And while some portions of his *Journalist's Creed* now seem naive and hopelessly dated ("I believe that no one should write as a journalist what he would not say as a gentleman"), the rest of it remains as pertinent and compelling today as it did three generations ago, when he called for a journalism that "is stoutly independent, unmoved by pride or opinion or greed of power, constructive, tolerant but never careless, self-controlled, patient; always respectful of its readers but always unafraid; is quickly indignant at injustice; is unswayed by the appeal of privilege or the clamor of the mob; seeks to give every man a chance and, as far as law and honest wage and recognition of human brotherhood can make so, an equal chance." It was this honorable belief, in journalism and in people, that won him such respect and affection wherever he went.

The Roaring Twenties and the Depression Thirties, when Williams was most visible on the world stage, were not the easiest periods in which to talk about ethics in journalism. But Williams did so anyway, and audiences listened. A columnist for the *Washington Post* wrote, "Dr. Williams not only gave journalism new mental and ethical standards, but kept alive its idealism at a time when it was floundering into cynicism . . ."[16]

His crusade for better education and stronger values would be delivered far and wide, in a way not unlike that of the preacher his family long ago thought he might have become. Realizing that the great journalistic leaders of the world were unlikely to travel to a tiny community in the middle of the American Midwest—though an astonishing number of them actually would do just that—he chose to visit them instead. Armed with travel grants from a variety of sources (and profits from the school's laboratory newspaper) Williams restlessly roamed the earth, on epic journeys that carried him to hundreds of newspaper offices in Europe, Asia, Africa, and Central and South America. Everywhere he went he was greeted with warmth and appreciation, and when he left he had made new friends—personal friends, to be sure, but often professional soul mates as well: that worldwide brotherhood of journalists

15. Walter Williams, undated speech text.
16. Malvina Lindsay column in the *Washington Post,* August 3, 1935.

he had envisioned as a teenaged editor back in Missouri seemed at times, if only for a few moments in a distant land, to be really happening. Dr. Ezequiel P. Paz, courageous editor of *La Prensa* in Buenos Aires, praised "the strength and justice of his principles and the efficacy of his exemplary teachings." In China, an editorial writer called him "the greatest journalist-educator of the modern age."[17] A columnist's eulogy in the *London Daily Telegraph* read:

> The greatest contribution made by Walter Williams to our common life was, I believe, the revelation of the remarkable personality of the man, and the expression of that personality in works he designed for the advancement of journalism. If, as we are told, true Americanism is a spiritual faith, independent of race, language and creed, our dear friend certainly represented all that is best in that faith, and if my reading is correct he was also at heart an "internationalist" in the true sense of the word.[18]

The Board of Curators went even further. "Walter Williams exerted a more potent influence for good on the newspaper profession than any other man since Gutenberg invented movable type . . . an opinion that is fortified by the adoption of his ideas and ideals in publishing plants on every continent and by the fact that the teaching of journalism in universities has, under his leadership, spread into nearly every country in the world."[19]

"Walter Williams was not born to greatness," a British journalist wrote, "neither was it thrust upon him. Literally, he achieved greatness."[20] That assessment is persuasive. Williams was born of modest circumstances in a pleasant but obscure town deep in middle America. Without a high school education he became a thoughtful writer and a serious editor. Without an agreeable speaking voice for much of his life, he became a compelling orator. Without a college education he became president of a great university. He was unimposing physically: "Perhaps five feet seven or eight inches tall," recalled one of his students, "probably tipping the scales at one hundred fifty-five or sixty pounds. Walking down the campus he would move along at a quick pace, short steps, straight as an Indian, looking straight ahead, arms dangling at his sides, fingers always working. His hat seemed to set on top of his head, never down over his head. He looked more like . . . a jurist than a country editor."[21] Whatever greatness he attained he earned the hard way. And on his

---

17. Paz's comments were made August 15, 1935. *Shanghai Evening Post and Mercury,* c. August 25, 1935.

18. Percy S. Bullen, *London Daily Telegraph,* August 3, 1935.

19. Statement issued July 30, 1935. Presidential Archive, University of Missouri.

20. Bullen, *London Daily Telegraph,* August 3, 1935.

21. E. A. McLaughlin, class of 1931, to the author, March 9, 1994.

own terms. Though he traveled far and wide, he never lived anywhere but in the rural heartland of America. He came to terms with the complexities of his personality that both helped and hindered him. He died in a home less than forty miles from the nurturing community where he was born.

At least part of his appeal can be attributed to charm, a charm so enduring that those who had known him longest idolized him most. His former students and faculty colleagues wrote poems and at least one song about him. Charlie Ross named his son after Walter Williams, as did a number of alumni. Governor Guy B. Park, who had slogged arm-in-arm with him through the Great Depression, called Williams "the greatest Missourian of his generation and certainly the best known of his time." Williams had charm all right, but as the *Kansas City Post* put it, "his charm was the real thing."[22]

But the secret to Williams's achievement had less to do with charm than with faith and conviction. From rural Missouri to the capitals of the world he was able to win and keep the confidence of his fellow journalists, perhaps because his high-minded campaign for professional values somehow reminded editors everywhere why they had gone into journalism in the first place. His idealism rekindled their own, making them glad again they had become journalists rather than real-estate agents or dentists or short-order fry cooks. He touched their souls, and they loved him for it. "Nothing is impossible to those whose hearts are young, whose faith is sure, and who have ever before them the profession of journalism," he told audience after audience of reporters and editors and publishers. "Journalism—the great unfinished, fascinating new adventure!" In his vision, journalism was nothing less than a calling "to serve the life of the world, and not to do disservice to those who live next door."[23] His faith and conviction, so evident to all who heard him speak or read what he wrote, inspired his audiences and, ultimately, ennobled him. His message played as well in Shanghai as it did in St. Louis, for the chord it struck was universal. He was a journalist to the world.

---

22. Among other sources, see Vernon Meyer, "Walter Williams," which says, in part, "His pen is dry, but what it wrote fades never/His fire is ash, but still remains the light;/His dream, grown real, will crown his name forever,/So long as men love verity and light." Also, Roberta Mansbarger, "To Walter Williams," etc. These are published in "In Memoriam: Walter Williams," University of Missouri Bulletin, February 10, 1936. The song is "A Salute to the Chief Silurian," with words and music by Hermann Almstedt. The Silurians in Columbia were an affable group of faculty who had been at the University of Missouri since Williams's days as a curator. On May 17, 1935, only weeks before his death, the Silurians performed the song at the President's House during what they knew would be a last meeting with him. Sung "with Paleozoic robustness," as its composer described it, the lyrics begin, "Silurians we with a pedigree." *Kansas City Post,* August 3, 1935.

23. Walter Williams, undated speech text.

Epilogue

Life went on. A grief-stricken Sara, whose eight-year marriage to Walter Williams had been her happiest dream come true, now confided that she "felt adrift."[1] To a friend on the Board of Curators she wrote:

> . . . my house and my life are in great confusion. Despite the long months of knowing that I would some day be alone, Walter's going left me so bewildered— everything seemed unstable. I loved him so dearly, we were such constant companions, our married life was so ideal that the terrible aloneness now seems almost unbearable. I realize this is selfish but that doesn't ease the hurt. His was such a full life. I have never known anyone who gave more or gained more from living. He was so useful, so joy-giving, so noble and generous, such a marvelous dreamer who could make dreams come true. How wonderful to have lived as he did, and what power his influence will continue to have through generations to come!
>
> He was my mentor, my inspiration and my confidant for more than twenty years. These eight years of living with him have been supremely happy, crowded years. He tried to build up happy memories. He studied to give me every advantage and joy possible. I know I have had in eight years what many people never have in a lifetime . . . I glory in the fact that he loved me and that I was able to help make his last years here happier and more comfortable. I know that I shall get over this numb terror of going on alone . . . [2]

Her sorrow and a need to rebuild her life would take her far from the campus of the University of Missouri, where the memories were now too painful to endure. She could no longer bear the sight of the President's House, and the tree-shaded sidewalks of Francis Quadrangle now seemed cold and unfriendly. "After the Dean married Sara Lockwood and he became president of the University," an undergraduate at the time recalled, "I saw them walking towards the President's House on several occasions, holding hands like young lovers." She hastily accepted a position as a visiting professor at Yenching University in Beijing, at a journalism program her husband, with an assist from *Missourian* profits, helped establish. The semester abroad, she hoped, would not only get her back into the swing of journalistic work again but also generate material she could use for magazine articles. She returned to the

---

1. Dains, ed., *Show Me Missouri Women,* 154–56.
2. Sara Lockwood Williams to Frank McDavid, September 19, 1935, Sara Lockwood Williams Papers.

United States in 1936, but not to Columbia, opting for a fresh start in St. Louis instead. She found work as a teacher of creative writing and did some lecturing and freelancing for magazines. She envisioned writing a biography of her late husband, and submitted a detailed outline to several book publishers and personally interviewed others during a disappointing stay of several weeks in New York. Their responses were polite but negative.[3] Perhaps editors sensed her manuscript would be too intimate and too adoring to be persuasive. Or maybe it was the economy. The country was still mired in the Great Depression, and as the book industry had been downsized and battered, its editors grew cautious; few would-be authors of that period got much encouragement. The following year, 1937, Sara was given her own radio program. Called "Sara Lockwood Williams's Scrapbook," the weekly talk show was broadcast from St. Louis on KSD and featured discussions of her travels and her observations on women in the news. She also wrote radio scripts, mostly dramatizations of incidents from Missouri history, for another big St. Louis station, KMOX. Soon that, too, played out, so she put in a year as a visiting professor of journalism at the University of Texas at Austin. By now she was finally able, emotionally, to return to Columbia. She lived quietly in the big home on South Glenwood, occupying her hours with various freelance writing projects. But her savings eventually ran out and she still had a living to make, so, in 1944, she moved to Rockford College in Illinois to be director of public relations and an associate professor of journalism. She went back to Columbia again in 1951, rejoined the School of Journalism faculty, and taught feature writing for ten years, still at the rank of assistant professor. As Walter Williams's widow, she was treated with deference by the administration and, though she was moving past the age of sixty-five, no one, so far as is known, suggested that she retire. She was, in fact, regarded as a capable teacher, though observers noted that she never seemed really comfortable, either with students or faculty colleagues. She gained some weight, which, given her short stature, made her appear even stockier, but her energy level remained high. She resumed her participation in various church groups and professional associations and served a term as president of the Missouri Women's Press Club. She had reached the age of seventy-two and had been a widow for twenty-six years when she died of cancer in 1961. She never remarried. Indeed, if she ever even considered doing so for a moment,

---

3. E. A. McLaughlin, who was graduated in 1931, to the author, March 9, 1994. Minutes of the Executive Committee of the University Missourian Association, January 20, 1928. Sara Lockwood Williams to Frank McDavid, September 19, 1935. In her papers are several letters to and from New York publishers reflecting regrets that the manuscript she proposed did not seem suitable.

the papers she left behind, so candid and complete in other respects, make no mention of it.

Frederick A. Middlebush, who had been handling the day-to-day business of the university during Williams's long illness, was unanimously elevated by the curators to the presidency. Though a national search was announced, Middlebush was the favorite from the beginning. He would prove an able steward, guiding the institution through the remainder of the Depression, more financial difficulties, world war, and a flood of war-veteran students. In all, he would hold the presidency for twenty years, longer than any other had served in that office. When he stepped down in 1955, he did so knowing faculty effectiveness and morale, his chief priorities, were in excellent shape.[4]

The World Press Congress, for all practical purposes, was finished even before Williams's death, though other regional and global organizations would come along later: the Inter-American Press Association and the International Press Institute among them. But there would be one last assemblage of the World Press Congress, in effect another tribute to the memory of Walter Williams. The congress convened in Columbia in 1959, commemorating the fiftieth anniversary of the School of Journalism. Representatives of some thirty-five nations showed up to deal with the Cold War theme, "A Stronger Free Press for a Better Free World." Former President Harry S. Truman was one of the speakers, and if the delegates thought "Give 'em Hell Harry" had mellowed, he soon set them straight. "I'd like to be the blue pencil man for a while in a newspaper office and cut out the things that ought to be cut out," he declared, while the delegates applauded, some of them uneasily.[5] Walter Williams would have approved.

Frank Lee Martin, who had spent a career quietly—and so far as is known, contentedly—preparing to head the School of Journalism, finally got the title of dean, a job he had in fact already been doing throughout the five years that Williams was president. While Martin had made several trips to the Orient and was credited with solidifying the school's China connection, he made his reputation by being a solid administrator who kept the school running smoothly. In all, he spent thirty-two years on the faculty, serving as dean in his own right for six years before his death in 1941. An affable, angular, low-key

---

4. Olson and Olson, *The University of Missouri,* 67. Stephens, *A History of the University of Missouri,* 622.
5. Taft, *Missouri Newspapers,* 314.

professional, Martin got on well with media people and, indeed, would be chosen for membership in the Missouri Newspaper Hall of Fame.[6] The School of Journalism was bigger and more complex by now, offering instruction in a wide range of mass communications courses, attracting students from far and wide. In 1936 a second building was constructed, joined to Neff Hall by a handsome arch that became the northeast entrance to Francis Quadrangle. The new journalism building virtually doubled the space for the school, and Martin happily presided at the dedication of it. The curators named the new building Walter Williams Hall.

Yet another loose end would be tied down more than fifty years later. This one did not involve Williams directly, but two people who had meant a very great deal to him, and whose story reached deep into the history of the School of Journalism. For years there had been hanging in Neff Hall a portrait of Charles G. Ross, the first person hired by Williams in 1908 as a member of the original faculty. Across the archway, in Walter Williams Hall, there was a portrait of Mary Paxton Keeley, who, in 1910, became the first woman to be graduated with a degree in journalism. Each had attained dazzling success in their careers. In Mary Pax's student days, she and Charlie Ross had fallen hopelessly in love but, because of circumstances, the wedding they had planned for themselves could not be. They drifted apart, and each eventually married someone else. But for Mary, Charlie Ross never really went away.[7] She wrote to him and he wrote back, hundreds of letters over nearly forty years. He died at his desk in the White House in 1950; she lived past her one hundredth birthday, until 1988. Not everyone knew of their enduring, star-crossed romance, but a latter-day successor to Walter Williams certainly did. He was James D. Atwater, dean of the school during the 1980s, a man who could be not only sensitive but decisive. One day he summarily ordered that the portraits of Charlie Ross and Mary Paxton Keeley be relocated and hung together in a prominent spot— in the Graduate Studies Center, as it turned out—facing each other, side by side, forever.

Walter Williams would have approved of that, too.

6. Olson and Olson, *The University of Missouri,* 70. Taft, *Missouri Newspapers,* 177.
7. Barbara Zang, "From Heart and Hand," *School of Journalism Alumni Magazine,* 1987, 11.

The History Quiz

While it is not known precisely what information was imparted in Walter Williams's History and Principles class, here are some reasonably plausible answers to the questions he posed in one of his final examinations (spring semester, 1915). The test appears on page 160:

Part A.

1. *Just what was it that Gutenberg invented?* If you said "the printing press," you're wrong. The press had been around since the ninth century, but the printing impressions had to be made from elaborately carved wood blocks, a page at a time. Gutenberg is credited with inventing movable type— that is, he used a combination of metals, chiefly lead, to create individual letters, which could then be swiftly assembled into words, locked into place on the press, printed, then replaced (distributed) into individual storage compartments for reuse again and again.

2. *Explain the point system of type measurement.* A system of sizing printing types. A "point" is 1/72 of an inch. In 36-point type, then, each letter would be 1/2 inch tall. Most publications use 8- or 10-point type for basic text, and up to 72-point type for headlines.

3. *Name the most striking two improvements in printing in the last fifty years.* The Linotype, a mechanical typesetting machine that molds an entire line of type at a time, would certainly be one. Other possibilities would include the Monotype, a then-modern typesetting machine much like the Linotype; the rotary press, which had just been introduced and which speeded up newspaper printing enormously; automatic press feeders; a new system of casting type by electrolysis; rapid improvements in photoengraving, which enhanced the use of photographs.

Part B.

Describe specifically the various restrictions placed upon the early English press and outline the struggle for freedom.

Most likely Williams wanted here a discussion of licensing, which was used by the Tudors to control the embryo printing industry in fifteenth-century England. After the Parliament dissolved the fearsome Star Chamber in 1641, more and more citizens began to speak out in favor of greater freedom of expression. John Milton's powerful *Areopagitica* was, in fact, an eloquent plea to abolish the licensing system in favor of an unfettered press.

Part C.

Write 150-word paragraphs on:

1. *John Peter Zenger.* New York Weekly Journal publisher who became a symbol of high-handed British justice in colonial America. Hauled into court in 1735 on a trumped-up charge of criminal libel (sedition, for criticizing royal authority), Zenger was brilliantly and successfully defended by Andrew Hamilton and acquitted by a defiant colonial jury. The spiritual impact of the trial was enormous and, indeed, helped escalate the resistance to British rule throughout the colonies.

2. *Prosecution of Harry Croswell.* Pathbreaking defamation case, tried in 1804, in which for the first time a court accepted truth as a defense in a libel suit. Alexander Hamilton, who defended Croswell in the politically charged courtroom, also argued that a jury could determine both the facts and the law in a libel action, positions previously denied by the courts. Hamilton lost the Croswell case, but his arguments so impressed the New York legislature that the law was eventually changed.

3. *John Wilkes.* Editor of *North Britain* (1762–1763) who attacked high British political leaders, including the king. He was ousted from his seat in the House of Commons and later convicted of seditious libel. "Wilkes and Liberty" became a rallying cry in the American colonies. The "Sons of Liberty" in Boston adopted him as a hero, and the South Carolina legislature appropriated fifteen hundred pounds to pay his debts and legal fees.

4. *Missouri Gazette.* First newspaper in Missouri, begun in St. Louis on July 12, 1808. Its publisher, Joseph Charless, is regarded by press historian William Howard Taft and others as "the father of Missouri journalism."

Part D.

Tell in a sentence or two each the important facts about the following:

1. *Horace Greeley.* Brilliant, if erratic, publisher of the *New York Tribune,* which he founded in 1841. His editorial page is considered the most important of the nineteenth century.

2. *Sarah J. Hale.* Longtime (1836 to 1877) editor of *Godey's Lady's Book,* a leading women's magazine. Though she was a quiet campaigner for

women's rights and wrote or edited fifty books, she is, alas, best remembered for the nursery rhyme she composed, "Mary Had a Little Lamb."

3. *Junius letters.* Anonymous, important essays published in the *London Public Advertiser* from 1769 to 1772, these letters were instrumental in advising citizens, both in England and in the turbulent colonies, of their rights.

4. *First daily newspaper in the United States.* There is considerable dispute about this, but Alfred McClung Lee, in *The Daily Newspaper in America* (Macmillan, 1937) makes a persuasive case for the *Philadelphia Evening Post and Daily Advertiser,* launched in 1783.

5. *First two newspapers in the American colonies.* Benjamin Harris's *Publick Occurrences* (1690) and John Campbell's *News-Letter* (1704), both published in Boston.

6. *First real English newspaper.* The *Oxford Gazette,* later renamed the *London Gazette,* written and edited by Henry Muddiman, 1665.

7. *First real daily in the world.* The *Acta,* also called *Acta Diurna* (daily record), also called *Acta Populi* (people's record), begun in 59 B.C. by order of Julius Caesar. Handwritten copies, prepared by teams of scribes, were posted throughout Rome and dispatched to commanders in the field.

8. *Early Washington newspapers.* The *Washington Federalist* (1800), the *National Intelligencer, Museum and Washington and Georgetown Advertiser,* and the *Cabinet of the United States,* all begun in 1800 when the capital was relocated to the District of Columbia.

9. *James Rivington.* "Jemmy" Rivington was the most influential Tory editor during the pre-Revolutionary period. His *New York Gazeteer and Weekly Advertiser,* though obviously unpopular with many readers for its political views, was nevertheless regarded as skillfully written and edited.

10. *Robert L'Estrange.* Became in 1662 the official licenser of the emergent British press, thus a symbol of authoritarian repression.

11. *Blanket sheets.* Name given to oversize pages of many nineteenth-century newspapers. Fearful that a tax would be levied on each newspaper page, some publishers shrewdly reconfigured their newspapers so as to provide the equivalent of eight normal pages of news and advertising on four "blanket-sized" sheets.

12. *Elizabeth Mallet.* Publisher, if only briefly, of the *London Daily Courant,* first daily newspaper in England, 1702.

13. *New Orleans Picayune.* Its editor-publisher, George W. Kendall, was acknowledged as probably the most effective correspondent covering the Mexican War. His vivid reporting, on all major battles throughout that

conflict, became the standard by which other war correspondence of the period was measured.

14. *Robert Hoe.* Beginning in the 1830s, his R. Hoe and Company manufactured steam presses that revolutionized American journalism, making possible fast, cheap production of newspapers that nearly everyone could afford.

15. *Acta Diurna.* See #7, above.

16. *Ottmar Mergenthaler.* Inventor of the Linotype, a remarkable typesetting machine capable of setting a full line at a time. The Linotype was first used in 1886 on the *New York Tribune.*

17. *Benjamin Franklin.* American statesman (1706–1790), scientist, inventor, postmaster, and, most especially, a printer. His journalistic empire, headquartered in Philadelphia, was composed of newspapers (including the country's first foreign-language paper), books, and magazines. He was, as historians have noted, not only eminently respectable but also prosperous, the first American to make a fortune in journalism.

18. *Henry J. Raymond.* Founder, in 1851, of the *New York Times* and one of the most brilliant and fair-minded writers of the era.

19. *James Gordon Bennett.* Publisher of the *New York Herald,* arguably the most successful of the penny press. Bennett's innovations changed American journalism forever, creating as he did a true press for the masses.

20. *George Jones.* A partner with Henry J. Raymond in establishing the *New York Times,* Jones carried on after Raymond's tragic early death. Under Jones's direction, and aided by the incisive editorial cartoons of Thomas Nast, the *Times* exposed and discredited the Tweed Ring, which dominated New York politics in the 1870s.

Index